CITIZEN INQUIRY

Citizen Inquiry: Synthesising Science and Inquiry Learning is the first book of its kind to bring together the concepts of citizen science and inquiry-based learning to illustrate the pedagogical advantages of this approach. It shifts the emphasis of scientific investigations from scientists to the general public, by educating learners of all ages to determine their own research agenda and devise their own investigations underpinned by a model of scientific inquiry.

'Citizen inquiry' is an original approach to research education that refers to mass participation of the public in joining inquiry-led scientific investigations. Using a range of practical case studies underpinned by the theory of inquiry-based learning, this book has significant implications for teaching and learning through exploration of how new technologies can be used to engage with scientific research. Key features include:

- a new perspective on science education and science practice through crowdsourced research
- explanation of the benefits of this innovative approach to teaching and learning
- a steady shift of emphasis from theory to application for readers to understand thoroughly the current state of research in the field and its applications to practice
- examples of practical applications of this approach and recommendations on how successful citizen inquiry applications can be developed.

This edited volume is essential reading for academic researchers and professional educators interested in the potential of online technology in all levels of education, from primary and secondary level through to further education and lifelong learning. It will be ideal reading on any undergraduate or postgraduate course involving research methods in education as well as developments in science education and educational software.

Christothea Herodotou is Lecturer in Innovating Pedagogy at the Open University, UK. She is interested in the evaluation of technology for learning and engagement through the use of innovative research methods, including crowdsourcing and learning analytics. She holds funding from the National Science Foundation (USA) and Wellcome Trust (UK) for evaluating online learning in museum-led citizen science projects. She is a Senior Fellow of the Higher Education Academy.

Mike Sharples is Professor of Educational Technology at the Open University, UK and Academic Lead at Futurelearn.com. He was Founding President of the International Association for Mobile Learning and is Associate Editor in Chief of *IEEE Transactions on Learning Technologies*. He has over 300 published papers on educational technology, mobile learning and inquiry science learning. His projects as principal investigator include nQuire: Young Citizen Inquiry, and Personal Inquiry to support inquiry-based learning of science topics between formal and non-formal settings. He co-edited *Orchestrating Enquiry Learning* (Routledge, 2012) with Karen Littleton and Eileen Scanlon.

Eileen Scanlon is Regius Professor of Open Education and Associate Director of Research and Innovation in the Institute of Educational Technology at the Open University, UK. Eileen completed her PhD in 1990 studying cognitive models of physics problem solving and has published extensively in the fields of technology-enhanced learning and science communication. She co-edited *Orchestrating Inquiry Learning* (Routledge, 2012) with Karen Littleton and Mike Sharples.

CITIZEN INQUIRY

Synthesising Science and Inquiry Learning

Edited by Christothea Herodotou,
Mike Sharples and Eileen Scanlon

Routledge
Taylor & Francis Group

LONDON AND NEW YORK

First published 2018
by Routledge
2 Park Square, Milton Park, Abingdon, Oxon OX14 4RN

and by Routledge
711 Third Avenue, New York, NY 10017

Routledge is an imprint of the Taylor & Francis Group, an informa business

British Library Cataloguing in Publication Data
A catalogue record for this book is available from the British Library

Library of Congress Cataloging in Publication Data
A catalog record for this book has been requested

ISBN: 978-1-138-20868-1 (hbk)
ISBN: 978-1-138-20869-8 (pbk)
ISBN: 978-1-315-45861-8 (ebk)

Typeset in Bembo
by Swales & Willis Ltd, Exeter, Devon, UK
Printed and bound by CPI Group (UK) Ltd, Croydon, CR0 4YY

CONTENTS

FIGURES

TABLES

CONTRIBUTORS

Janice Ansine is senior project manager – citizen science, in the Faculty of Science, Technology, Engineering and Mathematics (STEM) at the Open University (UK) and manages projects that facilitate learning journeys using innovative, easily accessible web-based tools and resources, including the award-winning iSpot (www.iSpotnature.org). This includes supporting informal to formal learning, engagement, communications, outreach and impact activities for STEM-related public-facing initiatives (see www.Treezilla.org, www.evolutionmegalab.org and www.opensciencelab.ac.uk). She has a comprehensive background, including postgraduate research in environmental change and ecological footprinting, biodiversity, sustainable development and science communications; experience as a newspaper reporter and environmental communications consultant; as well as expertise implementing and managing communications, public engagement, outreach and behaviour change projects and programmes around sustainability, biodiversity and the environment.

Maria Aristeidou is a technology-enhanced learning and community engagement researcher. Her interests revolve around community engagement for enhanced interaction and knowledge exchange, and the design of engaging learning technologies. She is a postdoctoral researcher in the Institute of Educational Technology of the Open University.

Rachel Becker-Klein, PhD has worked at PEER Associates for over a decade. She has a doctorate in community and developmental psychology from New York University. Her current work primarily includes research and evaluation of STEM education, citizen science and environmental education programmes.

Isabelle Bonhoure holds a PhD in materials science at the University of Paris-Sud (2000). Since then, she has combined research, science communication and scientific project management. She is currently project manager and researcher at the OpenSystems-Universitat de Barcelona research group where she is involved in several citizen science research projects related to formal education. She has acted as a project manager and researcher in the project Citizen Science: Education and Research, actively participating in the design of the pilots for the introduction of citizen science at 12 secondary schools; parts of the outcomes are presented in Chapter 9. She is a researcher in the H2020 project STEMForYouth, proposing innovative ways to make science education and scientific careers attractive to young people. In the frame of this project, she is involved in the co-creation and co-design of citizen science projects at school, in which the students are the central actors of this process.

Carol Boston holds a master's degree in education from the University of North Carolina and in human–computer interaction from the University of Maryland. Prior to joining the University of Maryland as a project manager on a National Science Foundation grant related to environmental education and informal science, she worked on contract with the US Department of Education to support ERIC, the Education Resources Information Center database. She was also a secondary education teacher.

Anne Bowser is a senior program associate with the Science and Technology Innovation Program at the Woodrow Wilson International Center for Scholars, Washington, DC. Her work focuses on increasing the use of citizen science in scientific research and policymaking.

Koula Charitonos is a Lecturer in the Institute of Educational Technology at the Open University with research interests in the field of mobile learning across formal and informal settings.

Gill Clough is a research fellow at the Institute of Educational Technology, Open University. She is currently researching evidence cafés with the Center for Policing Research and Learning. Evidence cafés offer an effective means for knowledge exchange between practising police officers and research academics, translating research evidence into policing practice.

Vickie Curtis is the public engagement manager at the Wellcome Trust Centre for Molecular Parasitology based at the University of Glasgow. She works with scientists to help them find opportunities to communicate about their research outside academia, and to find new ways to engage stakeholders with the Centre's research. Prior to working with the Wellcome Trust, she was at the Institute of Educational Technology at the Open University, where she carried out research on online citizen science and explored how scientists use digital technologies to engage with audiences outside of research. Her research publications are available at: http://oro.open.ac.uk/view/person/vc964.html.

Michael Dodd, PhD is the iSpot UK curator based in the Faculty of Science, Technology, Engineering and Mathematics (STEM). He has over 20 years' experience in teaching and research, including writing Open University (OU) science courses and playing a role in the development of iSpot and other OU citizen science initiatives (i.e. Evolution Megalab and Treezilla), as well the Floodplain Meadows Partnership project. Mike has a background in surveying, data analysis and geographic information systems (GIS) as well as expertise in a number of groups of organisms. His responsibilities with iSpot include provision of online support for website users; liaison with national recording schemes and other partners to develop community of experts and beginners using the site; data sharing and analysis.

Stuart Dunn is lecturer in the Department of Digital Humanities at King's College London. He teaches spatial humanities, digital archaeology and the history of network technologies, and one of his key foci in all these areas is the role of public participation and crowdsourcing. He has research interests in digital cartography and web gazetteers. He joined King's in 2006 as a research associate at the Arts and Humanities e-Science Support Centre, and research fellow in the Centre for e-Research. Stuart manages and contributes to several projects in the area of visualization, GIS and digital humanities.

Richard Edwards is emeritus professor in the Faculty of Social Sciences, University of Stirling, UK. He was previously professor and head of the School of Education at Stirling. He has researched and written extensively on lifelong learning and educational theory. He has researched learning through citizen science in projects funded by the British Academy and Wellcome Trust.

Núria Ferran-Ferrer has been lecturer at the Department of Information and Communication Sciences, Universitat Oberta de Catalunya (UOC), Spain, since 2005. She gained her European doctoral degree in 2010 at the Universitat de Barcelona, with a research stage at Sheffield University (2009). She was Assistant Professor of Information Management and User Studies from 2004 to 2008 in the Information Management and Journalism Bachelors at the Universitat Autònoma de Barcelona, and she is at present teaching at UOC research methodologies for user-centred design processes, user experience and human–computer interaction. She is currently involved in a research project on youth engagement and citizen science. Her research interests span from open content and participation, citizen science, to user experiences with digital media and mobile devices.

Salvador Ferré holds a biology degree and a biochemical and molecular biology PhD at the Universitat de Barcelona, Spain. He worked as editor of a science popularization book series by the Spanish publisher Omnis Cellula. He has written several science communication articles addressed to different public profiles (Omnis Cellula, Eureka, U-Divulga, etc.). He is the author of more than 25 science textbooks (both classical and digital, in which he designed all the interactive and audiovisual media). For 7 years he also coordinated a team of 80 multimedia experts to produce 100 multimedia interactive educational textbooks. He is one of the founders and codirectors of Eduscopi, a company that fosters educational innovation and science popularization.

Louise Francis is cofounder and managing director of Mapping for Change, University College London.

Amy Grack Nelson, MS, MA, is evaluation and research manager at the Science Museum of Minnesota. She is currently a doctoral candidate in quantitative methods in education at the University of Minnesota. Her work focuses on the development and validation of measures to advance the field of informal science education evaluation and research.

Muki Haklay is professor of Geographic Information Science (GIScience) and codirector of the Extreme Citizen Science group. He is a co-founder of Mapping for Change.

Jennifer Hammock is the project manager of the Encyclopedia of Life, Smithsonian Institution.

Derek L. Hansen is an associate professor at Brigham Young University's Information Technology program at the School of Technology. Prior to that, he taught at the University of Maryland's iSchool where he was a member of the Human Computer Interaction Lab. Dr Hansen completed his PhD from the University of Michigan's School of Information. His research and teaching focus on understanding and designing social technologies, tools and games for the public good. He has received over $2 million in grants (as a principal investigator or co-investigator) to help develop and test novel technical interventions with interdisciplinary collaborators, including educational alternate reality games, playable case studies, citizen science games and exercise games.

Yurong He is a PhD graduate from College of Information Studies at the University of Maryland. Prior to that she received a master's degree in cognitive psychology from the Institution of Psychology at Chinese Academy of Sciences and a bachelor's degree in psychology at the Beijing Forestry University, China.

Mark Hedges is a senior lecturer in the Department of Digital Humanities, King's College London, teaching on several modules in the MA in digital asset and media management. His original academic background was in mathematics and philosophy, and he gained a PhD in mathematics at University College London, before starting a 17-year career in the software and systems consultancy industry. Since joining King's in 2005, Mark has been involved in various research projects in the areas of digital archives and digital curation, computational methods, and crowdsourcing and public involvement in the humanities.

Christothea Herodotou, PhD is a lecturer in innovating pedagogy at the Open University, UK. She is interested in the use of innovative technologies, in particular web-based technologies, digital games and mobile applications for learning and their relationship to human motivation and cognition. She is also extensively involved in how learning analytics can inform understanding of the use of technologies and improve the learning experience.

Richard Holliman is professor of engaged research at the Open University, UK. He explores the ways that academic research is communicated via a range of media and genres, and how ideas about (upstream) public engagement with research may be shifting and extending social practices. From 2012 to 2015 he was the Open University's Champion for Public Engagement with Research, leading a programme of organisational change to embed the principles of engaged research across the university. More recently, he has codirected a school–university partnership in Milton Keynes designed to give children and young people opportunities to engage with contemporary research. He is an associate editor for *Research for All: Universities and Society* and a member of the Science and Technology Facilities Council's Advisory Panel for Public Engagement. His research publications are available from: http://oro.open.ac.uk/view/person/rmh47.html

Charlene Jennett is a research associate at the UCL Interaction Centre, UK. In the Citizen Cyberlab project, she carried out research exploring volunteers' motivations for participating in online citizen science projects, and their experiences of learning and creativity.

Ann Jones is a reader in the Institute of Educational Technology at the Open University. Her research interests include investigations into social and affective use of computers, mobile learning, technology-supported informal and semi-formal learning and the role of motivation in such contexts. She worked on the UK Research Councils-funded Personal Inquiry Project (2007–2010) which investigated supporting school children to conduct personally relevant scientific inquiries across different contexts, using mobile devices, including the formal curriculum and semi-formal contexts. She co-edits the *Journal of Interactive Media in Education*.

Laure Kloetzer is assistant professor in psychology and education at the University of Neuchâtel, Switzerland. She is interested in research methodologies for social innovation, as well as language and dialogue in lifelong learning and development. She is researching engagement and informal learning in Citizen Science, and chairing the European Citizen Science Association Working Group on Learning and Education in Citizen Science.

Patrick McAndrew is professor of open education and director of the Institute of Educational Technology (IET), Learning and Teaching Innovation. IET is a strategic academic unit carrying out research, supporting the university and offering postgraduate qualifications in online and distance education. IET's strategic programmes include developing learning analytics and learning design to drive quality enhancement processes in the university. Patrick has taken a leading part in the development of approaches to open and free learning. Recent projects in this area include iSpot, OpenLearn, OLnet, Bridge to Success and the OER Research Hub. These projects combine practice and research on the impact of openness. He has had an active role in over 40 funded projects across technology-enhanced learning.

Diarmuid McDonnell is a doctoral researcher at the Faculty of Social Sciences, University of Stirling, UK. His mixed-methods research explores the determinants of charity misconduct and vulnerability, and utilises linked administrative data derived from the Scottish Charity Regulator. He has contributed to a number of research projects in areas of education and social policy.

Josep Perelló holds a PhD in physics. He is currently associate professor at the Department of Condensed Matter Physics of the Universitat de Barcelona (UB), Spain, and expert in complex systems. In 2013, he created OpenSystems-UB, a research group that runs scientific research projects through citizen participation and artistic practices. He coordinates the Barcelona Citizen Science Office, a project promoted by the Institute of Culture of Barcelona-Barcelona City Council. He participates in citizen science public and collective experiments on human mobility, human behaviour and decision making through social dilemmas. He has also coordinated Sistemes Oberts, a teacher training programme in arts and science in collaboration with Barcelona Contemporary Art Museum (MACBA). He is currently developing several strategies to introduce citizen science at schools and to implement concrete citizen science projects within the particularities of a given neighbourhood. In both cases, the aim is to induce social change driven by a collective research practice.

Karen Peterman, PhD, is the president of Karen Peterman Consulting, Co. She holds a doctorate in developmental psychology from Duke University. Her current work focuses on evaluation of STEM programmes, and research on evaluation methods for informal learning environments.

Toni Pou holds a physics degree from the Universitat de Barcelona, Spain. He has worked as a science writer for several media, for which he has been recognised by the Spanish National Centre for Particle, Astronomy and Nuclear Physics (CPAN). As one of the winners of the Amundsen World Science Journalism competition, he spent a month on board a research icebreaker. As a result of this experience, he wrote a book entitled *Where the Day Sleeps with Open Eyes*, which was awarded the Godó Prize for Investigative Journalism and the Prisma Prize for the best popular science book published in Spain. The book was published originally in Catalan by the publisher Empúries (Grup 62) in 2011. The original title of the book was *On el dia dorm amb els ulls oberts*. Two years later, in 2013, the book was published in Spanish by the publisher Anagrama. The Spanish title of the book was *Donde el día duerme con los ojos abiertos*. He is also the curator of the science exhibition 'The Arctic is Breaking up'. He directed for 7 years a team of 80 multimedia experts to produce 100 multimedia interactive educational textbooks. He is one of the founders and codirectors of Eduscopi, a company that fosters educational innovation and science popularization.

Jennifer Preece is a professor and dean emerita at Maryland's Information School. Her research focuses on biodiversity citizen science, environmental education and motivation for community participation. Jennifer is a co-author of a leading human–computer interaction text entitled: *Interaction Design: Beyond Human–Computer Interaction* (4th edition, Wiley, 2015) and author of many research articles.

David Robinson, PhD is currently an honorary associate in the School of Environment, Earth and Ecosystem Sciences (EEES), holds a National Teaching Fellowship from the Higher Education Academy (UK) and is lead educator for Introduction to Ecosystems, the Futurelean/Open University (OU) Massive Open Online Course. He is a zoologist, specialising in acoustic behaviour and evolutionary biology, now researching insect ecology and ultrasonic communication, and has been committed to open and distance learning all his professional life using multimedia to excite learners about the natural world. A former senior lecturer in EEES at the OU, he was also academic advisor for iSpot's teaching and learning and a number of OU/BBC co-productions, including *Saving Species, Seasons, Life* and *The Great British Year*.

Eileen Scanlon is regius of open education and associate director of research and innovation in the Institute of Educational Technology at the Open University, UK. She is also honorary professor in Moray House School of Education, University of Edinburgh and a trustee of Bletchley Park. She has extensive research experience on educational technology projects. She is currently involved in research projects that explore aspects of digital scholarship to develop open educational resources; investigate science learning in formal and informal settings concentrating on the development of an inquiry learning pedagogy; and develop innovative approaches to evaluation of learning (e.g. games-based learning and citizen science). Professor Scanlon has published extensively in the field of technology-enhanced learning.

Mike Sharples is a professor of educational technology at the Open University. His research involves human-centred design of new technologies and environments for learning. He is author of over 300 papers in the areas of educational technology, science education, human-centred design of personal technologies, artificial intelligence and cognitive science.

Ian Simpson graduated from the University of Strathclyde with BSc and PhD degrees in geography and then worked from 1985 as a researcher on land use and environmental policy issues with the UK Government's Ministry of Agriculture. Joining the University of Stirling in 1990, he became professor of geography and environmental sciences in 2002. He has also held senior management posts of university deputy principal (research) and dean, Faculty of Natural Sciences. His major research interests are in soils and sediments as landscape history, considering soils and sediments as historical narratives that define land resource utilisation and organisation by early societies together with their environmental and landscape consequences. Within these themes he works on a range of research programmes in the North Atlantic region, South Asia and the Middle East.

Cathlyn Stylinski is tenured research faculty at the University of Maryland Center for Environmental Science. She holds a doctorate in ecology and has over 15 years of experience in designing, researching and evaluating science and environmental education projects within informal and K–12 settings.

Anna Wilson is a postdoctoral researcher in the Division of Sociology, Abertay University, UK. She worked as an academic physicist for more than 15 years before undertaking a PhD in education at the University of Stirling. She has worked previously in the UK, USA and Australia.

1

INTRODUCING CITIZEN INQUIRY

*Christothea Herodotou, Mike Sharples
and Eileen Scanlon*

The term 'citizen inquiry' was coined to describe ways that members of the public can learn by initiating or joining shared inquiry-led scientific investigations (Sharples et al., 2013). It merges learning through scientific investigation with mass collaborative participation exemplified in citizen science activities, altering the relationship most people have with research from being passive recipients to becoming actively engaged, and the relationship between scholarship and public understanding from dissemination towards cooperation. Through the presentation of empirical studies, this edited volume introduces concepts and practices of citizen inquiry.

In citizen science activities, members of the public (volunteers, non-expert individuals, amateurs) take part in research activities initiated by scientists, such as identification of invasive species, classification of natural history periodicals or identification of galaxies. The notion of public volunteering in the practices of science is central to citizen science. This is becoming a widespread method for conducting large-scale scientific research (Toerpe, 2013). The main reasons for the growth of citizen science include the availability of technical tools to analyse the large amounts of data collected and the realisation of the power behind this paradigm: involving the public can offer a freely available source of labour and skills that can overcome some financial and logistical constraints of doing large-scale science (Catlin-Groves, 2012; Silvertown, 2009). The Christmas Bird Count is a longstanding citizen science project, launched in 1900 and sustained by the observations of amateur birdwatchers (Havens & Henderson, 2013). Citizen science activities offer benefits to scientists and the participating public. Scientists generate large and long-term data series that would be labour-intensive and expensive to collect through traditional experiments. Members of the public have opportunities to educate themselves in scientific thinking and how science works, appreciate nature and contribute to science initiatives (Freitag & Pfeffer, 2013).

The degree of public engagement with citizen science varies. Most current initiatives engage the public in projects that are generated and guided by scientists. The role of the public is to contribute to data collection and analysis, such as making observations and measurements. Yet, in collaborative citizen science projects, members of the public take part in refining the design of the project, analysing data and disseminating findings. Co-created projects are designed in collaboration with the public, so citizens are engaged in all the aspects of a research project from defining the research questions to collecting, analysing and reporting data. In collegial projects, members of the public initiate and conduct their own research activities independently from scientists (Shirk et al., 2012). The greater the involvement of the public in research activities, the more challenges emerge, including the collection of valid data sets, identification of suitable participants to join the research and devising a sound process of data analysis and interpretation. Yet, extending participation in citizen science projects could address some of these challenges. There is evidence that continued systematic involvement in citizen science projects produces learning outcomes in terms of increasing accuracy and degree of self-correction of observations (Bonney et al., 2009).

In this book, the notion of citizen inquiry emphasises the active engagement of the public in scientific activities that are not restricted to processes of data collection and analysis, and includes examples of citizen science projects initiated and implemented by volunteers. In citizen inquiry, the focus shifts from scientists to members of the general public as active agents who define their own research agenda underpinned by models of scientific inquiry, producing identifiable learning benefits. Trained scientists may be recruited as advisors, co-investigators or assessors. Inquiry-based learning is a learning process by which participants pose questions about the natural and material world, collect and analyse data to address these questions, make and test hypotheses (de Jong, 2006). It is intended to develop thinking competences similar to those of scientists (Edelson, Gordin, & Pea, 1999). A recent approach to inquiry learning stresses the importance of devising personally meaningful scientific investigations by having learners setting their own research agendas that match their preferences and interests (Anastopoulou et al., 2012; Scanlon et al., 2011; Sharples et al., 2015).

Inquiry learning is a problem-based approach to learning that requires guidance, in the form of cognitive 'scaffolding', to make tasks manageable, support learners' understanding and encourage self-expression and reflection (Quintana et al., 2004). This guidance can be distributed across teaching material including educational software, teachers and mentors, and learners themselves (Puntambekar & Kolodner, 2005). Structured scaffolding facilitates cognitive apprenticeship whereby learners develop skills by working alongside more expert practitioners. It can enhance learners' problem-solving skills (Quintana et al., 2004) and decrease cognitive load by drawing learners' attention to aspects of the task that are relevant to the learning goals (Hmelo-Silver, 2006). In this respect, citizen inquiry points to extensive use of online social networks and mobile technologies, with professional scientists joining not to instruct but to facilitate and support massive participation of the public of any age in collective, inquiry-based activities.

In addition, citizen inquiry is a new approach to inquiry science learning which can be applicable across disciplines. While citizen science was originally used to refer to public participation in scientific activities in natural sciences such as physics, biology, chemistry and earth science, recent initiatives make reference to citizen science activities in disciplines such as the humanities. For example, citizen humanities aim to identify how public participation in research can enrich humanities and cultural heritage research. In this respect, citizen inquiry perceives science and scientific activities broadly, to encompass both natural and physical sciences, and social and applied sciences such as education, psychology, sociology and medicine. One example of how the public could engage with scientific activities in the field of education is the provision of personalised feedback to learners. Teachers could propose and gather together alternative methods to solve problems and help learners in choosing a method that matches their understanding and ability, thus tailoring learning to individual needs (Heffernan et al., 2016).

As an innovative approach to knowledge development, citizen inquiry is situated alongside participatory typologies of learning. Sfard (1998) makes an ontological distinction as to what learning is, drawing from two metaphors: the acquisition metaphor and the participation metaphor. In the former, knowledge acquisition is the unit of analysis; knowledge is 'out there' for the individual learner to acquire. The participation metaphor shifts the attention from concept and knowledge to activity, action, participation and a state of 'belonging and doing' rather than 'knowing'. In Sfard's term, the participation metaphor points to no clear end-point to the process of learning. It embraces participation in communities and a constant move from periphery to the centre. Learning through citizen inquiry is participatory in nature; the level of engagement with scientific activities varies – from data collection to initiation and implementation of personally meaningful projects. Yet, participation denotes a shared interest in the proposed scientific endeavour and communication with others to share and negotiate ideas. Systematic participation can lead to the development of scientific skills and expertise and a shared practice evidenced in shared experiences, stories and tools. Pointing to a third metaphor of learning – 'change as a person' (Marton, Dall'Alba, & Beaty, 1993) – learning through public participation in scientific activities may result in changes to individuals and how they identify themselves.

The chapters included in this edited volume present empirical evidence about the processes and outcomes of learning as they have been studied in a range of citizen inquiry projects, to illustrate how melding citizen science and inquiry learning holds certain pedagogical advantages, including massive participation by the public in initiating and implementing personally meaningful investigations, the strengths of collaborative learning and collective intelligence for identifying scientifically sound solutions to real-life phenomena and the long-term engagement of members of the public of any age with online lifelong learning endeavours. Each chapter has been designed to ensure a steady shift of emphasis from theory to application in order for readers to understand thoroughly the current state of research in the field and its applications to practice. The key aims are to describe a number of case studies of citizen inquiry and their pedagogical implications, specify the nature of citizen inquiry by drawing from concrete applications, identify learning contexts where citizen inquiry can most effectively be promoted and devise practical recommendations on how successful citizen inquiry applications can be developed.

In this edited volume, 11 citizen inquiry studies are described. These studies were conducted in both formal and informal learning contexts and the majority of them concerned examinations in the domains of natural and physical sciences.

Three chapters explore the concept of citizen inquiry in educational settings. In Chapter 8, He et al. present the motivations of university students to participate in citizen inquiry and how these relate to level of task difficulty. In Chapter 9, Perelló et al. describe the introduction of five citizen inquiry projects in secondary schools and their impact on scientific competences and student motivation. In Chapter 10, Charitonos details a small-scale implementation of citizen inquiry in language learning in community schools and introduces the concept of 'cultural citizen inquiry'.

Three chapters examine the concept of citizen inquiry in the domains of social and applied sciences, specifically education and humanities. These are Chapters 10 (see above), 3 and 7. In Chapter 3, Dunn and Hedges explore the kinds of knowledge created in citizen science projects with the aim of helping the design of citizen humanities projects. In Chapter 7, Clough describes how a community of Geocachers integrated inquiry learning into their practices, extending the concept of citizen inquiry beyond science to domains such as history, archaeology and cryptography.

Six studies draw evidence about citizen inquiry from the domain of natural and physical sciences. In Chapter 2, Curtis et al. investigate Foldit, Folding@home and Planet Hunters, discussing motivations to participate in these projects and how they relate to opportunities for informal learning. In Chapter 4, Kloetzer et al. report findings from the Science in the City air quality monitoring project, in particular how active engagement of community members led to rich and diverse learning outcomes. In Chapter 5, Peterman et al. integrated embedded assessment in three citizen science projects as a means of systematically capturing volunteers' scientific inquiry skills. In Chapter 6, Ansine et al. describe how iSpotnature, an active online citizen science community, supports processes of learning through a five-step process. In Chapter 11, Edwards et al., drawing evidence from two citizen science projects in ornithology, discuss how project design in citizen science may have an impact on learning while they raise the need for a sustained dialogue between citizen science and inquiry learning. In Chapter 12, Aristeidou et al. conclude this edited volume with a set of design elements that can engage the public with citizen inquiry projects and contribute to the development of sustainable citizen inquiry communities.

In this book we propose a new perspective on scientific practice through crowd-sourced science that involves citizens and scientists in shared explorations.

There are insights here of interest to an international audience, including: educational policy makers interested in public engagement and lifelong learning and aiming to improve the provision of education through the use of online technologies; researchers in academic and non-academic organisations investigating the potential of online technologies for learning and engagement; and practitioners in the field of learning and education, including undergraduate and postgraduate students in education and educational technology, pre-service and in-service teachers, and educational software developers and advisors. This book will be a significant asset to these audiences as it introduces and explains the new approach of citizen inquiry, provides examples of practical applications of this approach to diverse fields, and discusses the integration of citizen inquiry in formal and informal teaching practices.

References

Anastopoulou, A., Sharples, M., Ainsworth, S., Crook, C., O'Malley, C. & Wright, M. (2012). Creating personal meaning through technology-supported science learning across formal and informal settings. *International Journal of Science Education, 34*(2), 251–273.

Bonney, R., Cooper, C. B., Dickinson, J., Kelling, S., Phillips, T., Rosenberg, K. V., & Shirk, J. (2009). Citizen science: A developing tool for expanding science knowledge and scientific literacy. *BioScience, 59*(11), 977–984. http://doi.org/10.1525/bio.2009.59.11.9.

Catlin-Groves, C. L. (2012). The citizen science landscape: From volunteers to citizen sensors and beyond. *International Journal of Zoology,* 2012, 1–14. http://doi.org/10.1155/2012/349630.

de Jong, T. (2006). Computer simulations – Technological advances in inquiry learning. *Science, 312*(5773), 532–533.

Edelson, D., Gordin, D. & Pea, R. (1999). Addressing the challenges of inquiry-based learning through technology and curriculum design. *Journal of the Learning Sciences,* 8(3&4), 391–450.

Freitag, A. & Pfeffer, M. J. (2013). Process, not product: Investigating recommendations for improving citizen science "success". *PloS One, 8*(5), e64079. http://doi.org/10.1371/journal.pone.0064079.

Havens, K. & Henderson, S. (2013). Citizen science takes root. *American Scientist, 101,* 378–385.

Heffernan, N. T., Ostrow, K. S., Kelly, K., Selent, D., Van Inwegen, E. G., Xiong, X., & Williams, J. J. (2016). The future of adaptive learning: Does the crowd hold the key? *International Journal of Artificial Intelligence in Education, 26*(2), 615–644. http://doi.org/10.1007/s40593-016-0094-z.

Hmelo-Silver, C. E. (2006). Design principles for scaffolding technologybased inquiry. In A. M. O'Donnell, C. E. Hmelo-Silver & G. Erkens (Eds.), *Collaborative reasoning, learning and technology* (pp. 147–170). Mahwah, NJ: Erlbaum.

Marton, F., Dall'Alba, G. & Beaty, E. (1993). Conceptions of learning. *International Journal of Educational Research, 19,* 277–300.

Puntambekar, S. & Kolodner, J. L. (2005). Toward implementing distributed scaffolding: Helping students learn from design. *Journal of Research in Science Teaching, 42,* 185–217.

Quintana, C., Reiser, B. J., Davis, E. A., Krajcik, J., Fretz, E., Duncan, R. G., et al. (2004). A scaffolding design framework for software to support science inquiry. *Journal of the Learning Sciences, 13,* 337–386.

Scanlon, E., Anastopoulou, S., Kerawalla, L. & Mulholland, P. (2011). How technology can support the representation of inquiry learning across contexts *Journal of Computer Assisted Learning, 27*(6), 516–529.

Sfard, A. (1998). On two metaphors for learning and the dangers of choosing just one. *Educational Researcher, 27*(2).

Sharples, M., Scanlon, E., Ainsworth, S., Anastopoulou, S., Collins, T., Crook, C., Jones, A., Kerawalla, L., Littleton, K., Mulholland, P. & O'Malley, C. (2015). Personal inquiry: Orchestrating science investigations within and beyond the classroom. *Journal of the Learning Sciences, 2*(2), 308–341.

Sharples, M., McAndrew, P., Weller, M., Ferguson, R., FitzGerald, E., Hirst, T. & Gaved, M. (2013). *Innovating Pedagogy 2013.* Open University Innovation Report 2. Milton Keynes: The Open University.

Shirk, J. L., Ballard, H. L., Wilderman, C. C., Phillips, T., Wiggins, A., Jordan, R., McCallie, E., Minarchek, M., Lewenstein, B. V., Krasny, M. E. & Bonney, R. (2012). Public participation in scientific research: A framework for deliberate design. *Ecology and Society, 17*(2), 29.

Silvertown, J. (2009). A new dawn for citizen science. *Trends in Ecology and Evolution, 24*(9), 467–471.

Toerpe, K. (2013). The rise of citizen science. *The Futurist,* 25–40.

2

ONLINE CITIZEN SCIENCE

Participation, motivation and opportunities for informal learning

Vickie Curtis, Richard Holliman, Ann Jones and Eileen Scanlon

Introduction: Social technologies in use

Digital technologies are profoundly social in use. They are developed and defined by participants who learn through iterative processes of participation. This is the case with online citizen science projects. Typically, scientists propose a way of conducting their research in a distributed fashion. They seek out experts in information and communication technologies (ICT), and sometimes the citizens they wish to engage with, to work collaboratively in producing and testing a distributed, online research project. It is through this process of iterative collaborative design that these participants both learn from each other and through the development and use of technology. But the learning does not end there. Once the online citizen science project is launched, citizens will need to be recruited and trained in how to conduct the project task, use and potentially further develop the technology and, in some projects, interact with other participants in the activity. In some instances, this learning extends to include the governance of the project as a whole. Participants in citizen science learn about not only the science, but also the norms, conventions, rules and technologies of a given project. This chapter explores some of these issues, in particular focusing on why citizen scientists register on projects, but also, crucially, what makes them stay and become productive members of a distributed research project (Curtis, 2015a).

Informal learning and motivation

Citizen science projects, including those mediated in part by technology, are not new (Jones, 2014). However, it is clear that digital technologies have extended both the scope of what can be achieved in a distributed research project and the reach to those with the potential to participate (Hand, 2010). As a result of developments in ICT, and the resulting increase in data production and storage (also known as the 'data deluge') (Borgman, 2007), some citizen science projects are conducted entirely through the internet. Participants learn how to analyse sets of data that have been provided by the project scientists (Wiggins & Crowston, 2010), and/or help to collect data on behalf of an online community. These projects have been referred to as online citizen science (Curtis, 2015a; Holliman & Curtis, 2015). They are characterised by their ability to allow citizen scientists to participate whenever they have time, and wherever there is an internet connection.

Online citizen science projects operate through websites that serve as the public interface of the project. Participants must learn how to use these interfaces, in some cases developing skills in constructing and displaying their online identity. Many projects also have online forums where participants can interact with each other and (in some cases) with the project scientists or developers. Organisers need to draw on analogous projects to develop rules and regulations for effective online engagement, and learn how best to enforce them, whilst citizen scientists must learn how to work collaboratively and/or cooperatively as they communicate with other participants (Holliman & Scanlon, 2006). When they work well, these online forums enable participants to discuss the project, share problems they may be having with the tasks, offer help to others or ask questions to scientists and provide opportunities for cooperation and collaboration between project participants relating to project tasks (Paulos, Kim, & Kuznetsov, 2011). In other words, these forums can act as engines for informal learning in citizen science projects.

A small body of data exists exploring the motivation to participate in online citizen science projects (see Curtis, 2015a, for a review). Most of these studies have highlighted a desire to contribute to authentic science as an important motivation. Few have considered the role of informal science learning in initiating and maintaining involvement in online citizen science projects (Rotman et al., 2012). In this chapter we consider aspects of informal learning in online citizen science projects by exploring the motivation of citizens to participate. A mixed-methods case study approach was taken to investigate three online citizen science projects in detail: Foldit, Folding@home and Planet Hunters (Curtis, 2015a). Using an online survey, semi-structured interviews and participant observation, the following research questions were addressed: (a) What are some of the characteristics of project participants? (b) What motivations initiate and sustain participation in these projects? (c) What opportunities are there for informal learning? Drawing together the findings from these surveys, we will explore how online citizen science projects promote informal learning of science, of technology and of forms of distributed collaboration.

Brief description of the projects

Three projects were selected to explore in detail. A number of criteria were used to select the projects: each had a different type of task and represented a range of tasks currently on offer to participants in online citizen science projects (such as pattern recognition and spatial manipulation tasks); each is relatively well established with an active online community; and the projects were managed by a team of scientists keen to learn more about the project participants and what motivated their sustained involvement. By looking at three different projects, we could consider different formats, and levels of difficulty associated with the project task, and explore whether this in turn affected motivation to participate. While 'success' of the project was not a criterion for selection, each of them has resulted in publications based on the effort of participants (e.g., Khatib et al., 2011; Novick et al., 2012; Schwamb et al., 2013). In some cases, individual citizen scientists, or teams of citizen scientists, have been co-authors on these publications.[1]

Foldit (http://www.fold.it) was set up in 2007. It is a computer game that utilises the problem-solving and spatial awareness skills of its players in order to determine the three-dimensional structures of biologically important proteins (Figure 2.1). While many thousands of individuals have registered to play Foldit, very few complete all the tutorial puzzles and become regular players. As a result, this project has a small, but highly dedicated, core community of players numbering approximately 200–300 (Curtis, 2015b). Foldit players can play individually or within a team, and are able to communicate in real time via internet relay chat.

Folding@home (http://folding.stanford.edu) is a distributed computing project where participants can download software which runs protein-folding simulations (Figure 2.2). These simulations allow scientists to explore the nature of the folding process, and have resulted in over 100 publications. In addition to just running the software, smaller groups of participants with skills in computer software and hardware have contributed their learning and expertise, resulting in improvements to the processing capacity and outputs of the project (Curtis, 2015a). These have been

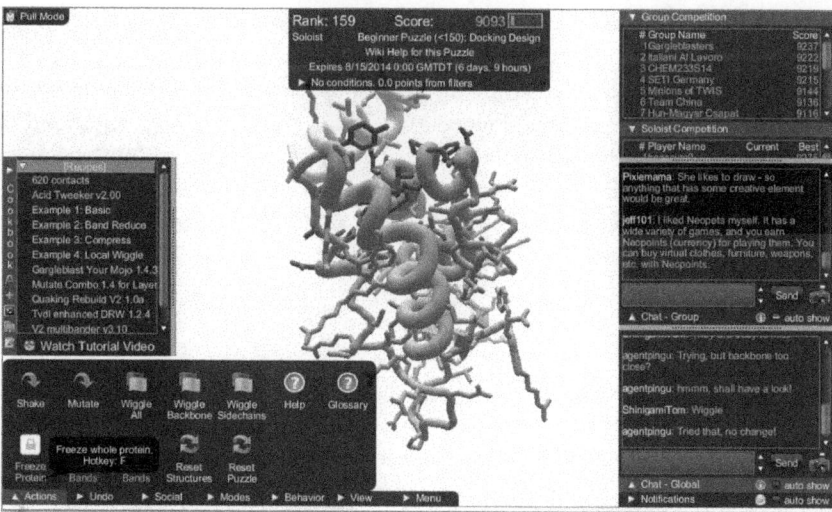

FIGURE 2.1 Screen image of a Foldit puzzle showing the puzzle tools on the left and internet relay chat window on the right (from first author's Foldit account).

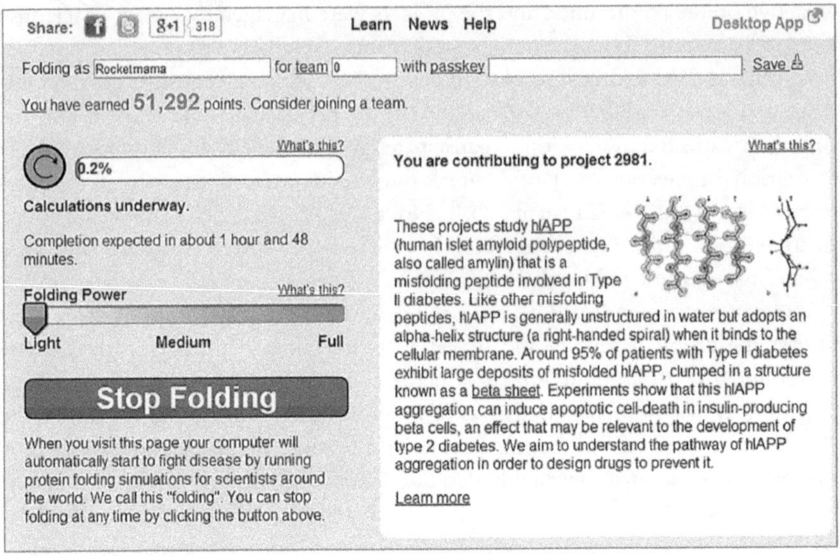

FIGURE 2.2   Folding@home participant progress page (from first author's Folding@home account).

considered the 'active' participants in Folding@home in this work and it is estimated that they may number 10,000. Participants are awarded points for the number of jobs they process, so there is also a competitive element to Folding@home. Discussions between participants take place on asynchronous chat forums.

Planet Hunters (https://www.planethunters.org) is one of the Zooniverse projects, a suite of online citizen science projects from a variety of disciplines. In this project, participants look for evidence of new extrasolar planets by analysing light curves obtained from the Kepler space telescope and looking for evidence of planetary transits (Figure 2.3). While thousands have registered to take part in Planet Hunters, a smaller number (approximately 300) have analysed most of the light curves in the dataset so far (Curtis, 2015a). Participants can interact with, and learn from, others via the 'talk' function, an asynchronous discussion forum.

Methods

The study took a mixed-methods approach and used participant observation, an online survey and semi-structured interviews to explore our research questions (Curtis, 2015a). Initially, participation in each project informed the development of the online survey, while the results of the survey as well as the continuing experiences of playing informed the development of the interview schedule. A protocol for participant observation was developed and strictly adhered to for all three projects (Table 2.1).

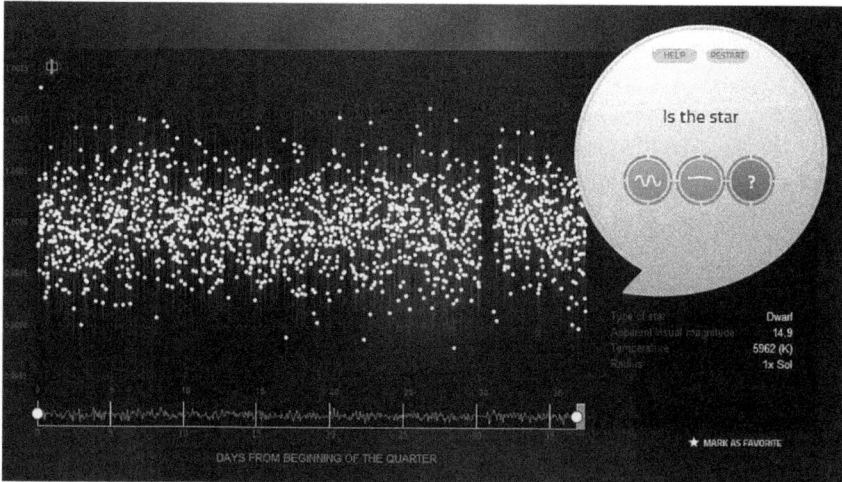

FIGURE 2.3 Screen image of light curve in Planet Hunters (from first author's Planet Hunters account).

TABLE 2.1 Participant observer protocol

1. Register with project
2. Download software, complete tutorials on project task
3. Register (when required) with online forum, and become familiar with project etiquette (e.g. online codes of conduct, presence of moderators)
4. Observe content and frequency of interactions between participants on online forum, internet relay chat (if available) and on project blogs. Identify key participants
5. Attempt to estimate active participants in the project
6. Take part in online forum discussions and internet relay chat when relevant or of interest (state research interests and affiliations on all first forum postings)
7. Explore other online project content produced by either participants or professional scientists (e.g. wikis, FAQs)
8. Participate regularly (4–5 times a week on average)
9. Write summaries of observations, reflections and any interactions in project diary during active participation
10. Compile a library of 'screen shots' to illustrate the online setting. These will supplement notes, and provide graphical illustrations of the areas where participants interact
11. Share research findings with participants

The online survey contained 28 questions which were a mixture of multiple-choice-based questions which related mainly to the demographic characteristics and playing habits of the respondents, and more open-ended questions that sought more detailed feedback relating to why they were participating, and what they liked best about the project. A link to the online survey was placed on each of the project forums with some background information about the research. Across the three projects, a total of 562 surveys were completed (37 from Foldit, 407 from Folding@home and 118 from Planet Hunters). At the end of the survey, respondents were asked if they would be interested in participating in further research which would involve taking part in an interview. Forty-three players agreed to take part in a semi-structured interview (10 from Foldit, 15 from Folding@home and 18 from Planet Hunters). These individuals were questioned once more about their motivations for joining and remaining with their respective projects in order to explore this area in more detail and to capture any responses or opinions that weren't given in the survey. Participants were offered the choice of interviews by email or via Skype, although only two participants opted for a Skype interview (each one lasting for approximately 1 hour).

Data analysis

Responses to the more quantitative survey questions were collated automatically by the survey tool, while the qualitative feedback from the open-ended survey questions was subjected to a content analysis. This analytical approach involves a close examination of textual data which is explored inductively for emerging themes relating to the same central meaning (Graneheim & Lundman, 2004). These themes were grouped into content or coding units, counted and illustrated graphically.

Interview responses were collated and subjected to a thematic analysis. This is a widely used method for identifying, analysing and reporting patterns (or themes) within data inductively (Guest, MacQueen, & Namey, 2012). In this study, the approach of Braun and Clarke (2006) was closely followed. The experiences of the participant observer were recorded in the form of field notes and internet screen shots. This material was reviewed and examined for emerging themes that also sought to address the research questions.

Sampling and representativeness

A potential problem with online surveys is that the response rate can be poor (O'Brien & Toms, 2010). Indeed, given the number of registered participants, the number of responses to the surveys was relatively low. However, the response rate needs to be considered within the context of active participants, and not necessarily the number of total registered participants. Observation of the three projects has shown that the number of participants who actively and regularly take part in these projects is a small percentage of the overall number of registered participants (Curtis, 2015a).

While this response rate may be better when viewed as a proportion of more active participants, it must be emphasised that the survey respondents may not be representative of the total population of active players, and can be considered unrepresentative of those who are inactive. The survey participants are a self-selected sample, and some individuals are more likely to respond to a questionnaire than others (Sterba & Foster, 2008; Tourangeau, Rips, & Rasinski, 2000).

The surveys could also be described as examples of 'convenience sampling', as they consist of individuals who were available and chose to make themselves accessible to the researcher (Battaglia, 2008; Castillo, 2009).

Those agreeing to take part in the interviews were self-selected and therefore the sample may be skewed towards those with stronger opinions about the projects who wanted to provide more detailed feedback. Given this context, however, it is important to note that this is a novel area of study that has provided significant insights into successful participation and learning in online citizen science projects.

Results

Characteristics of participants

Results from the three online surveys illustrate that respondents from all three projects have a number of shared demographic features. They are predominantly male (45 female respondents, or 8%, from a total of 562) and are mainly from developed countries (549 respondents, 98%). The next most notable feature of these three groups of respondents was how well educated they were, with 335 (60%) having a university education. Of the remaining 227 respondents, 97 were currently studying at a higher education institute. It follows that the majority of the citizen scientists in this study have graduate skills and competencies in independent learning. In effect, these participants had already learnt how to learn at an advanced level.

Many respondents (272, 48%) had formal qualifications in science, technology, engineering and mathematics (STEM) subjects, although there were very few respondents (36, 6.4% in total) who were employed as professional scientists or were in medicine. Individuals with a tertiary STEM education may bring pre-existing learning and expertise to the projects, either through their knowledge of the related science (e.g. two of the Planet Hunters interviewees had astronomy degrees), or knowledge of the 'scientific process' (e.g. the importance of rigorous data analysis, publication of results, collaboration).

The tasks associated with Planet Hunters and Folding@home were not especially complex, and there is no requirement for any previous knowledge or experience of scientific research in any of the projects investigated. As such, the barriers to participation in terms of the informal learning that was required were relatively low. However, Foldit is a difficult game to learn and play, and requires complex problem-solving skills and spatial awareness. This is borne out by the survey data. Of the three projects, Foldit respondents had a slightly higher percentage of both graduates and postgraduates, with a quarter of Foldit respondents educated to masters or PhD level (vs. 19% in Folding@home and 23% in Planet Hunters), raising questions about whether complex tasks like the ones in this project lend themselves to all citizens, or a smaller sub-set of previously successful learners.

Practically all of the respondents demonstrate a wider interest in science and report taking part in science-related activities and reading scientific publications and online content (only three respondents reported not taking part in any science-based activities in the previous year). More than half (52%, 293 respondents) had taken part in other citizen science projects. This high level of engagement with science may be indicative of the appeal of online citizen inquiry projects to those who have been described previously as 'confident engagers' (Ipsos MORI, 2011) or 'fans of science' (Priest, 2009). This reinforces the argument that citizen science projects, in particular those requiring significant levels of informal learning, are being populated from a pre-existing group of confident learners.

Motivation to participate

Table 2.2 presents a summary of the results obtained through the online surveys and lists the most important motivations that initiate and sustain participation for citizen scientist volunteers in each of the three projects. The number of individuals who gave these responses is in brackets. In most cases, two or three motivations are predominant.

Making a contribution to research is one of the most important motivations for initiating participation, followed by a background interest in science (or in computer hardware in the case of Folding@home participants). Planet Hunters and Folding@home participants admired the goals of the project, while Foldit players were curious and wanted to meet the intellectual challenge of playing.

TABLE 2.2 Summary of main motivations that initiate and sustain participation for citizen scientists from online surveys

	Foldit (n = 37)	Folding@home (n = 407)	Planet Hunters (n = 118)
Motivations that initiate participation	1. Contributing to research (22) 2. Interest in science (13) 3. Intellectual challenge (10) 4. Curiosity (8)	1. Making a contribution (to research or a worthy cause) (207) 2. Fully utilise computing power/hardware enthusiast (128) 3. Personal experience of diseases being researched by project (74) 4. Admire goals of the project (68)	1. Interest in the science (56) 2. Contributing to research (40) 3. Chance to make a discovery (26) 4. Goals of project important (11)
Motivations that sustain participation	1. Contributing to research (14) 2. Interaction with other players/ community (13) 3. Developing skills/learning (9) 4. Opportunity to be creative (8)	1. Making a contribution (150) 2. Ease of use/accessibility (75) 3. Overall idea/'concept' of project (54) 4. Competition (47)	1. Contributing to research (39) 2. Chance to make a discovery (29) 3. Easy to take part (21) 4. Community (10)

Making a contribution to research continued to be an important motivation for sustaining participation in all three projects. However, factors unique to a particular project continued to appeal to participants. In Foldit it was the chance to learn and develop skills relating to playing and interaction with other players. Folding@home participants liked the concept of distributed computing and found the project software accessible and easy to use. The possibility of discovery and the ease of participation sustained participation for many in Planet Hunters.

Feedback from the interviews with participants in Foldit and Planet Hunters mirrored the results of the online surveys, and participants re-stated their desire to make a contribution to scientific research, and an interest in the background science. The latter was especially true for the Planet Hunter interviewees, many of whom took part in amateur astronomy activities.

In Folding@home two groups of active participants were targeted in the interviews: those who were part of a group of participants (organised by the project developers) who helped to fix bugs in the project software, and those who identified as computer hardware enthusiasts making a significant contribution to the project through their greatly enhanced processing capacity. Those in the former group appeared to be motivated to join so that they could share their knowledge and expertise in order to make the project more successful. The hardware enthusiasts group wanted to make a contribution to the project, but also wanted to develop their technical knowledge through their interaction with other enthusiast participants. The results from the surveys and interviews suggest that both the research goals of an online citizen science project and the subject area are important considerations for potential participants.

Discussions relating to why people participate have also highlighted how participants view their contribution to their respective projects. For example, do they feel they are making a significant contribution to scientific research? How participants perceive their 'usefulness' may affect motivation to continue participating, and perhaps the quality of their efforts. Among those interviewed, there are differing views on individual contribution, as well as differences of opinion regarding the degree to which participating constitutes carrying out scientific research. Most of the interviewees clearly felt that they were contributing, and actively participating in scientific research. As participants explained:

> Love astronomy and science and it's great to get the chance to be part of some real science.
>
> *(Planet Hunters participant, male aged 46–50)*

> As a child, I would dream of being a scientist but as I grew up, that dream just remained a dream. Thus, when the opportunity presented itself to me to help scientists find a potential cure to cancer, Alzheimer's and other diseases, I was overjoyed and spent a considerable amount of time participating in the F@H project.
>
> *(Folding@home participant, male aged 31–35)*

> I feel like I'm doing core uncredentialed science when I'm doing Foldit, which I strongly feel is a valuable adjunct to science done by trained scientists.
>
> *(Foldit participant, male aged 61–65)*

Both the survey and interviews demonstrated that individuals are more likely to participate in a project that is also in an area of science that is of interest or relevance to them. While this was stated explicitly by a number of Foldit and Planet Hunter respondents in the surveys and interviews, and within discussion threads that were observed, it was more implicitly stated by Folding@home participants. The relevance of this project was illustrated in references by participants to loved ones who were suffering from the various diseases that are being investigated by the scientists associated with Folding@home (protein misfolding plays an important role in the development of Alzheimer's disease and Parkinson's disease).

Opportunities for informal learning

All three project websites contain background information about the science of the project that participants can refer to. These can be useful reference points for participants and help explain the rationale behind the project task. Interestingly, the opportunity to learn something new was only mentioned by 10 (out of 562) participants on the surveys as a reason why they decided to take part in a project. However, as participants get more involved, learning opportunities and working with other members of the project community become more important and were more widely given in the survey feedback for the things participants like best about their projects. Feedback from the interviews and participant observation were able to shed more light on the nature of informal learning in the three projects.

In Planet Hunters, interview participants spoke about what they had learned about the science associated with extra-solar planets, supporting previous findings that participation in citizen science can play a role in informal science learning (Evans et al., 2005, Jordan, Ballard, & Phillip, 2012, Jordan et al., 2011, Price and Lee, 2013). There is also some evidence that respondents may have learnt about the scientific research process. The tasks associated with Planet Hunters could be considered representative of aspects of data analysis in authentic scientific research. For example, in order to make a discovery a lot of data must be processed, which at times can be quite repetitive and may take many months.

Those involved in exoplanet discoveries (who constitute a very small number of participants, in the region of 50 or so) may get more of an insight into the various stages in scientific research and in dissemination of results. One respondent who had been involved in the discovery of an exoplanet talked about her experience sharing her findings with others and how she discussed her potential discovery with other project participants. This may have demonstrated to her the importance of verification, and of seeking out the opinion of one's colleagues or peers. A further insight for those involved in discoveries may involve an increased appreciation for the 'end-products' of science, and the collaborative nature of the effort required to produce results, and to produce publications – knowing that they are one of many involved in a single discovery.

Not only have some participants been acknowledged in publications or as co-authors in papers (e.g., Khatib et al., 2011; Schwamb et al., 2013), but some have found themselves talking to journalists about their experiences, as well as to other scientists and science communicators. This has given them direct experience of communicating about scientific research.

Through participation in Planet Hunters, discussion about the light curves took place asynchronously on a discussion forum with a dedicated participant moderator. However, these discussion boards did not appear to be used by many participants. Another route to communication was the 'talk' function where light curves of interest could be discussed with other participants. Again, only a few highly dedi-cated participants use this to compare observations and to learn from those more experienced. For the majority of Planet Hunters participants, their involvement is solitary, with minimal interaction with others.

In the Folding@home interviews, respondents refer to learning about the project software from members of the project development team and working collaboratively to fix bugs and make improvements to the project software. Other participants who are computer hardware enthusiasts talked about learning from others in sub-communities of enthusiasts. These participants came to the project with a high degree of knowledge and expertise and talk about the satisfaction they derive from being able to improve the project. While there is some educational material on the project website, very little of the discussion on the project forum is related to the science. Discussions between participants focus on the technical infrastructure of the project, and how participants can assemble their computer hardware in order to maximise their processing power.

Of the three projects, Foldit appears to demonstrate the greatest capacity for informal science learning. The difficulty of the game creates a high threshold for participation, and interviewees spoke extensively about how they learned to play. For some it was a case of trial and error, but the majority relied upon help from others. This help was derived from the real-time internet chat where any player can interact online. It is moderated by several long-term players who use it as an opportunity to help new players, and to facilitate collaboration. One interviewee saw herself as a 'teacher' of new players and posted instructions on guiding new players through the various game puzzles on the Foldit wiki. Foldit teams have their own live internet discussions which are visible only to other team members. This environment can play an important role in guiding and developing a new player. It is also where cooperation and collaboration between players can be witnessed as players work together to solve a particular puzzle.

In an interesting development, a group of Foldit players decided to automate a series of puzzle moves using the coding language Lua (https://www.lua.org). These players produced a series of 'recipes' that could be run to perform repeated steps, thus saving the players time. Certain players became known for this achieve-ment, and others soon learnt how to develop their own recipes. Some are shared with the wider playing community, while others were shared only with other team members.

The use of technical language on the Foldit forums was observed among players who have had no previous knowledge of protein biochemistry. A small core group of players (numbering approximately 20) have developed a high degree of specialist knowledge through playing Foldit and interact with the scientists and developers who manage the project regularly. In Foldit, the importance of the community and the intellectual challenge of the game become important as involvement becomes more established. Interaction with the community facilitates learning not just about the mechanics of the game, but with the underlying science. The immediacy of communication offered by internet relay chat is an important enabler.

Discussion

Motivation to participate

The reasons outlined by participants for their involvement in the projects were considered in light of a number of motivational frameworks that have been considered for other voluntary activities (Batson, Ahmad, & Tsang, 2002; Clary et al., 1998). However, the work of Ryan and Deci (2000) on intrinsic and extrinsic motivation was especially relevant. A basic distinction between *intrinsic* and *extrinsic* motivation has existed in the motivation literature since the 1950s (e.g. see White, 1959). These classic definitions were revisited by Ryan and Deci (2000) in the context of their Self-Determination Theory and their work has been particularly influential in psychology and education. They define and describe intrinsic motivation as: 'the doing of an activity for its inherent satisfactions rather than for some separable consequence. When intrinsically motivated a person is moved to act for the fun or challenge entailed rather than because of external prods, pressures, or rewards' (Ryan & Deci, 2000, p. 56).

They note that this is a particularly 'pervasive and important' form of motivation, and it has been increasingly of interest in understanding what drives people to engage in voluntary, informal activities such as online citizen science. They also write, however: 'it is critical to remember that intrinsic motivation will occur only for activities that hold intrinsic interest for an individual – those that have the appeal of novelty, challenge, or aesthetic value for that individual' (Ryan & Deci, 2000, p. 59).

By contrast, 'extrinsic motivation is a construct that pertains whenever an activity is done in order to attain some separable outcome' (Ryan & Deci, 2000, p. 59). In the context of online citizen science this could be becoming a co-author on a paper, or being identified as a discoverer of a new exoplanet.

While the approach of Ryan and Deci (2000, 2009) was relevant for many of the motivations for participation articulated by citizen scientists, some were not entirely explained by this framework. For example, one of the most commonly cited reasons for participation, the desire to help and to make a contribution to scientific or medical research, is based on an altruistic motivation or empathy that has more in common with other types of more general 'community-based' voluntary behaviour such as working with a charity, or volunteering at a local hospital (Batson et al., 2002; Clary et al., 1998). In addition to altruism, another important internal motivation is the desire to work with and be a part of a community; to cooperate and collaborate, in this instance as part of a distributed social group. This motive has been identified in previous work on those who write open-source software and Wikipedia articles (Hars & Shaosong, 2002; Kuznetsov, 2006).

Previous research on open-source software has also highlighted an important external motivator that relates to 'expected future returns' (Hars and Shaosong, 2002). Within the context of open-source software, this means that individuals may be rewarded for their involvement some time in the future in the form of revenues from related products and services, or career advancement through marketing and showcasing their technical skills (Hertel, Niedner, & Herrmann, 2003; Oreg & Nov, 2008). There appears to be a parallel to this motivation among some participants of the online citizen science investigated here, particularly those who have a more personal stake in the outcome of the research. For example, many respondents to the Folding@Home survey stated that their involvement in the project was the direct result of a loved one (or they themselves) being affected by one of the diseases being researched by the Folding@Home scientists. Some of the respondents to the Foldit survey also expressed this sentiment. Many of these individuals also hoped that their involvement would result in the development of a cure or therapies for these conditions.

A small number of studies have explored motivation to participate in citizen science projects (including online projects). As in this study, many have found that an interest in the science and a desire to help scientists were key motivators for participation (Krebs, 2010; Raddick et al., 2013; Reed et al., 2013; World Community Grid, 2013). Social interaction was also found to be an important motivator in some online citizen science projects (Nov, Arazy, & Anderson, 2011), as was a desire to learn from other participants (Holohan & Garg, 2005).

One of the more comprehensive studies to look at motivation and citizen science not only explored motivations for joining a number of conservation-based projects, but also explored motivations for remaining with the project (Rotman et al., 2012). The authors found that motivation was dynamic and temporal in nature. For example, an important primary motivator was a personal interest in the project combined with an interest in gaining something from the project (such as skills). As participants became more involved with the project over time, secondary motivations became more important. For example, factors relating to community involvement and the opportunity to develop a better understanding of conservation issues were key in sustaining their involvement with the project.

This desire for a deeper understanding of the science (often through the interaction with other participants as well as through interaction with the project scientists) was observed in Foldit and Folding@home participants. While learning as a motivation for participation was not often explicitly stated in the surveys, deeper questioning during the interviews revealed that learning more about the project, the accompanying science or technical aspects of the project, could result in sustained participation – sometimes over several years. In the case of Foldit, the knowledge acquired about the technical aspects of the game by some of the core participants has helped to drive its evolution and development, and has led to different sorts of scientific questions being posed by the scientists themselves.

Communities of practice

While individuals might be motivated to join a project, ultimately, the success of a project requires that participation is sustained over time – even if it is only a small number of participants that do the bulk of the work. This progression of participants from relatively inexperienced participants to experienced members of a core group of players who do much of the work provides an example of the 'reader-to-leader' framework in action. This framework, developed by Preece and Shneiderman (2009), describes the journey that some individuals make, from reading content, to contributing content, to collaborating with others, and eventually becoming a 'leader' of an online community. While the number of 'readers' may be large, the number of individuals moving to each successive stage rapidly decreases.

Some online citizen science projects eventually result in the establishment of an online 'community of practice' consisting of a small, highly motivated group of 'collaborators' and/or 'leaders'. A community of practice is a social or professional group that creates and promotes knowledge (Lave & Wenger, 1991). They can involve professional communities, and groups of hobbyists and enthusiasts. Learning takes place through legitimate peripheral participation in which new community members learn from experienced members through a fixed learning trajectory involving observation, feedback and movement through a set of increasingly specialised tasks. This was observed in Foldit and in Planet Hunters, with the emergence of a small community of core players who collaborate with each other, teach new participants about the project task and also have direct contact with the scientists and developers who manage the projects.

A community of practice was also observed in Folding@home, with the small group of participants who helped to improve and develop the project software. In these groups, participants are expected to become more involved and adept at the project task, or perhaps become involved in other project-related tasks such as moderating forums, teaching new participants, developing a project wiki resource or directly providing feedback and recommendations to the project scientists.

The findings of this research appear to corroborate the findings of other studies that have looked at online citizen science projects (Holohan & Garg, 2005; Krebs, 2010; Nov et al., 2011; Raddick et al., 2013; World Community Grid, 2013). Previous research on attitudes towards science has shown that those with a greater level of education are more interested and engaged with science (Ipsos MORI, 2011; RCUK, 2008). Such individuals may consume more science-related content and come into contact with sites and publications which promote and discuss online citizen science projects.

The citizens from the online inquiry projects investigated in this chapter appear to appeal to male, well-educated and scientifically engaged individuals who are also likely to be confident with computer technology. The lack of diversity in participants in some online citizen science projects may be related to a phenomenon known as 'threshold fear' (Gurian, 2005). This has been examined in relation to attendance at museums, art galleries and other public cultural institutions. It has been defined as the constraints people feel that prevent them from participating in activities that are targeted at them. In the case of physical spaces there may be tangible impediments that prevent some people from attending or participating (e.g. location or cost of entry), but there are also important socio-cultural factors such as gender, ethnicity, age, class background and personal history, that influence who takes part in these activities, and what kind of experience they have if they do participate (Dawson & Jensen, 2011).

One reason for the relatively small numbers of active participants observed may be unrelated to 'threshold fear', and may instead be related to something that has been referred to as 'participation bandwidth' (McGonigal, 2008). This refers to the total amount of time we have available for online activities. According to McGonigal (2008), there are ever-increasing numbers of social networks to join, new wikis to edit, new content to contribute and new games to play. We are exposed to more opportunities to contribute than we could possibly accept, and we only have so much time to contribute to online ventures. Therefore, online citizen science projects have to compete with other networks and online interests for the attention of those who are active online.

Conclusions

This study into online citizen science has shed light on what motivates and sustains participation. The opportunity to contribute to authentic scientific research is a powerful motivator that both initiates and sustains participation, as is a background interest in science. Opportunities for learning more about science were not widely expressed by survey respondents. However, participant observation and interview feedback demonstrated that participants learnt about the science underlying a project both through material provided by the project scientists and from other participants through their online interaction. Thus, scientists thinking about setting up an online citizen science project may need to consider what opportunities they will provide for informal learning and interaction with other participants, acknowledging that these may be key to motivating and sustaining participation. Opportunities for online collaboration were observed in all projects, but were most evident in Foldit. This was most likely the result of the complexity of the task, and the fact that synchronous communication was possible via the internet relay chat facility. The results of this research suggest that these three online citizen science projects have created opportunities for small groups of highly motivated 'confident engagers' to become involved in authentic scientific research.

These distributed volunteers have responded to a range of scientific challenges, and have self-organised into communities of practice to produce new knowledge and guide new generations of participants.

Acknowledgements

This research was funded by the Institute of Educational Technology at the Open University (United Kingdom).

Note

1 Questions remain about the most effective way of recognising the contributions of various participants in distributed research projects. We argue that some form of attribution is important, and this should be clearly stated when participants register their interest.

References

Batson, C. D., Ahmad, N., & Tsang, J. A. (2002). Four motives for community involvement. *Journal of Social Issues, 58*(3), 429–445. doi: 10.1111/1540-4560.00269.

Battaglia, M. (2008). Convenience sampling. In P. J. Lavrakas (Ed.), *Encyclopedia of Survey Research Methods*. Los Angeles: Sage Research Methods.

Borgman, C. L. (2007). *Scholarship in the Digital Age*. London: MIT Press.

Braun, V., & Clarke, V. (2006). Using thematic analysis in psychology. *Qualitative Research in Psychology, 3*, 77–101.

Castillo, J. J. (2009). Convenience sampling. Retrieved 3/12/16 from: http://explorable.com/conveniencesampling.

Clary, E. G., Snyder, M., Ridge, R. D., Copeland, J., Stukas, A. A., Haugen, J., & Miene, P. (1998). Understanding and assessing the motivations of volunteers: A functional approach. *Journal of Personality and Social Psychology, 74*(6), 1516–1530.

Curtis, V. (2015a). *Online citizen science projects: An exploration of motivation, contribution and participation*. PhD thesis. Milton Keynes: The Open University.

Curtis, V. (2015b). Motivation to participate in an online citizen science game: A study of Foldit. *Science Communication, 37*(6), 723–746. doi: 10.1177/1075547015609322.

Dawson, E., & Jensen, E. (2011). Towards a contextual turn in visitor studies: Evaluating visitor segmentation and identity-related motivations. *Visitor Studies, 14*(2), 127–140.

Evans, C., Abrams, E., Reitsma, R., Roux, K., Salmonsen, L., & Marra, P. P. (2005). The neighborhood nestwatch program: Participant outcomes of a citizen-science ecological research project. *Conservation Biology, 19*(3), 589–594.

Graneheim, U. H., & Lundman, B. (2004). Qualitative content analysis in nursing research: Concepts, procedures and measures to achieve trustworthiness. *Nurse Education Today, 24*(2), 105–112.

Guest, G., MacQueen, K. M., & Namey, E. E. (2012). *Applied Thematic Analysis*. Los Angeles: Sage.

Gurian, E. H. (2005). Threshold fear. In S. Macleod (Ed.), *Reshaping Museum Space*. London: Routledge.

Hand, E. (2010). People power. *Nature, 466*(5 August), 685–687.

Hars, A., & Shaosong, O. (2002). Working for free? Motivations for participating in open-source projects. *International Journal of Electronic Commerce, 6*(3), 25–39.

Hertel, G., Niedner, S., & Herrmann, S. (2003). Motivation of software developers in Open Source projects: An internet-based survey of contributors to the Linux kernel. *Research Policy, 32,* 1159–1177.

Holliman, R., & Curtis, V. (2015). Online media. In R. Gunstone (Ed.), *Encyclopedia of Science Education.* Dordrecht: Springer Reference.

Holliman, R., & Scanlon, E. (2006). Investigating cooperation and collaboration in near synchronous computer mediated conferences. *Computers & Education, 46*(3), 322–335.

Holohan, A., & Garg, A. (2005). Collaboration online: The example of distributed computing. *Journal of Computer-Mediated Communication, 10*(4), article 16.

Ipsos MORI. (2011). *Public Attitudes to Science.* London: Ipsos MORI; Department for Business, Innovation and Skills.

Jones, A. (2014). *'Science in the Making': A 1931/32 BBC experiment in citizen science.* Paper presented at the Sixth International Conference of the European Society for the History of Science, Lisbon, Portugal, 4–6 September.

Jordan, R. C., Ballard, H. L., & Phillips, T. B. (2012). Key issues and new approaches for evaluating citizen-science learning outcomes. *Frontiers in Ecology and the Environment, 10*(6), 307–309.

Jordan, R. C., Gray, S. A., Howe, D. V., Brooks, W. R., & Ehrenfeld, J. G. (2011). Knowledge gain and behavioral change in citizen-science programs. *Conservation Biology, 25*(6), 1148–1154.

Khatib, F., DiMaio, F., Contenders Group, F., Void Crushers Group, F., Cooper, S., Kaznierczyk, M., . . . Baker, D. (2011). Crystal structure of a monomeric retroviral protease solved by by protein folding game players. *Nature Structural & Molecular Biology, 18,* 1175–1177.

Krebs, V. (2010). Motivations of cybervolunteers in an applied distributed computing environment: MalariaControl.net as an example. *First Monday, 15*(2). Retrieved 3/12/16 from http://firstmonday.org/ojs/index.php/fm/article/view/2783/2452.

Kuznetsov, S. (2006). Motivations of contributors to Wikipedia. *SIGCAS Computers and Society, 36*(2).

Lave, J., & Wenger, E. (1991). *Situated Learning. Legitimate Peripheral Participation.* Cambridge: Cambridge University Press.

McGonigal, J. (2008). *Engagement Economy: The Future of Massively Scaled Collaboration and Participation.* Palo Alto, CA: Institute for the Future.

Nov, O., Arazy, O., & Anderson, D. (2011). *Dusting for science: Motivation and participation of digital citizen science volunteers.* Paper presented at the iConference 2011, Seattle, Washington.

Novick, P. A., Lopes, D. H., Branson, K. M., Esteras-Chopo, A., Graef, I. A., Bitan, G., & Pande, V. S. (2012). Design of β-amyloid aggregation inhibitors from a predicted structural motif. *Journal of Medicinal Chemistry, 55*(7), 3002–3010. doi: 10.1021/jm201332p.

O'Brien, H. L., & Toms, E. G. (2010). The development and evaluation of a survey to measure user engagement. *Journal of the American Society for Information Science and Technology, 61*(1), 50–69.

Oreg, S., & Nov, O. (2008). Exploring motivations for contributing to open source initiatives: The roles of contribution context and personal values. *Computers in Human Behavior, 24,* 2055–2073.

Paulos, E., Kim, S., & Kuznetsov, S. (2011). The rise of the expert amateur: Citizen science and microvolunteerism. In M. Foth, L. Forlano, C. Satchell & M. Gibbs (Eds.), *From Social Butterfly to Engaged Citizen* (pp. 167–196). Cambridge, MA: MIT Press.

Preece, J., & Shneiderman, B. (2009). The reader-to-leader framework: Motivating technology-mediated social participation. *AIS Transactions on Human–Computer Interaction, 1*(1), 13–32.

Price, C. A., & Lee, H. (2013). Changes in participants' scientific attitudes and epistemological beliefs during an astronomical citizen science project. *Journal of Research in Science Teaching, 50*(7), 773–801.

Priest, S. H. (2009). Reinterpreting the audiences for media messages about science. In R. Holliman, E. Whitelegg, E. Scanlon, S. Smidt & J. Thomas (Eds.), *Investigating Science Communication in the Information Age: Implications for Public Engagement and Popular Media.* Oxford: Oxford University Press.

Raddick, M. J., Bracey, G., Gay, P. L., Lintott, C. J., Cardamone, C., Murray, P., . . . Vandenberg, J. (2013). Galaxy Zoo: Motivations of citizen scientists. *Astronomy Education Review, 12*(1). Retrieved 3/12/16 from: http://dx.doi.org/10.3847/AER2011021.

RCUK. (2008). *Public Attitudes to Science 2008: A Guide.* Research Councils UK Department of Innovation, Unversities and Skills. Retrieved 3/12/16 from http://www.rcuk.ac.uk/publications/archive/publicattitude/.

Reed, J., Raddick, J., Lardner, A., & Carney, K. (2013). An exploratory factor analysis of motivations for participating in Zooniverse, a collection of virtual citizen science projects. *Proceedings of the 46th Annual Hawaii International Conference on Systems Sciences,* 7–11 January, Maui, HI.

Rotman, D., Preece, J., Hammock, J., Procita, K., Hansen, D., Parr, C., . . . Jacobs, D. (2012). *Dynamic changes in motivation in collaborative citizen-science projects.* Paper presented at the Proceedings of the ACM Conference on Computer Supported Cooperative Work, Seattle, Washington, USA, February 11–15.

Ryan, R. M., & Deci, E. L. (2000). Intrinsic and extrinsic motivations: Classic definitions and new directions. *Contemporary Educational Psychology, 25,* 54–67.

Ryan, R. M., & Deci, E. L. (2009). Promoting self-determined school engagement. Motivation, learning and well-being. In K. R. Wentzel & A. Wigfield (Eds.), *Handbook on Motivation at School.* New York: Routledge.

Schwamb, M. E., Orosz, J. A., Carter, J. A., Welsh, W. F., Fischer, D. A., Torres, G., . . . Lintott, C. J. (2013). Planet hunters: A transiting circumbinary planet in a quadruple star system. *The Astrophysical Journal, 768*(2), 127.

Sterba, S. K., & Foster, E. M. (2008). Self-selected sample. In P. J. Lavrakas (Ed.), *Encyclopedia of Survey Research Methods.* Los Angeles: Sage Reference.

Tourangeau, R., Rips, L. J., & Rasinski, K. (2000). *The Psychology of Survey Response.* Cambridge: Cambridge University Press.

White, R. W. (1959). Motivation reconsidered. *Psychological Review, 66,* 297–333.

Wiggins, A., & Crowston, K. (2010). *Distributed scientific collaboration: Research opportunities in citizen science.* Paper presented at the ACM CSCW Workshop on the Changing Dynamics of Scientific Collaborations, Savannah, GA.

World Community Grid. (2013). *Member study: Findings and next steps.* Retrieved 25/08/13 from: http://www.worldcommunitygrid.org/about_us/viewNewsArticle.do?articleId=323.

3

FROM THE WISDOM OF CROWDS TO GOING VIRAL

The creation and transmission of knowledge in the citizen humanities

Stuart Dunn and Mark Hedges

Introduction

Written in the mid-2000s, in the midst of the emergence of Web 2.0, *The Wisdom of Crowds* by James Surowiecki is an iconic and divisive study, which contends that – under certain conditions – collective decision making among groups of individuals is, on balance, better than decision making undertaken by individuals themselves, however expert they may be (Surowiecki, 2004). While this thesis, and the title which encapsulates it – a direct reaction to Charles Mackay's *Extraordinary Popular Delusions and the Madness of Crowds* (1841) – have polarised opinion, *The Wisdom of Crowds* undoubtedly forms an important part of the discourse on crowdsourcing, a term that emerged 2 years after Surowiecki's book, in an article in *Wired* by Jeff Howe. In noting that many companies in western countries were taking advantage of the emerging capabilities of the web to 'out-source' production tasks to cheaper labour markets overseas, Howe (2006) observed:

> All these companies grew up in the Internet age and were designed to take advantage of the networked world. . . . [I]t doesn't matter where the laborers are – they might be down the block, they might be in Indonesia – as long as they are connected to the network.
>
> Technological advances in everything from product design software to digital video cameras are breaking down the cost barriers that once separated amateurs from professionals. . . . The labor isn't always free, but it costs a lot less than paying traditional employees. It's not outsourcing; it's crowdsourcing.

Shortly after this, the long-established citizen science community began to capitalize on the benefits of 'crowdsourcing,' with Zooniverse[1] becoming one of the largest and most high-profile citizen science community platforms on the web (Simpson, Page, & De Roure, 2014).

The success of Zooniverse, which rested on a combination of a clean and attractive interface and simple, easy-to-grasp tasks, began to attract the attention of scholars working in the humanities, who reflected that the same kind of approach could be applied to the (otherwise costly) digitisation and enhancement of digital resources in their fields (Causer, Tonra, & Wallace, 2012; Lang & Rio-Ross, 2011). There were successes and failures in these early endeavours. For example, the *Transcribe Bentham* project at University College London offered a platform for the crowdsourced transcription of the handwritten works of the philosopher Jeremy Bentham; this was very successful, leading to the transcription of over 15,000 manuscript pages. Similarly successful was *Old Weather*, a project coordinated by the UK Meteorological Office to transcribe historic ships' logbooks with the aim of identifying historical climate data (Brohan et al., 2009). These are particularly prominent examples of successful early humanities crowdsourcing projects. However, key questions implicitly raised by Surowiecki (2004) remain: What sort of 'wisdom', or knowledge, is being produced by projects such as this? Is it comparable to knowledge produced in more conventional academic environments? Can the kinds of pedagogical structures embedded within those environments be applied in any way to crowdsourced knowledge, and if so how?

Context, rationale and objectives

We approached these questions in the context of our work on the PARTHENOS project (http://www.parthenos-project.eu/), a European project funded by the Horizon 2020 programme, which aims to strengthen the cohesion of research in the humanities in a broad sense by forming a cluster of research infrastructures and other initiatives across Europe, and thus building bridges across disciplines by identifying and strengthening commonalities and synergies. It aims to deliver guidelines, standards, methods, services and tools that can be used by its partners and by all the broad humanities research community.

The study discussed in this chapter forms part of a research activity tasked with developing a 'foresight study and interdisciplinary research agenda'. This activity concerns the evolution of the humanities research landscape over a 5–10-year period, and is addressing how digital research methods, infrastructures and tools in this field might develop, looking at the current state of the art, trends and requirements, and examining how organisations such as universities and funding bodies could help the potentiality become actual. The questions posed above, relating to how the public, and contributions made by the public, function in both the networked society and in academia, are extremely important to the project. The overall methodology involves a combination of literature reviews, interviews with researchers and other experts, and targeted focus groups and workshops.

The specific research addressed in this chapter addresses crowdsourcing, or 'citizen humanities', in the context of academic humanities or cultural heritage and memory institutions, which for our purposes we may define as the process of leveraging public participation in or contribution to projects and activities

(Dunn & Hedges, 2013), in particular for gathering, processing or interpreting information in some directed manner. As part of the present foresight study, 14 (to date) in-depth semi-structured qualitative interviews were conducted with key stakeholders from projects or organisations that are using crowdsourcing in humanities or social science contexts. Making use of the transformations that the web has brought to processes of collaboration and communication, these initiatives have harnessed public participation with a view to enhancing, augmenting or opening up cultural material, blurring the boundaries between the spaces occupied by professional and non-professional communities and transforming the relationship between cultural organisations and the wider community. Our aim was to explore this participation in greater qualitative depth, with the aim of delineating a future research agenda in the field.

The work built upon the results of an earlier Arts and Humanities Research Council-funded study, detailed in Dunn and Hedges (2013), which engaged with crowdsourcing project organisers and participants though a combination of survey, follow-up interviews and workshops, and sought to explore the rationale behind humanities crowdsourcing projects, and the motivations and experiences of those undertaking them. It also identified patterns within crowdsourcing communities and projects, and proposed a typology for describing different instances of crowdsourcing activities, which stressed the relationship of different kinds of tasks, assets, processes and outputs, some of which are discussed in more detail below.

Such public participation can take many forms, ranging from enhancing digitised documents through, for example, transcription of handwritten text (Brohan et al., 2009) or georeferencing of historical maps (Fleet et al., 2012); cataloguing, or more informally tagging or categorising, digital material to facilitate discovery and preservation (Greg, 2012); through to more complex activities such as commenting on or discussing content, adding contextual information such as personal experiences or memories, or constructing alternative narratives and interpretations. The activities thus range from independent 'microtasks' that are farmed out to individual participants – a model more akin to business crowdsourcing of the kind envisaged by Howe (2006) – through to participatory creation of complex information objects, or the 'social curation' of information (e.g. Hall & Zarro, 2012). It is noted that, while the term 'crowdsourcing' is frequently used as a catch-all for such activities, the group of active contributors may in fact be relatively small.

The study thus aimed to investigate such uses of crowdsourcing, to identify and examine emerging trends within crowdsourcing, to understand better how wider communities can collaborate with academia to create information and knowledge, and to examine issues that are raised by these practices. In this chapter, we develop this knowledge by examining the role of crowd decision making from citizen science to humanities crowdsourcing, which provokes the key question as to how learning works in relation to 'crowd wisdom'. The primary concern of this study, however, is the ways in which these activities create knowledge. As Dunn and Hedges (2012) found, the focus of most humanities crowdsourcing projects has been on the production and transformation of web-based content, rather than the generation of knowledge. With this first tranche of interviews from the PARTHENOS project, we aimed to gain a better understanding of how knowledge is created. Is this through the formal acquisition of detached and critical understandings which would be familiar in an academic environment (albeit one populated by participants who are, largely, not academics), or are the skills gathered by undertaking crowdsourcing tasks more generic in nature (Buehl & Alexander, 2001)?

Approaching humanities crowdsourcing in this way places it at the heart of contemporary debates on the role of networks and connectivity in contemporary society. Is it possible to identify, within the 'mass self-communication' described by Manuel Castells (1996), in which members of networked communities simply broadcast low-grade information incessantly to no one in particular, subsets in which the communications are directed and have an academic purpose? In such environments, individual pieces of information, or individual communications, can snowball in terms of their visibility: 'going viral'. The reasons for this happening are complex, and very hard to identify in individual cases (despite vast resources being spent on researching this, because of the commercial value of such information). Or is it possible to detect the kinds of 'co-production' trends identified by Bonney et al. (2009) in science education also in humanities crowdsourcing – or in 'citizen humanities'? The relationship between the research team of any particular project and its participant community is inevitably key (Ridge, 2014). The question of what attributes and characteristics such subsets of 'mass communicators' must have in order to produce useful knowledge remains unanswered.

A set of research questions were designed, drawing on the earlier investigation by Dunn and Hedges (2012). The overarching investigation had a broader range of research questions. However, the questions specifically related to learning were as follows:

- To what extent do participants learn through their participation in crowdsourcing projects?
- What sorts of thing are learned? For example, skills, domain knowledge, attitudes?
- How are the learning processes of participants facilitated and evaluated within crowdsourcing projects?
- Can these processes result in a demonstrable record of 'upskilling' that may be useful for future projects, or even for employment?
- Can crowdsourcing projects be designed with a view to building in concrete learning outcomes?

Methodology

The authors conducted a series of 14 semi-structured interviews with people having experience in humanities or cultural crowdsourcing. For the most part these were not academic faculty, but rather either practitioners from libraries, archives or museums who had been involved (in various roles, including operational staff as well as lead investigators) in the organisation or day-to-day running of crowd-sourcing activities, or researchers who had carried out studies into such activities and had a broader, albeit less detailed, overview of the subject. Each interview was conducted with a single interviewee (except for one case, which involved two interviewees from the same project), with one or both of the authors participating as interviewers. The interviews took place over a period of several months during January–August 2016. An audio recording was made of each interview and these were subsequently transcribed by an external company.

Individual extracts from the interview transcripts were entered into a spread-sheet (removing irrelevant 'filler' parts of the conversation) and were described and coded manually in terms of the following information (in accordance with a coding methodology drawn from Saldaña (2015):

- a sequence number
- an abbreviation indicating the interview from which the comment came:

  o Note that, although all information was anonymised, the characteristics of the interviewees' role(s) and the activities with which they had been involved were of relevance when analysing their opinions. Consequently, each interview was itself tagged with a number of codes that represented these aspects (although sufficiently non-specific to prevent identification).

- an abbreviation indicating the question to which the extract formed part of the response:

  o Note that, although the interviews were structured around questions addressing specific topics, sometimes information relevant to one ques-tion was provided during the response to another. Therefore, the set of extracts was analysed as a whole.

- the code itself, as described in Table 3.1.

These entries were then combined, sorted and clustered according to codes by the authors, and, alongside the full transcripts of the interviews, they formed the basis of our analysis. The analysis of this data was carried out by examining the codes for patterns and commonalities, interpreting the significance of what was coded and carrying out an initial categorisation, which forms the basis for the 'emerging themes' described in the following section. This analysis makes no claims for completeness – its aim was to identify issues or trends emerging from the data that could subsequently be investigated in more depth. Note that multiple codes could be associated with a single extract, and that the 'parity' codes '+' and '–' provided a simple classification of what is and what is not currently working in the areas under discussion during the interviews.

TABLE 3.1 Codes used in encoding the interviews

+	Corresponds to a positive comment about a particular topic, for example, '+ participants learned new skills'
–	Corresponds to a negative comment about a particular topic, for example '– not all participants learned new skills'
?	Corresponds to a question, for example '? How do we understand the process of learning?'
Keywords	A small number of codes corresponding to pre-defined keywords (or rather stems), for example, 'learn', 'skill'. While the overall objective was to identify issues that emerged from the data rather than to impose concepts upon it, this was useful for identifying parts of the data that were potentially relevant to the study (the interviews involved questions on other issues related to crowdsourcing)
In vivo codes	Codes corresponding to words or phrases extracted directly from the respective sections of the transcript
Open codes	Codes added by the authors to identify topics, issues and processes emerging from the transcripts. These were applied following an 'open' approach, which was deemed most appropriate at this exploratory initial stage of the research

Emerging themes

This analysis enabled us to identify a number of themes related to learning processes that emerged from the interviews, each of which is addressed in detail in Table 3.2.

Critical thinking versus connected thinking

All of the interviewees were involved in the production of knowledge of some form through the projects in which they participated. The types of knowledge

TABLE 3.2 Topics identified from the analysis of the interviews

Themes related to learning processes	*Brief explanation*
Critical thinking versus connected thinking	Discursive in-depth analysis of a particular element of content, as opposed to descriptive or non-critical synthesis across content (such as image tagging)
Use of generic platforms as learning tools	The extent to which generic web platforms may be used or adapted as learning platforms in the context of humanities crowdsourcing, and the limitations that are encountered
Use of primary sources	The opportunities that crowdsourcing can provide for users to engage with primary, documentary sources, and through this learn key historical research capabilities as well as attitudes required for critical thinking more generally
Upskilling and learning about processes	The potential for increasing skillsets in relation to processual activities

produced in crowdsourcing activities have not typically been widely addressed by the literature on the subject. Rather, the focus on crowdsourcing as a part of the research process in the 'citizen humanities' has been on the improvement and transformation of content from one type to another, the description of objects and the synthesis of information from different sources (Ridge, 2014: 23). This may be seen largely as a refinement both of Howe's description of crowdsourcing as a networked offshoot of outsourcing (Howe, 2006), and of Brabham's analysis, whereby crowdsourcing is a means of 'doing profitable business' (Brabham, 2008: 82). Significantly, in the cultural memory sector (museums, archives, libraries, etc.), much – but not all – of the focus has been on the production of unstructured knowledge content, such as blogs, social media and user-generated content, although this in itself has been hailed as a democratising paradigm in these sectors (Russo, Watkins, Kelly, & Chan, 2008). However, it is important to draw a distinction between democratisation and the freeing of content that would otherwise be stored with limited accessibility within an institutional framework, with the production of new knowledge based on that content. Following this distinction, it is also true that the purpose of academic crowdsourcing, at least in its earlier guises, has not been angled at the critical production of knowledge, as it would be understood in any of the pedagogical literature in the humanities and cultural heritage.

This production-based model, or rather set of models, was implicit in the typology of Dunn and Hedges (2012), which stressed the relationship of different kinds of tasks, assets, processes and outputs. The 'Asset' (or 'Input') categories for the typology concerned the different kinds of content that humanists work with, such as text, image, video and audio. The 'Output' category of the typology was described as 'the thing an activity produces as the result of the application of a process, using tasks of a particular task type, to an asset' (Dunn and Hedges, 2012: 37). In many cases, this involved dependencies of task types: for example, an output of the type 'structured data' would likely be a result of a project employing the process types of 'collaborative tagging' or 'linking'. This is perhaps inevitable, as the very act of structuring implies an act of coordination and agency; however, nearly all of the outputs described in Dunn and Hedges (2012) had the same forms of tangible properties as the inputs. The key exception to this was the output category 'Knowledge/Awareness', the description for which read: 'Increased knowledge of a subject (including practical skills), or increased awareness of a project or topic in the wider community'.

The early results of the current study make it clear that this description needs to be broken down further. As regards 'Knowledge of the subject', for example, Project C, which was concerned with the gathering of information from citizen archaeologists, noted a distinction between the development of generic practical skills such as time management and communication, and subject-specific aspects of knowledge, observing that participants 'may or may not get interested in the research itself'. In a similar vein, Project H spoke of 'really good training outcomes'. Project I, a transcription project, noted that the principles and practices of text encoding were a key skill that participants picked up in the course of their participation, but that they were aided in this acquisition. Statements such as these fit well with the 'practical skills' component of knowledge identified in the typology.

Other responses make it clear, however, that the distinction between 'practical skills' and less instrumental forms of knowledge is becoming blurred. Project N provides examples of this, speaking of the 'main intrinsic motivation [being] personal learning and some sort of personal growth'. This was a transcription project, of which this type of more reflexive learning is a by-product, but nonetheless one that was very valuable to individuals. Such knowledge can further be distinguished from the type of interest observed by Dunn and Hedges (2012), which found that some participants were *interested* in a subject such as climate change, and had a desire to make a difference by facilitating solutions to the problem of climate change, and from *academic* interest.

In the sample of projects investigated to date, the evidence for purely academic knowledge production remains anecdotal. As Project B noted, such knowledge production could easily extend to any kind of scale. However, we might at this stage propose a form of knowledge that connects the gaining of instrumentalist skills and practical competencies with 'pure' academic understanding, that of 'connected knowledge'. Many of the projects we surveyed stressed the importance of networks connecting the participants and those involved in running the projects. As Project D noted:

> I think it's more about the relationship then the technical side. So it's more about being open and responsive then about a specific . . . technical feature. Then obviously a very nice and user friendly interface helps as well. But . . . the core is this willingness to be open and responsive to the public.

What is not so apparent, as exemplified in the responses of Project I, is the importance of user forums, in marked contrast to significant citizen science projects, such as *Old Weather*, for which the importance of such forums was repeatedly raised by participants (Dunn & Hedges, 2012).

This appears to mark an interesting overlap with the focus of citizen science projects, which privilege intense collaborations between those who gather data about specific phenomena (of interest to the individual) in the wider world, and those who participate in projects on a formal and/or professional basis (Cohn, 2008). Such a perspective clearly privileges what one might call 'connected academic knowledge' over 'primary academic knowledge', where the type and quality of the knowledge gained are dependent on connections between those who are professionals and those who are not. The key distinction is that the tasks carried out by citizen scientists relate to the contemporary physical world. The tasks carried out by citizen humanists relate to different types of cultural content. When the *tasks* participants are carrying out are specifically aligned to types of *content* – as articulated in the typology of Dunn and Hedges (2012) – then the acquisition of content-specific skills can accompany the acquisition of primary knowledge, although the latter remains more nebulous, and less easy to document, than the former.

Use of generic platforms as learning tools

The use of generic web platforms and tools raises important questions for academic crowdsourcing, and in particular for the concept of 'connected learning', developed above. In particular, it speaks to the manner in which tasks and processes are determined (or not) by the capabilities of the contemporary web environment, and how these impact on the abilities of participants to gain skills which, in the general population, are becoming increasingly common, but which are not generally applied to academic problems. While the use of social media platforms can be a good way to engage communities with a particular project or subject, they only enable very particular kinds of (generic) task, such as the publication of bites of information. The lack of tools and platforms that can be easily customised for specific crowdsourcing processes is, arguably, a major barrier to the wider uptake of crowdsourcing in academic environments, and to their general utility even for the kinds of instrumentalist purposes envisaged by Brabham (2008), and extrapolated by Dunn and Hedges (2013) and Ridge (2014). The need for customisation to achieve the primary purposes of a project was highlighted in the interview responses. In their answers regarding the main challenges and opportunities for the future of the field, Project I stated that the absence of a transcription tool that was easily customisable and thus usable for different projects was a hindrance to wider uptake of their work. Also, in the same project, the respondents noted that there was a lack of collaboration among users of the platform: any communication tended to be with the project staff, rather than between or amongst themselves. This meant that there was no requirement for social media tools or forum platforms, which could enable mass communication. Project M discussed amateur researchers contributing to the Wikimedia platform, and what they learned in the process of adding content to such a synthesised environment:

> it's sort of deeper learning; learning by doing because you are very much involved in the topic itself, your interest for knowledge is guiding your activities and in doing so it's very practical, learning about the issue itself as well as perhaps any kind of tools and technologies that revolve around that. Yes and the motivation is sort of inbuilt into that.

However, Wikimedia is not a platform that might be considered 'generic' in the context of the present paper. Rather, it is a tool (or a set of tools) that facilitates collective endeavour (including, in the view of the interviewee expressed above, connected learning), which can be related directly to the following terms from the typology of Dunn and Hedges (2012): structured data, cataloguing and editing.

Another of the projects we have surveyed in this phase of the research has made use of a generic platform, namely Project M, which used Flickr to tag photos of botanical specimens with their correct names. This represented a two-pronged approach to the use of Flickr as an educational tool: firstly, the participants had to undertake independent research to discover the correct label to apply to a particular photo, and secondly they learned about the process of botanical taxonomy by the very act of making connections between tags and objects. That fact that K and M are the only projects in our sample that accord directly with a certain mode of crowdsourcing – that termed 'collaborative tagging', in the terminology of Dunn and Hedges (2012) – indicates the scale of the problem identified by Project I. Other online social tools – for example Twitter, Facebook or Instagram – do not have an explicit alignment of purpose, and thus do not feature in our respondents' accounts.

On the other hand, the emergence of academic crowdsourcing, and of the kind of aggregated data through what we describe in this chapter as 'connected learning', has *driven* the development of online tools in certain specialist areas. For example, crowdsourced maps and gazetteers created online by distributed groups of users/contributors are in fact composites of multiple individual perspectives, rendered through the digital medium into a convergent structure of points, lines and polygons. The desire to share contributions of a certain specific type ('geospatial data' in the 'Asset' terminology of Dunn & Hedges, 2012) has led to the emergence of tools dealing with specific content (asset) types but of generic application, such as OpenStreetMap (www.openstreetmap.org). Major corporations such as Google are making use of such local tools to crowdsource local knowledge, in the form of Google MapMaker (http://www.google.co.uk/mapmaker). MapMaker invites Google's users to upload data about areas with which they are directly familiar, to 'improve the map of places that matter to you'. Such tools have not displaced online digitisations of maps derived from a paper version, for example, Sylvia Ioannou's online map library (http://www.sylviaioannoufoundation.org), the well-known Rumsey Collection (http://www.davidrumsey.com), or the British Library's online maps processed by its Georeferencer project (http://bl.uk/maps).

Despite their divergent provenance – crowdsourced or not crowdsourced – all digital maps employ a common mode of representation, namely the same way of 'reading' the earth's surface, using the 'spatial primitives' of points, lines and polygons (Lock, 2010). This makes the tools more a function of data organisation, rather than representation. Several studies (e.g. Haklay, 2010) have suggested that such geodata-based tools derived from crowdsourced data are at least as good as those provided by official agencies. However, biases persist in aspects such as labelling and the attribution of significance to certain feature types. As several recent studies have shown, maps of the world derived from volunteered geographic information (VGI), such as OpenStreetMap (OSM), are conditioned by biases, sometimes extreme biases, in their contributor bases. Stephens, for example, has demonstrated that OSM's user base is overwhelmingly male, and that the platform is a male-dominated environment, both in terms of percentages of those contributing to it and in terms of the amenities included via OSM's user voting process (i.e. amenities of likely interest to a male audience are significantly more stable and thoroughly represented than those of likely interest to a female one) (Stephens, 2013). OSM therefore represents a primarily 'male reading' of the world. A base map may give an appearance of objectivity, but the psychological processes involved in its creation mean this is not so; and as an object, or rather a product, of 'connected learning', OSM is in fact extremely flawed.

Use of primary sources

The ability to work with primary documentary sources is of course a key research skill of the historian and one that is explicitly addressed in university-level education. There has in addition been for some years a body of research showing the value of engagement with primary sources as an educational practice at high school level, and that student performance is improved through these practices, given the close relationship between the skills and attitudes required for engaging with primary sources and those required for critical thinking in general when dealing with information processing and analysis activities in other contexts, for example in the work of Wineburg (2001). A study in which school students carried out document analysis with primary sources from the Library of Congress (Tally and Goldenberg, 2005) revealed the extent to which school students can learn 'historical thinking' through engaging with primary sources.

Research in humanities crowdsourcing has also revealed the learning effect of primary source engagement among a broader community. One of the key process types in this regard, according to the typology mentioned above, is *transcribing*, which is one of the most prominent forms of humanities crowdsourcing, and addresses the computational issue that handwritten text, in particular the older and unfamiliar forms of handwriting encountered in historical documents, cannot be transformed easily into searchable and machine-processable text files using current optical character recognition (OCR) technology, but requires human judgement and interpretation if sense is to be made of it.

Two crowdsourcing projects in recent years have contributed significantly to the prominence of transcription in this field: *Transcribe Bentham* and *Old Weather*. The aim of *Transcribe Bentham* was to encourage volunteers to transcribe and, more generally, engage with unpublished manuscripts (including philosophical works and, more recently, correspondence) by the philosopher and social reformer Jeremy Bentham (1748–1832). The project 'invites the public to play a part in academic research and attempts to break down traditional barriers' (Causer et al., 2012), by supporting them in the process of transcribing the documents into text marked up using the Text Encoding Initiative (TEI) XML standard, a format that has been widely adopted in the digital humanities community as the standard encoding for marking up textual data with structural and semantic information and for publishing digital scholarly editions (Mylonas & Renear, 1999; Pierazzo, 2011). The volunteers have thus been contributing to an online and searchable edition of the *Collected Works of Jeremy Bentham*.

Old Weather was also based on the need to digitise content that was not amenable to purely automated methods, in this case logbooks of ships of the British Royal Navy (Brohan et al., 2009). The initial aim was to transcribe the weather observations they contained, information of great significance for climate research, although as the project developed the participants transcribed a wide range of additional material from the logs, according to their own interests. In this case the output type was different from that in *Transcribe Bentham*, being plain text without additional mark-up.

The early results of the current study have provided some practical confirmation of concrete learning outcomes through engagement with primary historical sources, although this is still anecdotal, as only six projects had been involved in projects of this type. However, the results are suggestive as the target communities involved include not only school and university-level students, but also the broader community. Project I, for example, has incorporated their crowdsourcing interface into university classrooms, with students working on the transcription of a variety of historical document collections from the university library, and they note that students 'are definitely learning historical research using primary documents'. They additionally remark that, while the students of course learned such skills before, an advantage of using the crowdsourcing platform was that it provides 'a really hands on approach with a real tangible attachment to a real story'. The research skills go beyond transcription *per se*; in the case of some historical letters whose author was still living, they were able to contact the author and not only learn contextual information but also interviewing skills that were not possible previously.

As well as the fact of transcription itself, the transformation of the primary sources through crowdsourcing may require a degree of interpretation of the text, and the collection and assembly of contextual information necessary to understand the sources. For example, during the crowdsourced transcription of a set of 17th–20th-century culinary manuscripts,

> simply the act of transcribing has forced people to find alternative ways of measurement. There are all sorts of vernacular ways of measuring ingredients in the 1600s and so in order to accurately transcribe these materials, these transcribers would have to do historical research to find out actually how they measured and how they talked about different quantities and units of quantities.
>
> *(Project I)*

In other cases, the interpretation of certain words in letters required transcribers to:

> have to dig into the events surrounding the letter . . . in order to tease out some of the words that they couldn't understand. Once you have an understanding of the historical context, you're much easier able to figure out what these particular words are.

Project K also confirms that participants 'are motivated to learn new skills that aren't strictly related to the project because they want to do more with the things that they've found in the project', and also notes 'source familiarity' as a key outcome that facilitates learning, specifically because 'that process of looking at a lot of records of the same kind means that people have the skill to spot something that's unusual'.

Project K suggested that the learning outcomes can, with appropriate commitment of time and effort, be much more extensive. The *Marine Lives* transcription project, for example, is creating an academically respectable digital edition of 17th-century manuscripts originating in the High Court of Admiralty, London, through the participation of volunteers. Here, potential participants are required to commit themselves to dedicating the time and effort required to learn the required skills, which are significant in extent (including, for example, palaeography), in return for a guaranteed level of support from the project organisers. Participants have in this case come up with their own research questions and taken them further independently. There is thus a framework that builds in concrete learning outcomes from the start, rather (as in most crowdsourcing projects) than allowing them to develop organically in response to the circumstances that arise.

While 'learning behaviours are apparent in a lot of projects', as Project K observes, in most cases they emerge from the core activities of a project rather than being one of the core activities. The Project K interview also observes that from an analysis of:

> forums and social media and other kind of discussion about projects . . . you could see a lot of mutual support and that process of answering questions as well as asking questions. And even just the process of noting what you'd noticed shows a certain amount of learning.

The importance of a forum, or some other platform for mutual support and community development, has been flagged in other projects (e.g. *Old Weather*) as of extreme importance for learning, and indeed for the overall success of the project.

Upskilling and learning about processes

As the previous section suggests, in most academic contexts, the production of primary academic knowledge is dependent on the methodological treatment of primary research resources. The typology of Dunn and Hedges (2012) explicitly highlighted the role of identifiable processes as linking primary resources (or assets) with *outputs*. These processes were:

- collaborative tagging
- linking
- correcting/modifying content
- transcribing
- recording and creating content
- commenting, critical responses and stating preferences
- categorising
- cataloguing
- contextualisation

- mapping
- georeferencing
- translating.

From our interviews, it is clear that the learning operates very differently in relation to each of these process types. Collaborative tagging, for example, was described as having been used highly effectively by Project F, in relation to the classification of faunal specimens. Through this process, participants gain very specific knowledge about the species they are working with: 'they're learning where these species live, when they were first described, how they were first described, how their distribution has changed'. However, as noted above, it is interesting that this was also the only project we investigated that has made use of an existing web platform (Flickr), which is explicitly set up and designed to support this task type. Linking and correcting or modifying content are both generic skills, which, while of interest to projects such as Project M, do not relate to any particular academic discipline, or academic skillset.

Transcribing text, of course, remains one of the principal processes of the citizen humanities (Dunn & Hedges, 2013). However, among the projects that we interviewed, those that were most concerned with transcribing text – Projects N, J and H – stressed that the degree to which participants learned about the process was somewhat limited: 'I'm not sure that someone who's coming to the *Transcribe Bentham* is gaining new skills. I believe they're bringing their skills to that project'. Learning, where it happens, is serendipitous, as was made clear by Project J, in relation to comments made on transcribed archive material:

> '[I]t's very clear that the main intrinsic motivation of our volunteers is personal learning and some sort of personal growth. . . . When volunteers are communicating about personal learning goals they're usually describing really acts of discovery. Moments of discovery or something that has really stuck with them, surprised them. Serendipitous discovery as well as . . . expanding on sets of knowledge that they already have. I think I would probably say, I would argue that these kind of comments are 75% new discovery and 25% building on existing knowledge.

> The absence of other process elements of the typology from the interview samples, such as recording and creating content, categorising and cataloguing, are either too generic to support any kind of learning, and translating, of course, calls upon a very specific type of skill.

Conclusion

There is little doubt that citizen science projects such as Zooniverse are agents, facilitators and creators of new knowledge in the scientific domains (Cohn, 2008). However, projects such as Zooniverse do not rely on what Surowiecki (2004) would think of as the 'wisdom of crowds', but on well-managed and well-directed interactions between professional scientists and their citizen collaborators. While the PARTHENOS foresight study described in this chapter is still at an early stage, we have been able to gain some insights into how humanities crowdsourcing (which the community is increasingly coming to think of as 'citizen humanities' after the model of citizen science[2]) is starting to develop its own models of knowledge production, based on connective relationships between researchers and participants. Within these, learning outcomes can be based on domain knowledge, but more often they emerge from core activities and processes, and are, in and of themselves, peripheral to the design, implementation and research of the project itself.

This, we argue, is the key distinction that has emerged between citizen humanities and citizen science. In citizen science projects, such as Zooniverse, volunteers/participants are typically invested in the subject area. For example, Dunn and Hedges (2012) detected this pattern strongly in the *Old Weather* project, which was concerned with transcribing and encoding digitised log books of ships from the 18th to the 20th centuries from the UK National Archives. As such it was an activity that linked citizen science (as a means of investigating climate change) with citizen humanities (as a means of investigating naval history). Most of the participants were concerned either about climate change and climate history, or the histories of the ships themselves. In the latter case, some grew their roles to the point where they could produce sophisticated and detailed historical accounts, which were subsequently published.[3] Greater knowledge of these – academically traditional – subjects, we found, was the principal learning outcome, and most analyses of citizen scientist motivations concur (Simpson et al., 2014).

However, the networked society that Castells describes appears, in the context of our interviews, to be facilitating learning – where at all – more in the processes surrounding the humanities than in the humanities themselves. These are not linked explicitly to what one might think of as humanities research methods, but rather they are generic forms of process that take on a greater significance when applied, through crowdsourcing, to research materials in the humanities. Whereas citizen science involves a shared investment in the *topic* in question, citizen humanities involves a shared investment in the *material* in question, and in the methods for dealing with that material. This affects the type and range of skills available to participants in this type of project. The explicit exception to this was Project M, but in a way this exception demonstrates the point: the Wikimedia platform is a highly qualitative tool for the aggregation of *any* kind of knowledge, and therefore one would expect those engaging with it to be motivated by interest in that knowledge, rather than in the process.

Following the review we conducted in 2012, the lack of intra-community collaboration among participants, and thus the lack of shared learning experiences, in the citizen humanities projects we examined came as something of a surprise. The emergent trends we observed in 2012 suggested that increasing digital connectivity with society would lead to more of this kind of activity, with resulting shifts in the power and trust dynamics of citizen humanities (and, indeed, citizen science) activities. Yet, all of the projects we spoke to either have not used participant collaboration platforms such as forums, or they have explicitly rejected them. What our early research in the PARTHENOS foresight study has confirmed, however, is that the relationship between the (professional) researcher and the participant (volunteer) remains the key ingredient of a successful citizen humanities endeavour. All of the interviewees stressed this; indeed, it is the one factor that is common to all of them. The participation, time and effort that volunteers bring to citizen humanities projects are 'rewarded' by the time and attention of professional researchers, who are in turn rewarded by the engagement of the participants.

Neither citizen science nor citizen humanities has benefited significantly from 'The Wisdom of Crowds'. There is no evidence that collective decision making, or collective learning models, have had any great impact on either domain, either before or after Howe introduced the concept of 'crowdsourcing' in 2006. Similarly, neither has gained the kind of traction associated with the term 'going viral' in the creation or transmission of academic knowledge. However, from our investigations so far, we can suggest that both require direction and management in their knowledge creation and dissemination processes, but that the properties of that direction have important differences. Principal among these is the fact that citizen scientists tend to draw motivation from shared interest in the subject area. While, of course, there are always exceptions, citizen humanists, by contrast, tend to be interested in, and – where at all – develop skills in, the methodological treatment of materials. The investigation is currently in its early phases; subsequent research, based on a wider range of interviews and on an extension of the scope of the encoding beyond the lightweight approach deemed appropriate at this exploratory stage, will provide us with a more detailed and refined understanding of this important distinction.

Notes

1 https://www.zooniverse.org/.
2 See https://connected-communities.org/index.php/news/citizen-humanities-comes-of-age-crowdsourcing-for-the-humanities-in-the-21st-century-event-summary.
3 See http://www.naval-history.net.

References

Bonney, R., Ballard, H., Jordan, R., McCallie, E., Phillips, T., Shirk, J., & Wilderman, C. C. (2009). *Public Participation in Scientific Research: Defining the Field and Assessing its Potential for Informal Science Education. A CAISE Inquiry Group Report*. Retrieved January 17, 2017 from http://www.birds.cornell.edu/citscitoolkit/publications/CAISE-PPSR-report-2009.pdf.

Brabham, D. C. (2008). Crowdsourcing as a Model for Problem Solving: An Introduction and Cases. *Convergence: The International Journal of Research into New Media Technologies, 14*(1), 75–90. doi.org/10.1177/1354856507084420.

Brohan, P., Allan, R., Freeman, E., Waple, A., Wheeler, D., Wilkinson, C., & Woodruff, S. (2009). Marine Observations on Old Weather. *Bulletin of the American Meterological Society, 90*(2), 219–230.

Buehl, M. M., & Alexander, P. A. (2001). Beliefs about Academic Knowledge. *Educational Psychology Review, 13*(4), 385–418. doi.org/10.1023/A:1011917914756.

Causer, T., Tonra, J., & Wallace, V. (2012). Transcription Maximized; Expense Minimized? Crowdsourcing and Editing *The Collected Works of Jeremy Bentham. Literary and Linguistic Computing, 27*(2), 119–137.

Cohn, J. P. (2008). Citizen Science: Can Volunteers Do Real Research? *BioScience, 58*(3), 192–197. http://doi.org/10.1641/B580303.

Dunn, S., & Hedges, M. (2012). Crowd-Sourcing Scoping Study. *Engaging the Crowd with Humanities Research. UK Arts and Humanities Research Council Connected Communities Scheme.* Retrieved January 17, 2017 from http://crowds.cerch.kcl.ac.uk/wp-content/uploads/2012/12/Crowdsourcing-Connected-Communities.pdf.

Dunn, S., & Hedges, M. (2013). Crowd-sourcing as a Component of Humanities Research Infrastructures. *International Journal of Humanities and Arts Computing, 7*(1-2), 147–169.

Howe, J. (2006). The Rise of Crowdsourcing. *Wired Magazine, 14*(6), 1–4.

Lang, A., & Rio-Ross, J. (2011). Using Amazon Mechanical Turk to transcribe historical handwritten documents. *The Code4Lib Journal, 15.* Retrieved January, 17, 2017 from http://journal.code4lib.org/articles/6004.

Mackay, C. (1841). *Extraordinary Popular Delusions and the Madness of Crowds.* London: L. C. Page.

Ridge, M. M. (2014). *Crowdsourcing our cultural heritage.* Ashgate Publishing, Ltd.

Russo, A., Watkins, J., Kelly, L., & Chan, S. (2008). Participatory communication with social media. *Curator, 51*(1), 21–31.

Simpson, R., Page, K. R., & De Roure, D. (2014). Zooniverse: observing the world's largest citizen science platform. In *Proceedings of the 23rd International Conference on World Wide Web* (pp. 1049–1054).

Surowiecki, J. (2004). *The Wisdom of Crowds: Why the Many Are Smarter than The Few.* London: Little, Brown.

4

COMMUNITY ENGAGEMENT AROUND POOR AIR QUALITY IN LONDON

Citizen inquiry in a citizen science "Mapping for Change" project

Laure Kloetzer, Charlene Jennett, Louise Francis and Muki Haklay

Introduction

Poor air quality is recognised as a massive health issue in Europe, especially in big cities. Medical evidence suggests that air pollution contributes to the global burden of respiratory and allergic diseases, including asthma, chronic obstructive pulmonary disease, pneumonia and possibly tuberculosis (Laumbach & Kipen, 2012). Various long- and short-term studies also conclude that there is a positive association between poor air quality and mortality rates (Rückerl et al., 2011). As became evident from our data, some London (UK) residents are worried by poor air quality. To tackle this issue, a citizen science approach was adopted, which enabled local residents, many of whom had not been involved in a project of this kind before, to carry out grassroots data collection. Citizen science – here, engaging citizens in research design, data collection, mapping and interpretation – is seen as a way both to get rich local data, and to increase awareness and learning in environmental issues. In this chapter, we will first introduce the air quality monitoring (AQM) projects, especially in Barbican Estate, which was the largest community-based longitudinal citizen science AQM project to be carried out in the UK. Following this, we will define the research questions driving our analysis of participation patterns in the AQM projects, and present our findings from interviews with volunteer participants. Finally, we will discuss the emergence, conditions and transformations of citizen inquiry throughout the projects.

Science in the City: Air quality monitoring project

Science in the City, a project commissioned by the City of London Corporation and funded by the Department for Environment, Food and Rural Affairs (Defra) and the Mayor of London Air Quality Fund, was initiated with the aim to increase public understanding about air pollution, its causes and effects, and how concentrations of different pollutants vary over space and time, in the City of London area. The project was coordinated by Mapping for Change, an organisation that delivers mapping and sensing tools to empower local communities in improving their environment. The project focused on two of the major ambient air pollutants, nitrogen dioxide (NO_2) and particulates, both of which are considered harmful to health.

NO_2 is one of the major air pollutants found in our cities and is largely attributed to the burning of fossil fuels (coal, natural gas and oil) and vehicle emissions. Industry and road transport are primary sources of these emissions across the UK. As an irritant gas, NO_2 can damage cell membranes and proteins. High concentrations can produce airway inflammation (experienced as a cough, chest tightness and difficulty breathing) and may lead to narrowing of lung airways, particularly among people with pre-existing asthma. Particulates constitute another significant contributor to poor air quality and vary considerably in their composition, size and source. They are made up of organic and inorganic substances present in the atmosphere as both liquids and solids and are classified based on particle size. There are three classifications of particulates: PM10 (particles less than 10 micrometres in diameter), PM2.5 (particles less than 2.5 micrometres in diameter) and ultrafine (particles less than 100 nanometres in diameter). In urban areas the primary sources include diesel emissions, domestic solid-fuel burning, construction activities and non-exhaust traffic emissions such as brake and tyre wear. These particles are small enough to breathe in and can cause serious health problems, especially with the heart and lungs.

Science in the City started with an ambitious community-led study conducted over 1 year in the Barbican Estate, where citizens carried out an in-depth AQM project using both low and medium technical approaches. This was further extended to other shorter projects (1 month) that were initiated in other parts of London, such as Westway, Catford, Hackney, Streatham and Silvertown (Figure 4.1).

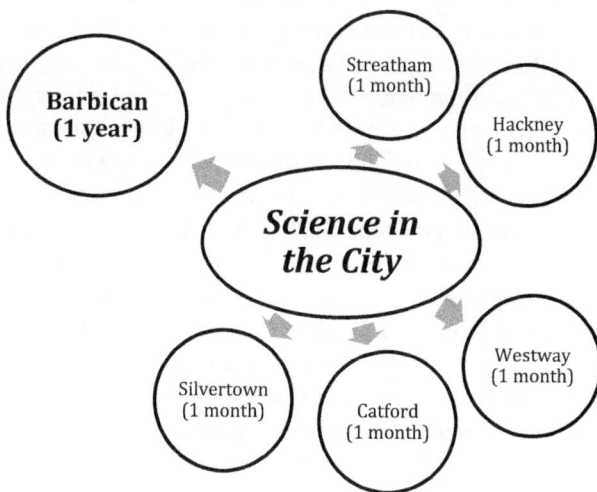

FIGURE 4.1 Science in the City.

The Barbican is a large residential estate within the busy "Square Mile" of the City of London. The Square Mile is known as a " pollution hotspot" and during periods of hot weather, health chiefs have advised the public to reduce their exposure to air pollution by choosing to travel on less-trafficked routes.[1] The City of London experiences some of the highest levels of air pollution in the country and recently it was reported that nearly 9,500 Londoners die each year from long-term exposure to NO_2 and fine particulates.[2] Informally it was known that a few Barbican residents had previously complained about air pollution to their local council, therefore it was viewed as an ideal starting point for the Science in the City project.

Mapping for Change started the Barbican project in October 2013. Residents were invited to attend a launch meeting at the Barbican Estate through various channels, including email, word of mouth, flyers and promotion by a local resident – a very active member of the community with a particular interest in air pollution. The meeting consisted of an introduction to the problem of air pollution in the City of London, current monitoring systems in place, the effects that poor air quality may have on health, measures currently in place to reduce air pollution and why this project was important. The meeting also included informal workshops to identify which areas the residents felt were the most polluted (hotspots) so these areas could be included in the monitoring programme. Residents were asked about what they felt could be done to reduce pollution. Two further meetings were held throughout the project to feedback results, maintain momentum and encourage discussion on key actions to take to improve local air quality.

With guidance from Mapping for Change, the Barbican residents put up diffusion tubes monitoring NO_2 in well-defined, specific sites. The diffusion tubes were left exposed for 4 weeks before being collected, re-capped and replaced with a new tube. The end time and date were recorded so that the exposure time, in hours, could be calculated. The tubes were collected by the local organiser and sent to the Mapping for Change research team and laboratory for analysis. This was repeated each month between October 2013 and September 2014, with the same pool of volunteers. Sixty-five NO_2 monitoring sites provided regular data over the 1-year period. All results for NO_2 monitoring were digitised using an interactive community map, plotted on graphs and shared via email with the residents involved. See Figure 4.2 for an example of the kind of maps that were produced.

In parallel, the participants had the opportunity to volunteer for monitoring their personal exposure to particulates (PM2.5). The routes and monitoring periods were selected by the residents so as to be more representative of their daily routines. These included static readings such as on the balcony outside their residence, journeys around the Barbican, their daily commute and several trips further afield. The SidePak aerosal monitor was charged up, switched on and calibrated prior to each use. Activity was recorded by participants in a diary. The GPS data were synchronised with the SidePak data using time as the constant to match the two datasets. Journeys and PM2.5 readings were mapped and shared with the resident surveyor. Once anonymised, the maps were shared with all the residents at a workshop and via the website.

FIGURE 4.2   Nitrogen dioxide annual mean at each monitoring site across the Barbican and height from street level (Francis & Stockwell, 2015).

From an environmental perspective, the project provided interesting scientific data. The results showed that NO_2 concentrations measured over the course of the year displayed seasonal variations in line with measurements taken over previous years from local authority-managed monitoring stations. A number of locations, such as Beech Street Tunnel and London Wall, were found to have concentration levels exceeding the EU annual targets (Figure 4.3). The interior of the estate, however, proved to be less exposed to the same poor air quality as that at street level, although residents living in the towers overlooking Beech Street were still exposed to potentially harmful concentrations of pollutants, even up to a height of 60 metres (Francis & Stockwell, 2015).[3] Mapping for Change took on a similar advisory role with the other shorter projects (in Catford, Hackney, etc.) – introducing residents to monitoring tools and mapping methods and helping them to get started with AQM in their local areas.

Mapping for Change have carried out surveys to gain a better understanding of the demographics of volunteers. For example, in 2014 (Francis & Stockwell, 2015), they surveyed 31 Barbican residents and found that the majority of participants were female (65%), the most popular age category was 64+ years (37%), the majority had lived in the Barbican for more than 3 years (81%), most had heard about the project via email (71%) and most thought air quality was "often very poor" (40%) or "sometimes bad" (33%). A complementary research project was set up to investigate further the experience and motivations of the participants, as well as the different kinds of learning and creativity that volunteers encounter.

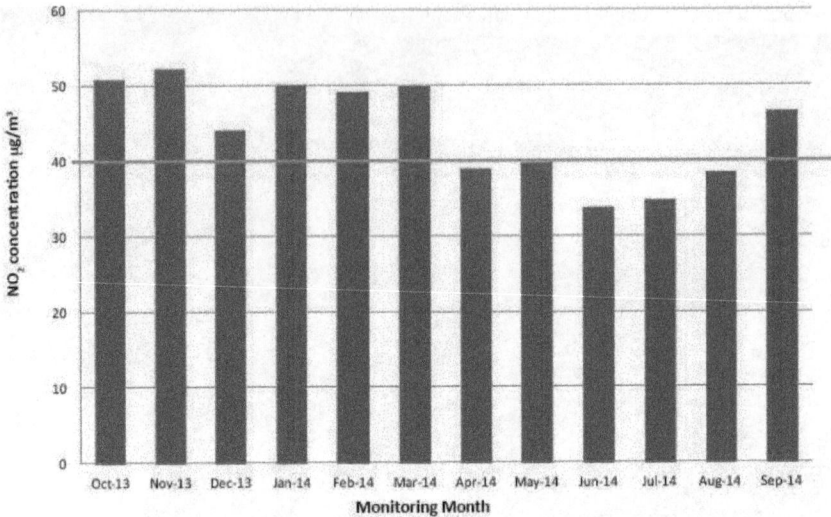

FIGURE 4.3 Monthly average reading of nitrogen dioxide (NO_2) across the Barbican Estate October 2013–September 2014. The line indicates the EU target of 40 $\mu g/m^3$ (Francis & Stockwell, 2015).

Motivation, learning and creativity in citizen science

In citizen science, volunteers work with professional scientists to carry out scientific projects. Examples include naturalistic, fieldwork projects like the Cornell's lab ornithology projects, or the famous Christmas Bird Count, as well as online projects, such as Galaxy Zoo (where volunteers categorise images of stars) and Eyewire (where volunteers colour in images of retina neurons). The Science in the City AQM projects can also be thought of as citizen science projects. However, rather than the scientists leading the project direction with help from volunteers, it is the volunteers (local residents) who are leading the project direction with help from the Mapping for Change science team. These projects are refered to as "extreme citizen science" (Haklay, 2010, 2013). By definition, citizen science projects pursue scientific goals. However, they also display specific social dynamics. A research focus on the participation patterns and experience of the volunteers is emerging in the community of scholars interested in these new forms of collaboration between citizens and scientists, as well as a more recent research interest for the educational opportunities that they may offer.

From an educational perspective, participation in citizen science projects has been demonstrated to trigger environmental awareness and improvement in scientific literacy (Ballard & Belsky, 2010; Bonney et al., 2009a, 2009b ; Crall et al., 2012 ; Cronje et al., 2011; Jordan et al., 2011), topic-specific content knowledge

(Crall et al., 2012 ; Jordan et al., 2011) and changes in everyday behavior (Crall et al., 2012; Jordan et al., 2011). Recently, some researchers have also argued that participants may experience a much wider range of learning outcomes, depending on their engagement in the projects (Jennett et al., 2016; Kloetzer et al., 2013, 2016). They have also highlighted that learning in a social community of volunteers supports sustained participation in citizen science projects (see also Curtis, 2015; Price & Lee, 2013; Rotman et al., 2012, 2014). The balance of scientific and educational goals in citizen science is therefore complex.

In parallel, educational researchers and teachers working on science education have investigated authentic science as a way to convey scientific literacy and passion among students. Inquiry-based learning approches, for example, create situations in which students can mimic and experience the scientific reasoning. Well-structured approaches based on authentic science – or science-mediated scaffolding of student investigation – have proved useful for science education (see, for example, a synthesis in Hmelo-Silver et al., 2007). As also demonstrated in other chapters of this book, there are good reasons to think that citizen science, which allows volunteers to be engaged in authentic scientific activities, may therefore provide good opportunities for learning and science education.

In our previous work (Jennett et al., 2016), we interviewed 28 volunteers and 11 scientists from several online citizen science projects (including Old Weather, BOINC, Eyewire, Bat Detective) to find out more about their motivations for taking part and their experiences of learning and creativity. Our thematic analysis revealed that volunteers are motivated to keep contributing to a project if they feel like they have an aptitude for the task, they enjoy the task and/or they enjoy participating in the activities surrounding the project (forums, chats). The most dedicated volunteers appear to get into a rhythm of regular contributions and they become increasingly familiar with other volunteers over time, becoming part of the core community.

Activities through which volunteers learn can be categorised according to two levels: at a micro level, that is direct participation in the task; and at a macro level, for example, use of project documentation, personal research on the internet, and practising specific roles in project communities. Generally, the more aspects volunteers participate in for the project, the more they learn. See Figure 4.4 for a full typology of the different ways in which participants learn and what they learn.

Creativity is an important and controversial aspect of participation and learning in online citizen science projects. Although volunteers feel that strict compliance with the scientific process guarantees the quality of their contribution, they sometimes offer powerful suggestions or creations to improve the project. Therefore, at the microlevel, engaged volunteers tend to follow the scientific protocol strictly and "uncreatively", whereas at the macro level, they might develop and share personal creations, as they are motivated by their sense of belonging to a community, and their desire to improve the project. Community-enhanced gamification, forum discussions, sharing of interesting or amusing pictures, creation of artwork provided excitement and enhanced the life of the community. Volunteers also

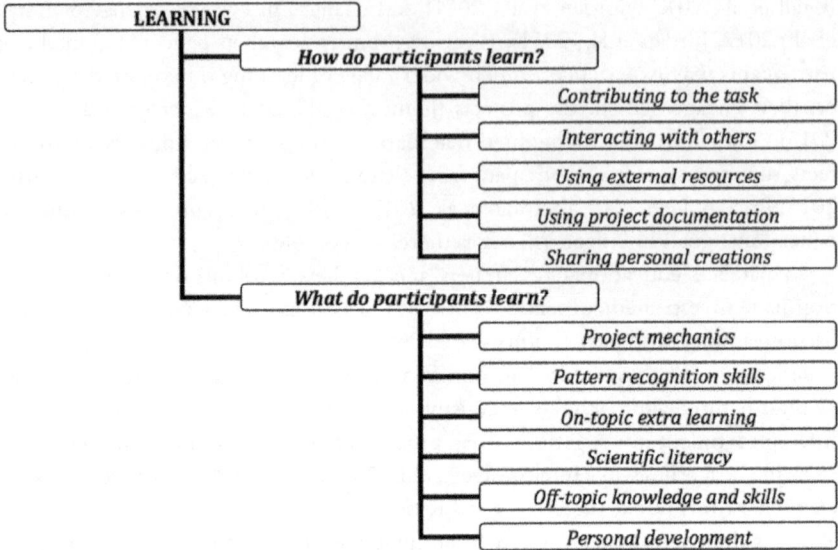

FIGURE 4.4 Thematic map of volunteers' learning (Jennett et al., 2016).

shared the project with others via outreach activities, providing new ways for the community to grow.

Based on our findings, we proposed the MLC model (Jennett et al., 2016), where we explain that motivations, learning and creativity are connected. The more volunteers participate in different aspects of a project (at micro and macro levels), the more they learn and the more their identity as a project volunteer deepens. Identifying as a project volunteer involves three aspects: self-confidence, feeling that they are contributing to research, and feeling that they belong to the project community. Learning is then connected to sustained participation through these mediations. Some participants may also produce some personal creations as a way to solve various challenges emerging in the course of participation, which also increases their motivation to participate and impacts recognition of the importance of their contribution in the community. Therefore, creativity seems to be strongly related to engagement: it can optimise both an individual's activity and the project itself.

Exploring motivation, learning and creativity in AQM

Building upon our previous work and the MLC model (Jennett et al., 2016), we decided to carry out a similar interview study with volunteers of the Science in the City AQM projects. Will we uncover similar themes for motivation, learning and creativity in the context of Science in the City? Or will we uncover different themes because these are local community-driven citizen science projects, as opposed to online scientist-led citizen science projects?

The research questions of the study were as follows:

- Which are the motivations of the participants to the AQM projects?
- Are there initially any learning expectations among the volunteers, and how do they evolve during the project?
- Which are the learning outcomes they experience from participating in the AQM projects?
- Which kind of activities and processes contribute most to these learning outcomes?
- Are there creative outcomes related to participation in the AQM projects, and how do they relate to motivation and learning?

Fourteen participants were recruited via an opportunity sample. Mapping for Change sent an email to participants of all of the Science in the City AQM projects, explaining that we were interested in interviewing participants about their experiences of AQM. Fourteen participants replied to the email, volunteering to take part: nine participants (52–87 years old, mostly retired people and independent workers) participated for 12 months in the Barbican project (2013–2014); five participants (30–44 years old) participated in 1-month-long replications and extensions of the Barbican project, in various areas of London (Westway, Catford, Hackney, Streatham, Silvertown) in 2014 and 2015. It is probable that these participants may be more engaged than average participants, as they were confident enough to volunteer to be interviewed (i.e. self-selection bias). However, we emphasised that we were interested in hearing about people's bad experiences of the project as well as their good experiences.

The interviews were carried out either face to face or by Skype. They were audio recorded and lasted between 30 minutes and 1 hour. The resulting transcripts were analysed using thematic analysis (Braun & Clarke, 2006).

Motivation to participate

In our analysis we distinguished between motivations for initial participation and motivations for sustained participation. See Table 4.1 for an overview of the different themes.

We comment here on two main findings. Firstly, the bedrock to participation in AQM projects is previous sensitivity to environmental issues. This personal sensitivity can be grounded in various personal experiences, for example, some participants complained about respiratory problems, including asthma, in their family. As two interviewees explained: "I'm interested in air quality because I've had respiratory problems and I have a young child and you know there are problems" (participant, Barbican project) and "I have chronic asthma and I have found that the traffic . . . the traffic pollution makes it worse. I had found that even with the inhalers, it seems to be a constant problem" (participant, AQM project).

TABLE 4.1 Motivation themes in the air quality monitoring (AQM) interviews

Level of participation	Motivation for the AQM project
Participation involved	• Hosting an air monitor for several months, every month sending data and replacing monitor, optional meetings • Additionally for those leading the project: bid for funding, coordinating with Mapping for Change, meetings with residents, writing magazine updates and local newsletter, email reminders to residents, forums, social media, liaising with press, setting up meetings with MP and council
Initial participation	*Personal health* • Suffer with asthma or respiratory problems, or have a family member who suffers • Worried about effects of pollution on young children *Interest in environment* • Involved in local Green Party • Building on an earlier campaign, want to expand this work and engage more people • Interest in recycling, pollution, conservation, green urban spaces • Raising awareness about air quality – "you can feel it is polluted" *Helping others in local area* • Asked by friends to help put up tubes • Read an advert in the residential newsletter, forum • Nice to live in a place where people take care of the environment *Lobbying for change* • Interested in improving things • Want to collect real evidence to persuade authorities to do something, help to build up a case – "it's good to have data" • Want specific improvements – e.g. "I want the council to do more monitoring", "I want Transport for London to change buses to hybrids"
Sustained participation	*Practical* • Doesn't require much effort to host a monitor *Community* • Nice feeling that everyone is working together • Enjoy publicising the project and engaging with others • Positive feedback from the community • Status – becoming more well known to residents • Feeling empowered, that you can make a difference *Research* • Sense of agency – we choose where to put up the monitors, which area to cover • Excited by the idea of citizen science, that you can do it by yourself

- Want to play a part in collecting good data, contributing to a bigger study
- Learning the results increases motivation

Accessibility

- Easy to understand, no intimidating jargon
- Like that it involves people who are not usually involved in science experiments

This existing environmental sensitivity is reinforced by existing local networks and social connections, which enable potential participants to hear about the project. Therefore, participation is triggered by a wish for efficient political action, in which scientifically grounded data play an instrumental function. As one participant explains: "I was obviously very interested to ensure that we were getting . . . collecting real evidence to try and persuade the authorities to do something about improving air pollution" (participant, Barbican project).

Secondly, consistent with what we observed in other citizen science projects, participants' initial motivations were found to evolve throughout the project. Feelings of contributing efficiently in a community, varied unexpected informal learning experiences and social dynamics, played a critical role in sustained participation. As two participants note: "I really enjoyed meeting a whole new roster of people on the estate . . . And it's a very nice feeling when everybody is working for a common objective" (participant, Barbican project); "What was really nice, it's a citizen science project, to get more and more people involved and it's something that you can do yourself" (participant, Barbican project).

Learning through citizen science

In their internal survey with Barbican residents, Mapping for Change found subjective evidence for air pollution awareness in the project. Over 90% of respondents agreed that their understanding of the health impacts of air pollution had improved as a result of participating in the project. Residents were asked how they felt about air quality around the Barbican Estate. The responses showed that at the start of the project 40% of residents felt it was often very poor and 20% always very bad, whereas 59% and 14%, respectively, felt this way at the end of the project. Only 7% believed air pollution was not really a problem at the start of the project. When asked if the project had made residents aware of any measures the local authority undertakes to monitor and improve air quality in the city, 92% agreed it had; however, only 23% felt "sufficiently" informed about its work to reduce air pollution.

This survey also provided evidence for some behavioural change: 82% of respondents agreed they would make changes to reduce their personal exposure and contribution to air pollution as a result of the project, including "greening up" their balconies with air-filtering plants, avoiding Beech Street tunnel and other hotspots, reducing their use of private transport and collecting parcels rather than having them delivered. As a direct result of the NO_2 monitoring, some residents have decided only to open the windows of their flat that face inwards into the Estate rather than a roadside window or avoid opening windows and vents at peak traffic times. The project also supported the residents in making various structured suggestions to the City Corporation (the local government), including "greening up" the area with more trees, plants and living walls, closing Beech Street tunnel to traffic or improving its ventilation, introducing penalties for idling taxis, delivery vehicles and buses, encouraging the use of electric buses and private vehicles by promoting and installing more charging points in the area and extending the Ultra Low Emission Zone.

We found that our interview study complemented these survey findings, while at the same time providing a more in-depth understanding of the wide variety of learning outcomes that AQM volunteers experience. See Table 4.2 for a summary of the main learning outcomes and main learning processes from participation in AQM projects.

First, people mostly enjoyed the experience, especially the feeling of being able to contribute efficiently as a community, although they had no prior experience in the field. As one participant explained:

> It just felt great that a group of volunteers that had no experience of collecting pollution data were just able to go out there and run a project and then you send it off and get some real data that's valuable, you can put it to good use and you can deliver some results from it. So I really enjoyed that aspect of this, I keep mentioning citizen science, but I just think it's really exciting that more and more things can be done from this approach.
>
> *(participant, Vauxhall project)*

Second, participants' learning expectations were connected to their main motivations for participating in this project, i.e. building a strong case backed up with scientific data to support their political action as a community. Reinforcement of the community feeling also contributes to empowerment of the community in this activist stance, and is therefore perceived as valuable. As two participants explain:

> I wanted to learn more about the mechanics of setting up an air quality monitoring system with a bunch of neighbours.
>
> *(participant, Westway project)*

> I was so interested in the final results. I think, we all thought that air quality was going to be very poor just around personal experience, and that it was a real issue. And it was very nice to be able to actually get data to have us back that up because when you're asking questions in the meeting, you don't have an idea of what to say. . . . It's nice to have the data up your sleeves to be able to present a case. So yes, I mean, I did learn a lot over the course of this, and I mean you're constantly picking up articles, people are sending links to you about other air quality incidents or data that's coming in from some other academic study or Mapping for Change type study. So you do get very much more up to speed over the course of the project.
>
> *(participant, Barbican project)*

TABLE 4.2 Learning themes in the air quality monitoring (AQM) interviews

Learning outcomes and processes	*Learning in the AQM project*
Learning outcomes	*Topic knowledge*
	• Distribution of pollution in time, space and height
	• Day-to-day variations of pollution according to atmospheric and traffic conditions
	• Different kinds of pollutants
	• Accepted pollution levels in Europe and effects on health
	• Link between taxi and car traffic and air pollution
	Awareness and community engagement
	• Raising awareness of the issues of air quality
	• Strengthening community feeling and community engagement
	• Better knowledge of the neighbourhood
	Public participation and citizen science
	• Understanding how citizens can be involved in air quality monitoring
	• Increasing political expectations of the City Council
	• Nurturing political claims by local communities
	For the coordinators
	• Communication and coordination, interpreting scientific results, mapping, writing synthesis
	• Using the tools and software
	• Leading a campaign through social media
	For some engaged participants
	• Creative ways of raising awareness and communicating findings
Learning processes	• Physical engagement ("I carry a ladder")
	• Collective project (they do it as a community)
	• Cross-fertilization of the local residents' community and the project community; therefore, pre-existence of a strong local community helps a lot
	• Collaboration with scientists

Third, the project triggered learning about air pollution, including a more complete and precise view of its components, risks for health and day-to-day variations, as well as personal environmental awareness. As these were two expected educational outcomes of the project, the project can be considered successful on its educational dimension. For example, the project brought a more detailed and nuanced understanding of air pollution:

> I think I learned that rather than a generic term "air quality" that there are lots of different components, so looking at the Mapping for Change website, there were lots of different layers that you could switch on and off. It made

you more aware of beyond nitrogen dioxide being a pollutant, that you also are looking at different particulates, so I think it gave you more of an in-depth insight and particularly which things might make you short of breath as a cyclist. . . . And why these different components of the air quality have a different effect and why some are more important than others to focus on.

(participant, Barbican project)

Another participant explained how the project changed the initial "modelling" in the community of air pollution concentration and diffusion:

And because it lasted for a year, we actually got some very meaningful data, which could be used hopefully to change some of the modelling of the air quality model where it shows that there's very high concentrations along roads and then it drops off quite markedly into the spaces, sort of a few hundred metres away. We found that that actually wasn't the case. That even at height, 34th floor, looking away from the road on some of the tower blocks, the concentration was high or if not higher than down at street level. And in the garden, some flats that have slowed down for the rise in greenery had levels of nitrogen dioxide below the safe levels for health. But there were an awful lot across the estate where the really average level was well above the safety limit for health. So it probably has changed people's views of the original modelling that was done.

(participant, Barbican project, emphasis added)

Fourth, as observed in other citizen science projects, the project triggered a host of diverse, unexpected learning outcomes, related to the specific roles that some highly engaged participants had in the project, especially as local coordinators. As explained by one participant:

In terms of leading the campaign, I've learned loads about social media and marketing. I wasn't on Twitter before, I'm on Twitter, I now have a community group page on Facebook. I've learned loads about marketing and media generally as well, I've been on Radio 4, Radio 5, BBC London Tonight, Channel 4, so local and national media, mostly national actually, and that has been really exciting to learn more about how the whole thing works. So I've learned about marketing and so on.

(participant, Hackney project)

Fifth, local, physical engagement in the project, mediated by simple tasks (like installing, checking and changing the diffusion tubes), seems to be a fundamental aspect of the whole engagement process. By providing emotional, collective engagement within the city, it impacts both one's view on one's neighbourhood, and relations with others in the local community. As one participant details:

This participation in the air quality monitor project was different because it was actually *physically being involved* whereas in the past that's mainly just listing emails to people and . . . I mean it's actually important *learning to have to do it together in the community* and it's definitely *changed the nature of the engagement* to being just *more people orientated*. . . . *I learned about the neighbourhood*. I mean I learned more about the neighbourhood and details of where all the schools are and where all the playing pitches are and where the community is most affected by bad air and the level of pollution, dust pollution from local construction sites and that they're not always following the rules around air quality management. . . . There was certainly a tangible lesson in how people can actually be involved in monitoring the environment. . . . I enjoyed meeting the other people and seeing that there's some shared concern about these issues.

(participant, Westway project, emphasis added)

Creativity in the AQM projects

Creative outputs are interesting, as they offer specific windows on the strong engagement of some volunteers in the project. In the AQM projects, the creative activities spontaneously carried out by the volunteers were orientated towards promoting the project, communicating its findings and using them in air quality lobbying. As shown in Table 4.3, these were driven by the activist stance of participants.

Volunteers wrote newsletters and press releases to promote their projects. For example, they organised a community fair and created a newsletter to publicise this event. Creative outputs were driven by the challenges of the project, here,

TABLE 4.3 Creativity themes in the air quality monitoring (AQM) interviews

Activities	Examples of creativity in the AQM project
Creative activities	*Promoting the project* • Coming up with ideas to raise awareness • Designing promotional materials: posters, flyers, t-shirts • Communicating findings: posters, flyers, newsletters, press releases • Organising events : " Air Champion Fair" • Incentives – e.g. time credits *Presenting the data in a different way* • Creating own Google map with different colour scheme • Creating posters and flyers to feedback results of project to community *Lobbying against air pollution* • Thinking of ways to use data to lobby against air pollution • Suggesting ways to improve air quality

engaging others with scientific data which might appear as not too engaging for non-scientists. As exemplified in these quotes, the efforts of volunteers focused on communication and engagement issues in creative ways:

> We've got t-shirts we produce for kids to wear, and we distribute flyers at events. So the kids all wear these black and white t-shirts with "smog off" and "diesel no tar" and "clean air tastes good", and they pass these out to passers-by while the parents just hang around. So that's good, one of our big events we do to raise awareness around the public, and if you invite press to it they come because it's cute kids dressed up as super heroes raising awareness.
>
> *(participant, Hackney project*[4]*)*

> And then once you get the data, the greatest creativity from us comes in the production of the flyer. The flyer is critical, it's the point of communication between us and the parents we want to reach, so what we do is produce a flyer and we also produce a poster as well. The maps are alright but the maps to be honest are data heavy. They are interesting to parents that walk around those schools, because they want to see where the most polluted roads are, but if someone is just walking past a poster they're not necessarily going to stop and look at that. So you need to make the whole thing really attractive and eye-catching.
>
> *(participant, Hackney project)*

One of the most interesting cases demonstrates how volunteers improved in data visualisation and interpretation by changing the colour codes of a map to highlight relevant information. They highlighted the high levels of pollution by coding it from orange to black instead of using the more neutral colour code chosen by the team at Mapping for Change. This case is interesting as it highlights the tensions around a shared object, here, the pollution map, used by stakeholders and participants with diverse intentions. The rather neutral colour code chosen by the scientists aims to display the results in the clearest, most readable way (readability being understood here as continuum and contrast) whereas the emergency colour code (orange-red-black) chosen by the participants highlighted the overall poor air quality. Thanks to this new colour code, the volunteers highlighted that even the lowest measures done in the local area are close to or above the European safety level (Figure 4.5).

Discussion: Function and transformations of citizen inquiry in AQM projects

Based on our empirical findings, we can now discuss the function and transformations of citizen inquiry in the project. To do so, we first update the thematic maps of motivation, learning and creativity that we presented earlier in this chapter, for the specific case of the community-centred AQM projects. Our interviews

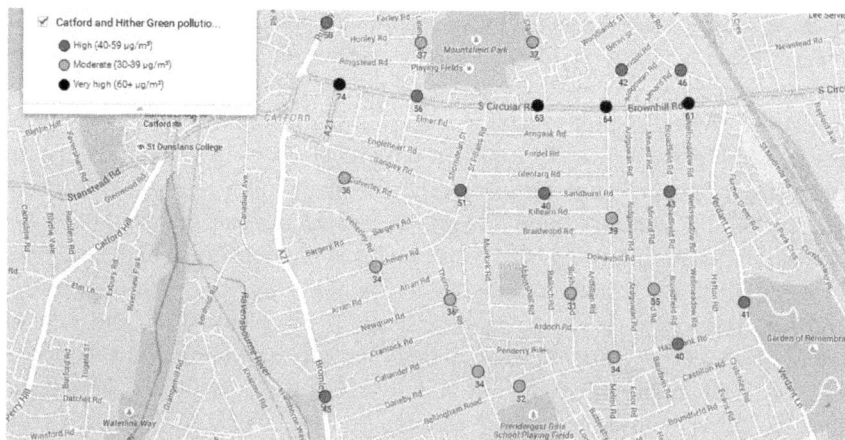

FIGURE 4.5   Google map created by a volunteer in Catford project.

Map data: Google

allowed us to specify the kind of motivations, learning outcomes, learning processes and creative outputs that can be expected in an AQM project. Although the
sample was quite limited (14 interviews), we believe that it covers a large set of
the potential outcomes of this kind of project, as the volunteers interviewed were
most probably engaged volunteers with a broad range of experiences. We added
in grey in Figure 4.6 the major changes between this community-centred project
and more scientists-centred online citizen science projects (presented in the section on motivation, learning and creativity in citizen science, above). The major
change is in the profile of motivations: curiosity, interest in science and desire
to contribute to scientific research, which are the usual initial drivers for online
citizen science project volunteers, are replaced by more specific interests: personal

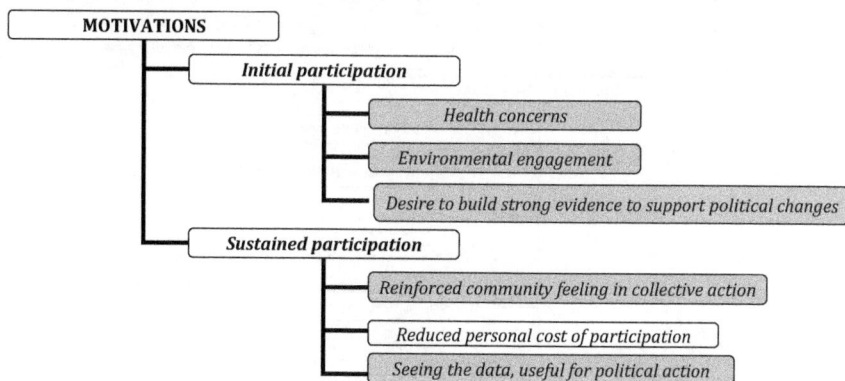

FIGURE 4.6   Thematic map of volunteers' motivations in a community-centred air
quality monitoring citizen science project.

or family health concerns linked to air pollution in the City of London, environmental engagement, desire to build strong evidence to support political change. Sustained motivation is also connected to the potential of data analysis for political action. Therefore, project participation is strongly grounded in the interest of the participants for increased air quality; our volunteers were found to engage in personally meaningful scientific investigations (Figure 4.6).

How did this personal significance affect the learning outcomes and processes at stake? Interestingly, it did not change much of the type of learning outcomes experienced by the volunteers, nor of the type of learning processes (Figures 4.7 and 4.8). However, these experiences seem to be mediated, in the case of AQM volunteers, by three specific dimensions: physical engagement, community engagement and direct interaction with scientists – these three dimensions themselves get transformed in the research process. Refraction of one's own experience in a local community of neighbours, with at least partially shared concerns, reinforces both the personal experience and the community. Personal physical connection with the city is enhanced and transformed by the scientific protocol that volunteers aggreed to follow, by the resulting maps and by their discussions in the local community. Interactions with scientists may bare the contradictions of different projects, as the case of the recolouring of the final map shows. Compared to other citizen science projects, the AQM project seems therefore to be different because it is directly connected to the everyday life and concerns of the volunteers.

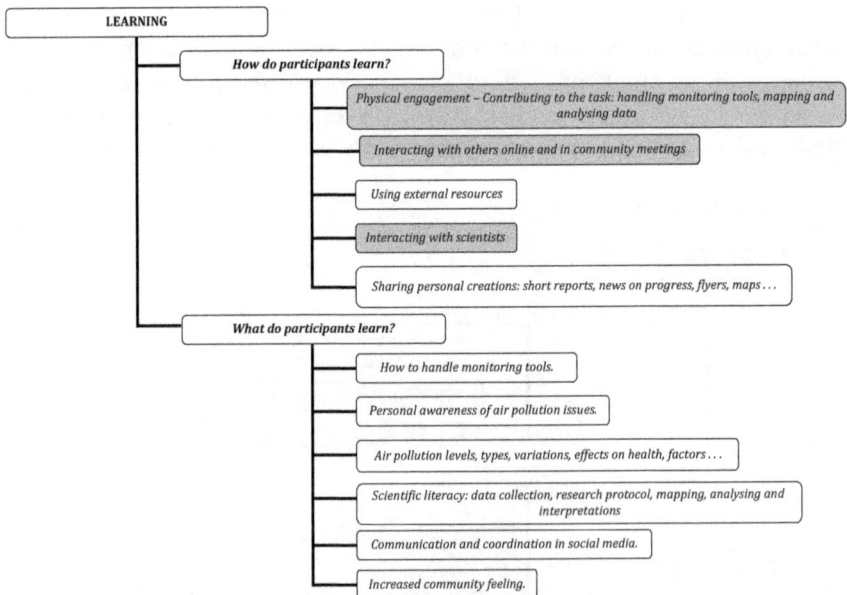

FIGURE 4.7 Thematic map of volunteers' learning in a community-centred citizen air quality monitoring science project.

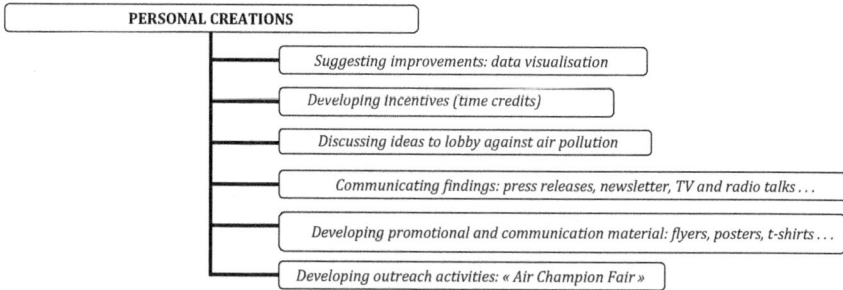

FIGURE 4.8 Thematic map of volunteers' creations in a community-centred air quality monitoring citizen science project.

Citizen inquiry initiates and grounds the whole citizen science process. The personal meaningful inquiry is transformed through collaboration in the citizen science projects. The process of carrying out the research involves personal engagement performed in structured collaboration with community leaders, neighbours and scientists, within a network of volunteers.

This personal impulse turns into a meaningful scientific activity by the mediation of the scientists providing tools, methodologies, standards, literature, background information, concepts, framing discourse, powerful and valuable ways of doing. We have here a scientific empowerment, in the sense of empowerment by science.

The personal impulse also gets collective. Volunteers discover that their concerns are shared by friendly, active neighbours. They collaborate by setting research questions, defining the methodological design, collecting data, analysing and mapping data, interpreting them, sharing findings and reflections in short reports and meetings, and suggesting and taking actions. They create outreach events, innovative ways of communicating and gathering people. Volunteers experience stronger community feeling through shared concerns, shared fun activities and shared findings. This is a kind of community empowerment, in the sense of empowerment of and by the community.

Although learning outcomes and creative activities may look similar to what has been observed in other types of online citizen science projects, the kind of personal inquiry which grounds the project impacts all their experience. Volunteers evaluate data collection, scientific findings, their own learning and creative engagement with the project, against their strong personal interest in improving air quality.

Citizen inquiry, from personally meaningful, gets transformed in the process of participating in the citizen science AQM project by a double empowerment (Figure 4.9): scientific empowerment, and empowerment by the community. Citizen inquiry can then contribute to transforming these two mediations, innovating in the scientific process and strengthening the local community. However, our analysis highlights the critical role of the existing local communities and networks of interests in this virtuous circle. Existing local communities mediate the encounter

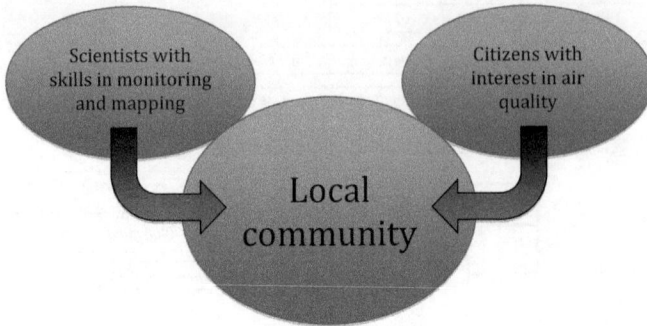

FIGURE 4.9 Dynamic double empowerment process through air quality monitoring project.

of personally meaningful topics and scientific knowledge, tools and research methodologies. They play a role in the carrying out and diffusion of the project. They are transformed and strenghtened in the process through learning and an increased feeling of belonging of their individual members. However, without these pre-existing local communities, the whole process of engagement in citizen inquiry turns out to be more difficult. The emergence and existence of the project are allowed by the joint efforts and engagement of the local citizens (providing initial interest, local knowledge, time and a lot of ideas), the scientists (providing scientific expertise, technical support in the choice and use of monitoring tools, laboratory analyses, mapping techniques, co-design of research protocol, analysis and interpretation of the data, scientific writing, scientific literature) and the City of London authorities (providing funding and interest for the findings) – grounded in local networks and communities.

Conclusion

In this chapter, we reported on the Science in the City AQM project, facilitated by Mapping for Change, and dedicated to collaboratively gathering and mapping data on air pollution. Design of the research, data collection and mapping, interpretations of the findings, reporting and communication on the project were performed by local volunteers collaborating with scientists. The initial citizen inquiry, driven by local concerns about pollution levels that were subjectively experienced as high, led to the implementation of a monitoring protocol of NO_2 and particulates, which triggered rich scientific findings, highlighting high levels of pollution as well as its variability. It also triggered diverse and sometimes unexpected learning among participants, depending on the activities endorsed by volunteers, including increased knowledge of air pollution in the city (understanding of the distribution of pollution in time, space and height as well as of the main effects of pollution and factors affecting it), increased environmental awareness, increased community identity and sometimes development of communication skills on various media.

We show how personally meaningful inquiry grounds participation in the whole project, how it gets transformed in the process thanks to a double empowerment, by the scientific team and by the local community, and finally how it drives the subjective evaluation of the whole project, including its scientific findings and the volunteer experience, which are evaluated against citizens' strong personal interest in improving air quality. Our chapter finally highlights the critical role of local communities in mediating the encounter between scientists and volunteers around partly shared interests.

Acknowledgements

We would like to thank all of the community members who participated in the Science in the City research project, led in the Barbican Estate by Mapping for Change in 2013–2014, as well as its following extensions in other parts of London. Special thanks to those who participated in our interviews. We also warmly thank our colleagues, Emily Collins (postdoctoral research associate at UCL), Mattia Fritz (at that time master student at University of Geneva) and Hannah Stockwell (Mapping for Change), who helped us with the organisation and conduct of the interviews, as well as Anna L. Cox (UCL) and Daniel Schneider (University of Geneva) for their support throughout the project.

Science in the City was funded by Defra and the Mayor of London Air Quality Fund and commissioned by the City of London Corporation. The Citizen Cyberlab research project was funded by an EU FP7 grant (no 317705).

Notes

1 See, for example, this news article : http://www.standard.co.uk/news/health/city-pollu tion-blackspots-revealed-amid-warnings-square-miles-air-is-too-toxic-for-joggers-10299351.html.
2 http://www.standard.co.uk/news/london/farringdon-street-in-the-city-is-the-worst-place-for-toxic-pollution-in-london-a3270791.html.
3 Mapping for Change project report is available online : http://mappingforchange.org.uk/wp-content/uploads/2015/08/Barbican-Final-Report-draft_12012015_edited.pdf.
4 Here is the website of their project : http://www.ilikecleanair.org.uk/home/.

References

Ballard, H. L., & Belsky, J. M. (2010). Participatory action research and environmental learning: Implications for resilient forests and communities. *Environmental Education Research, 16*(5–6), 611–627.
Bonney, R., Cooper, C. B., Dickinson, J., Kelling, S., Phillips, T., Rosenberg, K. V., & Shirk, J. (2009a). Citizen science: A developing tool for expanding science knowledge and scientific literacy. *BioScience, 59*(11), 977–984.
Bonney, R., Ballard, H., Jordan, R., McCallie, E., Phillips, T., Shirk, J., & Wilderman, C. (2009b). *Public participation in scientific research: Defining the field and assessing its potential for informal science education*. Washington, D.C.: Center for Advancement of Informal Science Education. Retrieved on December 12, 2016 from http://www.birds.cornell.edu/citscitoolkit/publications/CAISE-PPSR-report-2009.pdf.

Braun, V., & Clarke, V. (2006). Using thematic analysis in psychology. *Qualitative Research in Psychology, 3*(2), 77–101.

Crall, A. W., Jordan, R., Holfelder, K., Newman, G. J., Graham, J., & Waller, D. (2012). The impacts of an invasive species citizen science raining program on participant attitudes, behavior and science literacy. *Public Understanding of Science, 22*(6), 745–764.

Cronje, R., Rohlinger, S., Crall, A., & Newman, G. (2011). Does participation in citizen science improve scientific literacy? A study to compare assessment methods. *Applied Environmental Education & Communication, 10*(3), 135–145.

Curtis, V. (2015). Online citizen science projects: An exploration of motivation, contribution and participation. PhD thesis. The Open University. Retrieved December 12, 2016 from http://oro.open.ac.uk/42239/.

Francis, L., & Stockwell, H. (2015). *Science in the City. Monitoring Air Quality in the Barbican.* Final Report, Mapping for Change. Retrieved December 12, 2016, from http://mapping forchange.org.uk/projects/science-in-the-city/.

Haklay, M. (2010). *'Extreme' Citizen Science.* Paper presented at London Citizen Cyberscience Summit, Kings College London, London, UK, September 2–3, 2010.

Haklay, M. (2013). Citizen science and volunteered geographic information: Overview and typology of participation. In D. Sui, S. Elwood, & M. Goodchild (Eds.), *Crowdsourcing Geographic Knowledge. Volunteered Geographic Information (VGI) in Theory and Practice* (pp. 105–122). The Netherlands : Springer.

Hmelo-Silver, C. E., Duncan, R. G., & Chinn, C. A. (2007). Scaffolding and achievement in problem-based and inquiry learning: A response to Kirschner, Sweller, and Clark (2006). *Educational Psychologist, 42*(2), 99–107.

Jennett, C., Kloetzer, L., Schneider, D., Iacovides, I., Cox, A., Gold, M., Fuchs, B., Eveleigh, A., Mathieu, K., Ajani, Z., & Talsi, Y. (2016). Motivations, learning and creativity in online citizen science. *Journal of Science Communication, 15*(3), 1–23.

Jordan, R. C., Gray, S. A., Howe, D. V., Brooks, W. R., Ehrenfeld, J. G. (2011). Knowledge gain and behavioral change in citizen-science programs. *Conservation Biology, 25*(6), 1148–1154.

Kloetzer, L., Schneider, D., Jennett, C., Iacovides, I., Eveleigh, A., Cox, A. L., & Gold, M. (2013). *Learning by volunteer computing, thinking and gaming: What and how are volunteers learning by participating in Virtual Citizen Science?* Proceedings of ESREA 2013: Changing Configurations of Adult Education in Transitional. Retrieved December 12, 2016 from http://ebwb.hu-berlin.de/aktuelles/esrea/conference-programme/esrea-book-of-abstracts.

Kloetzer, L., Schneider, D., & da Costa, J. (2016). Not so passive: Engagement and learning in Volunteer Computing projects. *Human Computation, 3*(1), 25–68.

Laumbach, R. J., & Kipen, H. M. (2012). Respiratory health effects of air pollution: Update on biomass smoke and traffic pollution. *Journal of Allergy and Clinical Immunology, 129*(1), 3–11.

Price, C. A., & Lee, H. S. (2013). Changes in participants' scientific attitudes and epistemological beliefs during an astronomical citizen science project. *Journal of Research in Science Teaching, 50*(7), 773–801.

Rotman, D., Preece, J., Hammock, J., Procita, K., Hansen, D., Parr, C., Lewis, D., & Jacobs, D. (2012). Dynamic changes in motivation in collaborative citizen-science projects. *Proceedings of CSCW 2012*, ACM Press, 217–226.

Rotman, D., Hammock, J., Preece, J., Hansen, D., Boston, C., Bowser, A., & He, Y. (2014). Motivations affecting initial and long term participation in citizien science projects in three countries. *Proceedings of iConference 2014*, Berlin, March 4–7, 2014.

Rückerl, R., Schneider, A., Breitner, S., Cyrys, J., & Peters, A. (2011). Health effects of particulate air pollution: A review of epidemiological evidence. *Inhalation Toxicology, 23*(10), 555–592.

5

EXPLORING EMBEDDED ASSESSMENT TO DOCUMENT SCIENTIFIC INQUIRY SKILLS WITHIN CITIZEN SCIENCE

Karen Peterman, Rachel Becker-Klein,
Cathlyn Stylinski and Amy Grack Nelson

Introduction

Scientific inquiry is inherent in citizen science (CS), and perhaps for this reason has been used to distinguish between contributory, collaborative and co-created models of public participation in CS (Bonney et al., 2009; Shirk et al., 2012). Despite the fact that inquiry can be seen as a defining characteristic, methods for demonstrating the impact of CS on volunteers' scientific inquiry skills are limited (Phillips, Bonney, & Shirk, 2012). This assessment challenge is not unique to CS. Indeed, both formal and informal science education have seen recent calls encouraging researchers and evaluators to begin using *performance* as a key metric of scientific inquiry skill (Bell, Lewenstein, Shouse, & Feder, 2009; Fenichel & Schweingruber, 2010; National Research Council, 2014). The field of CS is poised to make a significant contribution to our understanding of how to measure science inquiry learning via performance-based measures.

As CS begins to focus directly on inquiry learning as an outcome, it is imperative that authentic measures of that skill be developed as well. Embedded assessments (EA) offer one such solution, though the process for developing these assessments is not well understood. EA has been defined, in the context of classrooms, as "opportunities to assess student progress and performance [that] are integrated into the instructional materials and are virtually indistinguishable from the day-to-day classroom activities" (Wilson & Sloane, 2000, p. 182). For the purposes of the current study, we define EA in more general terms as assessment activities that are integrated into a learning experience and that allow learners to demonstrate their competencies. These demonstrations could be captured through the observation of CS volunteers performing a skill or through products that are created during a CS activity and coded later. EAs can be developed as part of a program's inception or added later.

Many of the tasks included in CS projects could serve as performance assessments in which participants demonstrate their inquiry skills (Rural School and Community Trust, 2001; Wilson & Sloane, 2000). Though the opportunity exists, we have found only one published example that used performance tasks or outputs as evaluation measures. Crall et al. (2011) compared skills related to plant identification, GPS use, and sampling between CS volunteers and professionals. Data validation procedures are more commonly used to assess volunteer skills, as well as data quality (Bonter & Cooper, 2012; Dickinson & Bonney, 2012; Havens, Vitt, & Masi, 2012).

A recent scan of the CS field provides specific details about the range of scientific inquiry skills being evaluated (Stylinski, Phillips, Peterman, Becker-Klein, & Linhart, in preparation). The study determined that many projects focus on a narrow array of skills (primarily around data collection). Their evaluation of volunteers often does not include skill assessment and even rarer is direct assessment of these skills (e.g., more typical is self-reflection). The focus on data collection is intuitive given that high-quality data are paramount for CS projects. It also hints at the potential for new scholarship by expanding evaluation to capture volunteers' learning across the full range of scientific inquiry skills. Authentic measures of CS volunteers' abilities to use scientific inquiry skills and skill growth over time are needed to provide evidence of the learning that occurs through participation in CS (Becker-Klein, Peterman, & Stylinski, 2016).

Much of what we know about EAs to date is based on research conducted on performance assessments used in formal learning environments. A recent essay summarized the value of EA for CS, and ways to address the common challenges associated with these kinds of measures (Becker-Klein et al., 2016). The purpose of this chapter is to provide empirical evidence to support the use of EA as a measure of scientific inquiry skill. In so doing, we respond to two of the common challenges with EA, namely the lack of a standard EA development process and the lack of validity and reliability evidence for these types of instruments (Becker-Klein et al., 2016). Given these, the study was conducted with two aims in mind: (1) to document whether and how an exploratory development process could be used to create EAs across three CS contexts; and (2) to document the opportunities and challenges present in developing and administering EA tools for CS.

Method

The current investigation used case studies to implement and study an exploratory approach for creating EAs. Three environmentally based CS projects were selected as case studies. All had clearly defined target audiences, and each included at least one learning goal related to scientific inquiry skill development. All three included in-person training and interaction between CS staff and volunteers.

The case studies were selected to reflect variations that are common to the CS community. Two focused on youths, and one on adults. Each was operated by a different type of parent organization: a museum, a partnership between a federal agency and a university, and environmental education-focused community centers. Two projects had a history of implementation prior to the study, and one was a new CS project.

Exploratory approach for developing embedded assessments

Our exploratory approach for developing EAs for CS included strategies that are common to rigorous evaluation and instrument development practice and that were tailored to our needs (American Educational Research Association, American Psychological Association, & National Council on Measurement in Education, 2014; Johnson, Penny, & Gordon, 2009; Rural School and Community Trust, 2001). The process consisted of six components, each of which culminated in the creation of a product. Most of the individual components included in the exploratory approach have their own history in the literature. The combination of these specific strategies and products was unique, and thus a focus for our research.

The exploratory process is depicted in Figure 5.1. Generally speaking, the EA development process included three stages of inter-related components, and the potential for an iterative cycle between stages two and three. The first stage of the process included two components. Stage two consisted of an iterative process that was used to develop multiple drafts of each EA. Near-final drafts were then field tested. The findings from the field test resulted in either the replication of at least one component from stage two or a finalized EA. Each stage and its associated product is described in the figure.

Articulate program goals and activities

Work with each case study began with a series of meetings that were designed to identify and clarify project goals related to scientific inquiry skill development.

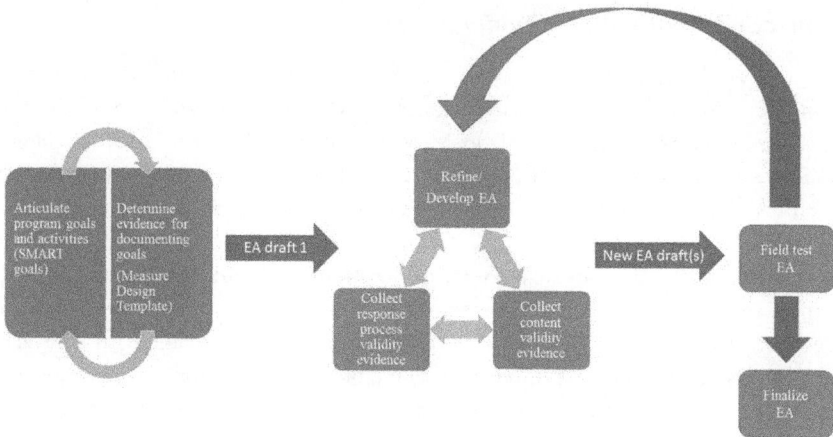

FIGURE 5.1 Exploratory embedded assessment (EA) development process.

Early meetings focused on existing documentation that described project goals, and collecting information from each team about existing activities that featured scientific inquiry skills. The culminating product of these conversations was a SMART goals document that detailed the goal(s) of interest for the EA. SMART goals are specific, measurable, attainable, relevant, and timely (Doran, 1981). Completing this document helped to articulate a comprehensive set of goals for scientific inquiry skill development for each project.

Determine evidence for documenting goals

Initial meetings also focused on the kinds of outputs or products that could demonstrate scientific inquiry skill proficiency or development. Conversations focused on both the activities that were already part of the CS project and new ways to demonstrate scientific inquiry skills within the context of the project. The culminating product of these conversations was a complete measure design template (Barr, 2011 in Smith, 2013, p. 41) that identified the scientific inquiry skills that were most relevant for the SMART goal(s) identified, as well as the kinds of evidence that would serve as feasible and meaningful indicators for the case study team.

Refine or develop EA tools

A key advantage of EAs is the way in which they integrate assessment tasks into project activities. This component of the process identified: (1) opportunities for integrating EAs into the program; (2) the specific roles that we and case study teams would play in either refining existing activities or developing new activities for the purposes of EA; and (3) the frequency with which data would be collected. The culminating product of these interactions was a draft EA, with accompanying scoring procedures.

Collect content validity evidence

Content validity is defined as the extent to which a measure adequately covers a given construct (American Educational Research Association, American Psychological Association, & National Council on Measurement in Education, 2014). Content validity evidence was gathered from a small panel of three to five experts who reviewed each EA. All panels included at least one evaluator, one education researcher, and a CS educator.

For two of the EAs, an adapted version of Newman, Lim, and Pineda's (2013) expert review process was used; experts reviewed a table of specifications that described the proposed alignment of each assessment item or task with the various aspects of the construct of interest. The table of specifications process was not appropriate for the format of one case study since the assessment was composed of a single data collection task. Instead, experts reviewed a detailed description of the assessment and responded to general questions about the alignment of the task with the construct.

In all cases, the panel provided feedback on construct definitions, administration information, scoring procedures, and data analysis and interpretation plans. These results were used to refine the constructs being measured and the EA tool, as needed, resulting in an EA that was ready for additional validity testing.

Collect response process validity evidence

Response process validity evidence was gathered through an adapted think–aloud method to understand how CS volunteers interpreted and responded to assessment tasks (American Educational Research Association, American Psychological Association, & National Council on Measurement in Education, 2014). In all instances, the researcher also observed the EA to provide context for the response process validity evidence gathered.

Two EAs used worksheets to collect assessment data from groups of volunteers. In these cases, response process validity evidence was gathered by recording volunteers' conversations as they thought out loud while completing the worksheet with their group. Individual volunteers also completed a reflection form afterward to share suggestions for specific revisions to the EA task and worksheet.

The third EA was not conducive to think–aloud conversations during the EA because conversation would have detracted from the task itself. Instead, a researcher interviewed volunteers immediately after they completed the assessment task to understand how they interpreted the task's directions and the procedures they followed during the task.

The results were used to verify that the EA tasks were interpreted as intended. Revisions were made to an EA when this was not the case. This process resulted in EAs ready to be field tested by each case study team.

Field testing the EA

To field test the EA, each case study administered their EA to at least one group of CS volunteers and then scored the results. A debrief meeting was held afterward to review the results and determine next steps in the development process. Conversations have focused on the administration of the EA, the content of the EA, and scoring procedures. In some cases, the field test data were used to begin establishing reliable scoring procedures that could be used to scale up use of the EA.

Each case study circled back to stage two of the process to refine the EA after their first field test. Currently, the concept and focus of each EA are considered final for all three case studies; the procedures for collecting the EA data are still being optimized. The culminating product from the field test will be a finalized EA that can be used for summative evaluation purposes.

Results

This section presents the development process for each case study and describes each EA. Examples of products created at different stages are scattered throughout. The development process itself resulted in formative changes to each CS project, and these results are shared. Each description ends with a discussion of the opportunities and challenges for using the EA to document inquiry learning in the context of that project. Table 5.1 provides a summary of the sample for each stage of the EA development process.

Case study 1: Nature's Notebook and paying close attention

Project description

Nature's Notebook (NN) is a national, online monitoring program where amateur and professional naturalists of all ages record observations of plants and animals to help generate long-term datasets. Operated by the USA National Phenology Network, NN began in 2009.

NN participants observe nature in their yards or in nearby areas on a weekly basis and then record their observations online. The EA for NN was created to help evaluate the project's goal of having volunteers contribute to scientific discovery.

This case study focused on a series of in-person workshops conducted by NN to train some of their volunteers. During the first workshop, volunteers learn about phenology and record keeping. They also practice their observation skills by collecting data about flora and fauna at the training site.

Assessment description

This EA took advantage of the workshop's journal and observation worksheet. To complete the worksheet, CS volunteers work in teams to explore the outdoor space surrounding them. To begin, teams answered three questions about their overall data collection approach and location (Figure 5.2). Next, groups chose two of five specimen options to observe and describe by answering questions on the worksheet. The options included: plant with green leaves, plant in bloom, plant bearing fruit, pollinator, and insect.

TABLE 5.1 Summary of embedded assessment development process, by case study

Project	Inquiry skill	# expert reviewers	# think-aloud interviews	# field test participants
Nature's Notebook	Paying close attention	5	13 (6 groups)	14 (8 groups)
Young Scientist Club Driven to Discover	Interpreting graphs Drawing conclusions	4	8 (3 groups)	
Dragonfly Detectives	Precise data collection	4	11 (4 groups)	37 (12 groups)

nature's notebook

A project of the USA-NPN

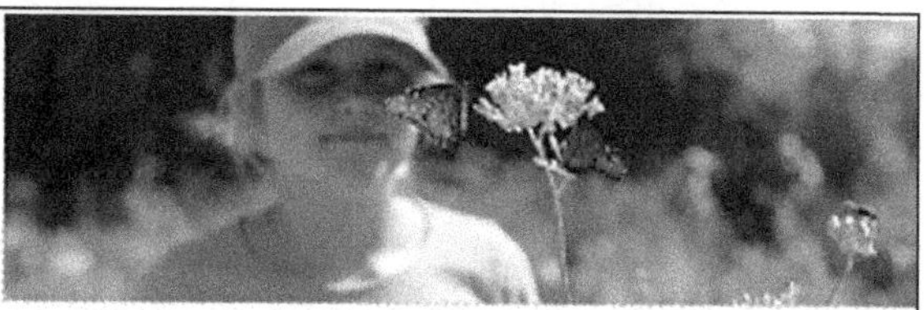

Provide a detailed description tell us where you are and describe the site characteristics. For example, if you are in a demonstration garden at a nature center, describe it and draw a map if you can. Be sure to provide enough information such that someone who is not familiar with the site could easily locate it from your description. If you can, draw what you see as well as describe it.

Assignment: SELECT TWO suites of plant and animal questions below to complete for this assignment. Answer the questions as thoroughly as you can in the allotted time. Indicate with an * next to the number the ones you have chosen for review. If time permits, you can answer other questions below.

1. **Find a plant that has green leaves.**

   a. Describe the location of the plant within the site, referencing your description of the site above, so you, or someone else, can find it again.

   b. Describe or draw the leaves of this plant as best as you can. Be sure to include as much information as you can about the size and shape of the leaves.

   e. Describe or draw the entire plant as best as you can. Be sure to include as much information as you can about the size of the plant.

FIGURE 5.2 Sample questions for paying close attention.

Groups completed the worksheet together, one worksheet per group. Completed worksheets were scored based on the quality of responses. For the overall questions, credit was given for paying attention to birds and to providing details that could be used to find the exact location where data were collected. Location data were also required for each species observed, as well as drawings or written descriptions to document three of the specimen's key features. Each species characteristic received a score of 1 if sufficient detail was provided according to the codebook (for a total of 4 points).

EA development process

To begin the process, the program's curricular materials were reviewed. NN staff shared an interest in focusing on the scientific inquiry skill of observation in the first meeting. Over three subsequent meetings, *paying close attention* was identified as the skill that would be targeted through the EA. NN staff considered paying close attention to be an essential precursor for making accurate and reliable observations. In addition, this skill was already featured in the journaling and observation worksheet.

The SMART goals sheet was completed, and the program's journaling and observation worksheet was revised to function as an EA. Revisions included attending to consistency, so that the same questions were asked in the same way for each category.

The SMART goals and the revised worksheet were used to complete the measure design template. The gaps identified by completing the template led to a final set of revisions for the worksheet and the creation of a checklist for scoring the worksheets. These were reviewed by the expert panel.

The content validation process resulted in meaningful feedback about each item on the worksheet, and the extent to which that item measured paying close attention. Some items were removed and others were edited to ensure that volunteers provided the kinds of responses that would be indicative of the construct. With these revisions completed, response process validity testing was conducted during the next NN workshop.

Think-aloud data were gathered from a total of 13 workshop participants working in six groups to complete the EA. The response process data revealed that some questions were measuring two constructs: paying close attention and the volunteer's knowledge. The results also highlighted challenges with having volunteers estimate certain features, such as the number of leaves on a plant. The EA was revised again to remove questions that relied on prior knowledge and to provide additional support for volunteers around estimation.

Completed worksheets were used to field test the scoring checklist and issues that might affect inter-rater reliability. Multiple raters scored the completed worksheets, compared their scores, and discussed areas of disagreement. These conversations resulted in the inclusion of new examples in the scoring checklist codebook, as well as revisions to the worksheet questions and checklist details.

Formative results

Observations of the NN workshop highlighted the fact that the workshop itself does not include instructions for how to pay close attention prior to completing the activity. The focus of this EA was reframed at this point to be considered a baseline measure of the skill that volunteers will need to sharpen in order to be successful with NN.

Defining the journaling and observation worksheet as the EA also helped the NN team think critically about how program activities before the EA prepared volunteers to be successful during the assessment, and how subsequent activities could build on the EA experience and results. The first workshop now describes the connection between the kinds of data that will be submitted online via NN and the kinds of information documented on the journaling and observation worksheet to provide volunteers with additional context for the worksheet. NN has also added more explicit training to the second workshop to ensure that volunteers have the requisite skills to conduct quality observations.

Opportunities and challenges for documenting inquiry learning

To date, the EA has provided a baseline measure of volunteers' ability to pay close attention. Overall, the level of detail provided by volunteers has been lower than expected. Average scores on the worksheet were 5.4 out of 10, with a range of 2–9. Scores for location were particularly low; only half included a level of detail that would allow someone else to find a specimen's location. This skill is particularly important to NN, given that it is ideal for the same specimen to be tracked across time.

NN staff are currently exploring the use of the EA as a pre–post measure, collecting data from volunteers across two workshops. Debrief conversations with the NN team have focused on two challenges in moving toward a pre–post measure. First, the groups from the first workshop do not necessarily attend the second workshop together. Second, once in the field, NN data are typically collected by individuals rather than groups. The NN team is exploring the possibility of setting a benchmark score that can be used as a success metric for individual-level worksheets collected during the second workshop.

Case study 2: Young Scientist Club and formulating conclusions

Project description

Operated out of the Urban Ecology Center in Milwaukee, Wisconsin, the Young Scientist Club's Driven to Discover (YSC-D2D) program utilizes CS projects such as eBird to introduce youths aged 8–13 to scientific research.

YSC-D2D includes a unit that challenges youths to design an inquiry project connected to science, and CS in particular. The unit begins with instruction on a number of scientific inquiry skills. Youths then complete a 30-minute inquiry activity that is used to guide the development of questions that students will investigate as part of a CS project. This activity served as the context for the EA.

The EA was designed to assess youths' ability to interpret graphs and formulate conclusions in order to gain a better understanding of youths' skills overall, and whether those skills changed over time.

Assessment description

The 30-minute inquiry worksheet was used to collect the data needed for the EA (http://www.extension.umn.edu/b-assets/extyouth/driven-to-discover-citizen-science/mini-inquiry-blank.pdf). The worksheet pictures a circular inquiry process that begins and ends with questions that the student has about the CS project.

Hypotheses are developed to answer one of the questions listed. Next, students brainstorm data collection procedures. The hypothetical data from this step are then recorded in a graph, and students respond to three prompts to summarize and interpret their results.

The final two sections of youths' worksheets were scored for the EA, using a checklist that was developed to align to the literature used by YSC-D2D to formulate the 30-minute inquiry activity. Carpenter and Shah's (1998) categorization of graph comprehension was used to score descriptions of the relationship between independent and dependent variables. Responses were scored from least to most complex as: nominal (includes name of variables, but nothing about relationship between variables), ordinal (mentions relationships between variables), or metric (more detailed quantitative explanation of relationships between variables).

Three components from the RERUN method for drafting conclusion statements were used to score EA responses. The RERUN method reminds students to: (1) describe their study briefly; (2) explain the purpose of the study; (3) state the results of the study, including which hypothesis was supported; (4) describe uncertainties or limitations of the study; and (5) write two new things that were learned.[1] The final three steps of this process were those identified as most relevant for the EA; 1 point was awarded for the inclusion of details related to each step (for a total of 3 points).

EA development process

When the EA development process began YSC-D2D did not have a standard set of written curricular materials that could be used as a reference point for identifying specific goals and project activities. As such, initial conversations included a range of staff members, including those in charge of the day-to-day activities conducted with youths and the CS director, to ensure that the EA would be of interest to those from all levels of the organization. Two common interests emerged from these conversations: *interpreting graphs* and *formulating conclusions*. YSC-D2D staff considered these skills to be particularly challenging for youths. In addition, these skills were already featured in their 30-minute inquiry activity.

The SMART goals sheet was completed at this point in the process (Table 5.2). Revisions were made to the 30-minute inquiry worksheet based on the SMART goals. A checklist was also created to score the worksheets for EA purposes. Using each of these resources, the measure design template was completed and final revisions were made to the worksheet.

The content validity process helped confirm that the items on the worksheet covered the two constructs adequately. The expert panel suggested revisions to one item, as well as points of clarification in the scoring checklist to establish additional parameters for scoring a correct response. Some also shared concerns about group scores potentially masking individual-level learning.

Response process validity data were collected from a total of eight youths who were split into three groups. The results revealed that youths were not interpreting

TABLE 5.2 SMART goals for interpreting data

Specific	What do I want to accomplish?	Youth identify independent and dependent variables (by deciding which goes on which axis)
	Benefits of accomplishing the goal	For program: Identify strengths and weaknesses in leading of the CS component of YSC
		For participants: Document that youth are learning what the program set out to teach them, *and* are gaining science skills that would be useful to them in school and beyond
	Identify requirements and constraints	Requirements: CS component of YSC-D2D; 30-minute inquiry worksheet; a score sheet/ rubric; collection of completed worksheets; scoring of worksheets; database to enter and sum participant scores
		Constraints: 30-minute inquiry would need to be done at least twice; requires simple questions since data are collected within a short time frame
Measurable	How much/how many?	2+ administrations of the 30-minute inquiry, with 1 graph accompanying each administration
Attainable	How can this goal be accomplished?	Standardize the process for conducting 30-minute science inquiry administration; create a data collection sheet template; create a scoring guide/ rubric template; create an online form for data entry; after pilot testing, create a guide that can be used for scale-up
Relevant	Does this goal match our other efforts/ needs?	Yes, we are working on graphing with them
	Is the goal applicable to your organization?	Yes, we are trying to ramp up evaluation across the board, and interest in improving students' science skills
Time-Bound	When?	By fall 2015
	What can I do 6 months from now?	Be ready for validation work and/or first field test
	What can I do 6 weeks from now?	Have a template score sheet/rubric created and work with EA4CS team to create a system for data collection, data entry, and scoring

Source: CS, citizen science; YSC-D2D, Young Scientist Club's Driven to Discover; EA4CS, Embedded Assessment for Citizen Science.

the items related to the *interpreting graphs* as intended, and thus revisions were made to the worksheet. Data from this stage of the process were also used to refine two of the questions related to the construct *formulating conclusions* to improve alignment between the worksheet and the scoring checklist.

The data also confirmed experts' concerns about group-level data collection. All three groups included at least one instance in which a response on the worksheet was not representative of all members of the group.

Formative results

YSC-D2D staff acknowledged that using this EA provided the opportunity to reflect on and revise their teaching practices. The low worksheet scores helped staff realize that youths' baseline understanding of both constructs were even lower than expected. YSC-D2D staff are in the process of reassessing their approach for teaching scientific inquiry in order to meet student needs.

The group-level responses have also resulted in new plans. In the future, EAs will be administered to homogeneous groups in an effort to encourage group rather than individual-level participation.

Opportunities and challenges for documenting inquiry learning

The EA was successful at measuring each construct and provided YSC-D2D with some of the first data they have had to begin documenting the challenges that students have describing data in graphs and formulating conclusions. Indeed, the baseline scores from the pilot test reflected much room for growth: scores ranged from 0 to 7 (out of 7 points), with an average score of 2.3 for describing graphs. Scores were slightly higher for formulating conclusions, with an average of 2.7 out of 5 (range 2–3). The specific questions that students miss consistently on the baseline assessment provide the opportunity for YSC-D2D to target instruction toward those areas. Collecting the post data will also provide the opportunity to document what students have learned through the program.

The primary challenge associated with this EA was the group-level administration of the activity. Group scores can mask evidence of individual learning and this was observed to be the case. When one group was pressed for time, for example, each youth answered one individual item instead of discussing the sections and filling them out together. In a group of mixed ages, the older youth answered the worksheet, leaving the younger youth out. As a result, the worksheet responses represented the older youths' knowledge and not that of the group as a whole.

Case study 3: Dragonfly Detectives and precision in data collection

Project description

Dragonfly Detectives (DD) was designed as a CS project for 9–13-year-olds. The project is operated out of the North Carolina Museum of Natural Sciences, and was designed to collect data that can be used to document the relation between the white-tail dragonfly's flight behavior and weather.

Data collection for DD involves counting the number of dragonflies that cross a youth's field of vision during a series of data collection intervals. Weather data are collected during the same time period using a Kestrel sensor and a light meter. The EA for DD was created to help evaluate the success of the project's goal to introduce children to scientific inquiry through a real-world CS project.

Assessment description

The DD team believes strongly that youths can be good citizen scientists who collect high-quality data. Though accuracy of data collection would have been an ideal measure, the logistics of the DD program (and many others) are such that accuracy cannot be determined for each individual volunteer. *Precision of data collection* was identified as an alternate measure that could be used to serve the evaluation's intended purposes.

Students collected data in groups of three, according to the DD procedures. Each group picked a spot to conduct their count. They stood shoulder to shoulder during the data collection period, looking straight ahead over the water. All youths conducted a separate dragonfly count and then recorded the number of dragonflies on their own individual data sheet.

The EA was designed to measure the precision with which youths collected data over time. Precision scores were created for each youth by comparing the number of dragonflies that the youth counted to the number counted by his/her partners during the same time period. Using this process, a score of 0 reflects perfect agreement.

A range of scores less than or equal to three were considered in the acceptable range. This range was determined by video-based counts that were conducted by the project's founder, a dragonfly expert. A total of 96 intervals were video-recorded and scored by the expert. Half of the sample ($n = 47$) was then coded a second time to document intra-rater reliability at the expert level. The expert's count varied by an average of 1.3 dragonflies across the 47 sessions, with a range of 0–11 and a mode of 0 (i.e., perfect agreement).

EA development process

Initial meetings with the DD team focused on the program's existing goals, and plans for program activities that would provide opportunities for assessment. Decisions related to the EA were made while discussing these program components and the SMART goals sheet and measure design template were completed toward the end of the decision-making process (Table 5.3).

The EA development process was initiated right before DD began, which did not allow time for the entire process to be completed. Even so, early pilot testing and response process validity testing were conducted with the draft EA. Reflections from those experiences were then used to create the version of the EA that was used for the content validity test the next year.

The content validity process resulted in additional validation work. While the expert reviewers understood the rationale for focusing on precision, they also

TABLE 5.3 Completed measure design template

Begin with the end in mind	• We want to measure students' ability to collect quality citizen science data for the Dragonfly Detectives project • We want to demonstrate that students' skill with data collection improves over the life of the program • We want to demonstrate that students' skill level is comparable to that of adults who do the same data collection task
Be sensory-specific	If this outcome actually happened: • Students would become better at identifying the white-tail (and only the white-tail) during the data collection period • Students would become better at conducting accurate counts of white-tails

Find potential measures	*Potential measures*	*Strength*	*Feasibility*
	1. Accuracy of counts – not possible	High	Low
	2. Dragonfly quiz – available as a PowerPoint quiz but not authentic to data collection setting	Medium	High
	3. Precision task – groups of three collect data together on the same day, and scores are compared	High	High

Check the bigger picture	We have already discovered that having students work in pairs is not effective because we don't know which student is "accurate" when counts vary widely. [We have shifted to a three-person group to respond to this challenge, as our adult groups of three show patterns that allow us to assume which people are precise and which people are still a bit "off" in their counts] We could find out that students have not learned to collect quality data in the time provided. [This result cannot be prevented or managed, as it is related to the way the program is organized; it might result in recommendations for changing the program's time scale and/or delivery so that these outcomes could be achieved]
Name the measure(s)	A precision task will be used to generate scores that serve as an indicator that the data collection skills needed for the project have been fostered in students

Source: Measure design template (Barr, 2011 in Smith, 2013).

shared skepticism about measuring precision when the accuracy of youths' dragonfly counts was unknown. A second procedure was added to document the accuracy of youths' dragonfly counts. Video cameras were installed at each viewing area of the pond, and teams were assigned to a camera each day. A dragonfly expert reviewed the videos at the end of each program to conduct independent dragonfly counts. These counts were then compared to those from each youth to document an accuracy rate.

Response process validity data were collected from 11 students working in four small groups. These results indicated that youths understood the purpose of the activity but that they were not consistently using the DD data collection procedures to conduct their counts. In some cases, the youths were unaware of these procedures.

Formative results

The program observations and think-aloud results indicated that variation in how the assessment was administered introduced unnecessary measurement error into youths' dragonfly counts. Based on these results, a detailed administration checklist was created to ensure that assessment administration instructions were presented consistently from week to week, and before each data collection session. This addition has increased our confidence that youths' scores reflect the precision with which they conduct their dragonfly counts and not differences related to the assessment's administration (Johnson et al., 2009).

One specific recommendation from the checklist was to standardize and shorten the length of the observation period for each data collection session. This change was motivated by two observations. First, 5 minutes of data collection seemed to stretch the attention spans of the youths taking part in the project (particularly when there were no dragonflies to observe). Second, narrowing the data collection window ensured that the CS leaders had time in the schedule for teams to compare their dragonfly counts and reflect on any differences that were found. This time was considered important if youths were expected to reflect on and improve the precision of their data collection over time.

Opportunities and challenges for documenting inquiry learning

Three rounds of data collection have been conducted to date. The results have provided the opportunity to explore the quality of youths' data collection skills by comparing scores to those of the dragonfly expert to determine accuracy and with other youths to determine precision. In both cases, agreement was defined as dragonfly counts of within three. The expert was considered to be the accurate count, based on the inter-rater reliability data presented earlier in this section.

Agreement was low during round 1; youths agreed with the expert for 22% of the observations and with their peers in 33% of cases. The administration checklist was implemented starting with round 2. Scores improved under these conditions, though the results indicated that students were precise with each other (76%), but not with the expert (38% agreement). Agreement improved markedly in round 3, with accuracy rates with the expert at 86% and precision rates with peers at 89%.

One challenge that is particular to this EA, and to species counts in general, is that it may be easier to be accurate and precise when fewer individuals are present. Two-thirds of the observations in round 3, for example, included zero dragonflies. Youth accuracy in these instances was 98% compared to 64% when dragonflies were present. On the other end of the continuum, the range of what is considered accurate and precise might widen as the number of individuals increases. DD plans to use data from the EA in the future to determine whether differential scores should be used for accuracy and precision, given the number of specimens available at the time of the observation.

Discussion

As noted, this study was conducted with two aims in mind. First, we explored whether a common development process could be used to create EAs across CS projects. Our EA development approach married best practices in evaluation with the use of specific products that were created at each stage of the process. Using this approach, we were successful at creating an EA for each of three case study sites.

The EA development process had the flexibility to accommodate the needs of each environmentally based case study to generate EAs that included a range of methods and scientific inquiry skills. Two EAs were developed to score volunteer-created products, and the third scored data collection records. Each EA was designed to provide evidence of learning in relation to a different scientific inquiry skill: paying close attention, data interpretation, and precise data collection. The EAs targeted either youth or adult audiences. We believe that the success of our approach across projects and the variability in the EAs produced provides initial evidence to support the use of the EA development process.

Though originally envisioned as a series of steps, the actual implementation of the EA development process unfolded in three stages, with the potential for iteration between stages two and three. For the seasoned evaluators who led this effort, the SMART goal sheet and measure design template were often completed toward the end of the decision-making process as a way to ensure that our discussion with each case study team was comprehensive. We suspect that novice evaluators and those who do not have experience with EA will find these tools to be useful earlier in the process as a way to guide the articulation of project goals/activities and the identification of meaningful ways to document evidence of inquiry learning.

Both the SMART goals and measure design template proved invaluable in preparing the test specifications for the expert review panel. The test specifications expanded key information from earlier products through the inclusion of construct definitions, administration information, and how to interpret EA scores. The experts were then able to review and verify our theory of action for the entire process of each EA, from the goals of the assessment itself through the analysis of the data generated. Though considered a best practice in instrument development (American Educational Research Association, American Psychological Association, & National Council on Measurement in Education, 2014), in reality many CS projects will not have the time and resources to engage an expert review panel. Even in cases that do not allow for this step, we believe that preparing test specifications can serve as a useful reflection tool.

The response process validity component resulted in key changes to each EA. Changes to the assessment itself included removing additional items from the NN activity, revising the 30-minute inquiry worksheet for YSC-D2D, and having youths conduct dragonfly counts for 3 rather than 5 minutes. Scoring procedures were also improved as the result of this process: the organization of the NN checklist was revised to include two sections, the checklist scoring process was expanded for YSC-D2D, and the precision range for DD was revised. In each case, the goal of the assessment and the scientific inquiry skill(s) being measured remained unchanged. Instead, iterative revisions focused on the procedural aspects related to the activities in which the EA was embedded and the assessment procedures themselves.

The second aim of this study was to document the opportunities and challenges present in developing and administering EA tools for CS projects. Two primary opportunities have been identified. In relation to the development of EAs, it is noteworthy that all three case studies opted to modify existing activities. This consistency reiterates the goodness-of-fit between existing CS project activities and the EA method, and indicates an opportunity to develop EAs that may be inherent in CS projects. The scientific inquiry skills selected are also an indication of the development opportunities of EA, given that the range of skills targeted in the current study extends beyond the data collection skills that are evaluated currently by most CS projects (Stylinski et al., in preparation).

The second primary opportunity results from both the development and administration processes. EAs have the potential to simultaneously strengthen the CS activities that feature scientific inquiry skills and the evaluation of those skills. Because a true EA is indistinguishable from the program itself, the development process often resulted in strengthened project activities.

This opportunity also relates to one of the primary challenges in developing EAs. If an EA is truly indistinguishable from the project activity itself, it can be difficult for CS leaders and evaluators to determine where the program ends and the assessment begins. This ambiguity can create tension in cases where volunteers are not performing scientific inquiry skills as expected, making it difficult to disentangle whether the results were due to shortcomings of the program or a failing of the EA designed to evaluate the program. In response to this challenge, it may be necessary to draw artificial parameters to constrain the project's implementation and/or the EA. Reflecting on the NN project activities that preceded and followed the journaling and observation worksheet EA and the administration checklist created for DD are both examples of this strategy.

A final set of challenges for administering EAs relates to the group-based implementation of some CS projects. Group scores may not represent the skills of the entire group, as was the case with YSC-D2D, making the results biased and difficult to interpret. In cases such as NN, group administration of EAs may compete with goals related to documenting learning or proficiency at the individual level.

Conclusion

Using EAs to measure scientific inquiry skills offers an important strategy to advance the evidence base of knowledge about the impact of CS experiences on volunteers. EAs are an innovative way of capturing volunteers' skills that are particularly appropriate for informal learning environments such as CS. Even so, there is much to learn about how to use EAs effectively. Many authentic assessment approaches "rely on qualitative interpretations of evidence, in part because researchers are still in the stages of exploring features of the phenomena rather than quantitatively test-ing hypotheses" (Bell et al., 2009, p. 57). The case studies in this chapter begin to bridge this gap by investigating a process for developing and using EA methods to test hypotheses about inquiry learning in CS.

Our exploratory development process demonstrated that there are opportuni-ties in CS projects for creating and using EAs to document volunteers' scientific inquiry skills. The EA development approach has great potential as a tool for strengthening inquiry-oriented CS project activities. The formative impact of the EA development process was an unintended outcome of our work. That said, this result seems intuitive with hindsight. Each case study took advantage of an exist-ing activity to create an EA of scientific inquiry skills. EA requires an individual project activity to be aligned directly with the project's theory of action and to produce an action or product that reflects a project outcome. Given that individual activities are not often developed with these dual goals in mind, it is not surprising that applying this different and more tailored perspective results in different and stronger activities overall.

It is important to note that the case studies were all environmentally based CS projects, and that each focused on in-person rather than online program com-ponents as the contexts for their EA. Because the EA development approach is comprised of many existing best practices in instrument development, we expect it to be applicable across context. Even so, future research should determine whether this is the case. Studying the approach in the context of new disciplines and apply-ing the approach to online EAs have the potential to result in refinements to the EA development process.

The challenges highlighted in this chapter set the stage for continued scholar-ship about the use of EA to measure the impact of CS projects on volunteers. Future work should study the use of the EA development approach within narrow constraints that have the potential to limit program-related challenges. For example, ideal CS projects would include established programs that have already been implemented and evaluated multiple times. This context would pro-vide a stable program environment through which to study the development and use of EA for summative purposes, and allow each EA to build on and supplement existing evaluation measures. Further, we believe that CS projects that collect data to answer a specific scientific question are particularly suited for the use of EA because the procedures for these projects are likely to have narrow constraints that limit project variability. Studies on the use of EA might also focus on adult-based programs, given that adults participate in CS projects as true volunteers who are motivated to take part in the CS project and the scientific inquiry skills inherent in that project.

Though the results of this study are promising, we are at the earliest stages of understanding how to capture authentic evidence to document learning related to scientific inquiry skills. CS represents one of the greatest opportunities for the public to experience scientific inquiry skills in real-world contexts, and thus provides some of the greatest potential for future research on EAs designed to document inquiry learning. The use of a common EA development process, with common products, has the potential to generate new research to address the challenges of using EAs to measure inquiry learning in the context of CS projects and beyond.

Acknowledgments

We would like to thank our case study partners, LoriAnne Barnett from Nature's Notebook; Chris Goforth, Tanessa Schulte, and Julie Hall from Dragonfly Detectives; and Erick Anderson from the Young Scientist Club. This work was supported by the National Science Foundation under grant number DRL#1422099. Any opinions, findings, and conclusions or recommendations expressed in this material are those of the author(s) and do not necessarily reflect the views of the National Science Foundation.

Note

1 For a description of the RERUN method, see http://monarchlab.org/education-and-gardening/how-to/the-process-of-science/.

References

American Educational Research Association, American Psychological Association, & National Council on Measurement in Education. (2014). *Standards for educational and psychological testing*. Washington, DC: American Educational Research Association.

Becker-Klein, R., Peterman, K., & Stylinski, C. (2016). Embedded assessment as an essential method for understanding public engagement in citizen science. *Citizen Science: Theory and Practice, 1*(1), 8. http://doi.org/10.5334/cstp.15.

Bell, P., Lewenstein, B., Shouse, A. W., & Feder, M. A. (Eds.). (2009). *Learning science in informal environments: People, places, and pursuits*. Washington, DC: National Academies Press.

Bonney, R., Ballard, H., Jordan, R., McCallie, E., Phillips, T., Shirk, J., & Wilderman, C.C. (2009). *Public participation in scientific research: Defining the field and assessing its potential for informal science education*. A CAISE Inquiry Group Report. Washington, DC: Center for Advancement of Informal Science Education (CAISE).

Bonter, D. N., & Cooper, C. B. (2012). Data validation in citizen science: A case study from Project FeederWatch. *Frontiers in Ecology and the Environment, 10*(6), 305–307.

Carpenter, P. A., & Shah, P. (1998). A model of the perceptual and conceptual processes in graph comprehension. *Journal of Experimental Psychology: Applied, 4*(2), 75.

Crall, A. W., Newman, G. J., Stohlgren, T. J., Holfelder, K. A., Graham, J., & Waller, D. M. (2011). Assessing citizen science data quality: An invasive species case study. *Conservation Letters, 4*(6), 433–442.

Dickinson, J. L., & Bonney, R. (2012). *Citizen science: Public participation in environmental research*. Ithaca, NY: Cornell University Press.

Doran, G. T. (1981). There's a S.M.A.R.T. way to write management's goals and objectives. *Management Review, 70*(11: AMA FORUM), 35–36.

Fenichel, M., & Schweingruber, H. A. (2010). *Surrounded by science: Learning science in informal environments*. Board on Science Education, Center for Education, Division of Behavioral and Social Sciences and Education. Washington, DC: The National Academies Press.

Havens, K., Vitt, P., & Masi, S. (2012). Citizen science on a local scale: the Plants of Concern program. *Frontiers in Ecology and the Environment, 10*(6), 321–323.

Johnson, R. L., Penny, J. A., & Gordon, B. (2009). *Assessing performance: Designing, scoring, and validating performance tasks.* New York, NY: The Guilford Press.

National Research Council. (2014). *Developing assessments for the next generation science standards.* Committee on Developing Assessments of Science Proficiency in K-12. Washington, DC: The National Academies Press.

Newman, I., Lim, J., & Pineda, F. (2013). Content validity using a mixed methods approach: Its application and development through the use of a table of specifications methodology. *Journal of Mixed Methods Research, 7*(3), 243–260.

Phillips, T., Bonney, R., & Shirk, J. L. (2012). What is our impact? Toward a unified framework for evaluating outcomes of citizen science participation. In Dickinson, J. L., & Bonney, R. (Eds.). *Citizen science: Public participation in environmental research* (pp. 82–96). Ithaca, NY: Cornell University Press.

Rural School and Community Trust. (2001). *Assessing student work.* Retrieved January 17, 2017 from http://www.ruraledu.org/user_uploads/file/Assessing_Student_Work.pdf.

Shirk, J. L., Ballard, H. L., Wilderman, C. C., Phillips, T., Wiggins, A., Jordan, R., & Bonney, R. (2012). Public participation in scientific research: A framework for deliberate design. *Ecology and Society, 17*(2), 207–227.

Smith, V. S. (2013). Data dashboard as evaluation and research communication tool. *New Directions for Evaluation, 2013* (140), 21–45.

Stylinski, C. D., Phillips, T., Peterman, K., Becker-Klein, R., & Linhart, J. (in prepation). Supporting and assessing scientific inquiry skills of citizen science volunteers.

Wilson, M., & Sloane, K. (2000). From principles to practice: An embedded assessment system. *Applied Measurement in Education, 13*(2), 181–208.

6

EXPLORING CITIZEN SCIENCE AND INQUIRY LEARNING THROUGH ISPOTNATURE.ORG

Janice Ansine, Michael Dodd, David Robinson and Patrick McAndrew

Introduction

Citizen science enables members of the public to contribute to scientific knowledge, and is recognised as playing a role in the science learning experience of many across informal and formal learning contexts (Bonney et al., 2009b). Unpaid volunteers have a long history of making significant contributions to science, among whom even Charles Darwin can be numbered (Silvertown, 2009), while in the USA, lighthouse keepers were a notable source of data on birds as far back as 1880 (Bonney et al., 2009a). Supported by technology, citizen science now involves a much wider audience, engaging volunteers in the collection and/or processing of data on a mass scale (Newman et al., 2012). The ability to involve the public in a process of scientific inquiry, while also advancing scientific literacy, is also an important outcome (Miller-Rushing et al., 2012; Silvertown, 2009).

Citizen science is interdisciplinary and unique; it has the ability to provide citizen participation in authentic research; it "relies on cooperation between a range of experts and nonexperts", "involves some sort of public engagement, education and data collection" and this provides possibilities for more autonomous/participatory scientific inquiry (Jordan et al., 2015; p. 208). This is aptly demonstrated by www.iSpotnature.org (iSpot), an online citizen science platform which combines learning technology with crowdsourcing, linking beginners and experts. Anyone can build their species identification skills while learning more about wildlife through either individualised or group participation which is demonstrated as one's expertise develops (Silvertown et al., 2015).

iSpot provides a multifaceted experience, incorporating participatory science research with innovative educational technology; communications, public engagement and outreach initiatives further facilitate a unique learning journey (Ansine, 2013). Developed by the Open University (OU) and launched in 2009, iSpot has become an extended platform with international partners (i.e. South Africa, Chile and Hong Kong) and is part of the OU's OpenScience Laboratory (www.opensciencelab.ac.uk), an online centre for cutting-edge science education. With the growth of the site, additional features were integrated in response to user feedback, funding and project priorities to improve the site's information architecture and capabilities. The resulting redesign and rebrand of the site to iSpotnature.org in 2014 (Figure 6.1), with a design-based research methodology, improved usability and capacity for engagement with learning, i.e. the participant learning journey, in a more holistic way (Scanlon et al., 2014; Woods et al., 2016).

The research and development behind iSpot's "technology-mediated citizen science learning" (Woods et al., 2016, p. 70) make it on a par with related project approaches with a focus on inquiry-based learning outside of a classroom setting and learning approaches embedding the inquiry process into science curricula (Jones et al., 2013). The design and functionality of the platform, both in terms of

FIGURE 6.1   The www.iSpotnature.org website.

technology and pedagogy, include the development of key tools and features such as iSpot projects and quizzes (see below). iSpot has been noted as helping to build natural history skills (Silvertown et al., 2015), which are currently missing from science education at varying levels (Tewksbury et al., 2014). The framework and design of the site and how it is used emphasise its role in learning: "By focussing on learning, iSpot not only helps participants generate valid scientific observations, but it also trains them to become the biological recorders on whom future data collection will depend" (Silvertown et al., 2015, p. 127).

This chapter illustrates the scope for citizen science and how it can support inquiry from informal to formal learning. The chapter demonstrates iSpot's approaches to, and experiences of, learning, which are authentic, the experience of real scientific research (Chinn & Hmelo-Silver, 2002) and personalised, meaningful and relevant to the individual (Anastopoulou et al., 2012). A five-step methodology for citizen inquiry through iSpot (Figure 6.2) is outlined using examples, results and outcomes from participant activity. Each stage demonstrates how inquiry in a citizen science initiative leads to learning.

First is participatory learning though exploring the site; and second, informal learning from identifying an observation and getting help from the community.

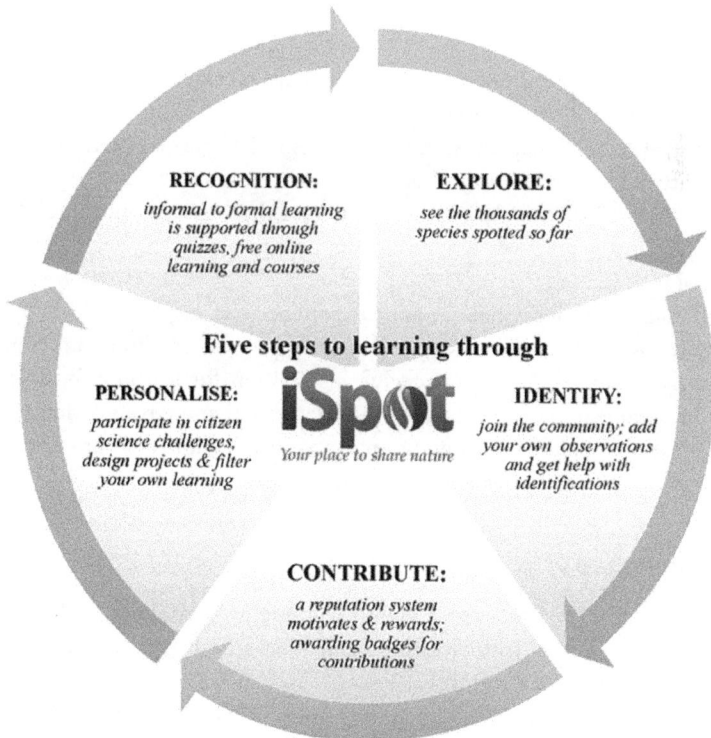

RECOGNITION:
informal to formal learning is supported through quizzes, free online learning and courses

EXPLORE:
see the thousands of species spotted so far

Five steps to learning through

iSpøt
Your place to share nature

PERSONALISE:
participate in citizen science challenges, design projects & filter your own learning

IDENTIFY:
join the community; add your own observations and get help with identifications

CONTRIBUTE:
a reputation system motivates & rewards; awarding badges for contributions

FIGURE 6.2 The iSpot five steps to learning methodology.

Third, there is the user reputation system which badges and rewards how participants contribute; while fourth is the role and impact of iSpot personalised inquiry features such as project filters. The fifth and final stage focuses on more experiential learning, presented in two parts: a preliminary analysis of the iSpot quiz, the assessment process for iSpot's informal learning; and a review of the use of iSpot in more structured, formalised learning, as in the OU Massive Open Online Course (MOOC) *Introduction to Ecosystems* and the practical activities designed to encourage learners to take on the role of citizen scientists using iSpot. In conclusion, the results and impact of these five steps to learning are discussed, highlighting iSpot as an exemplar, through this multi-faceted approach, that demonstrates how a citizen science initiative broadens the scope for inquiry-based learning.

Citizen inquiry through iSpotnature.org – a five-step methodology

iSpotnature.org is a citizen science initiative that facilitates citizen inquiry in practice, promoting a view that, in addition to the value of the data from citizen scientists, the process of inquiry and the way learning is supported are key. The methodology outlined here is centred on iSpot's approach: a learning design framed by a five-step model, leading from exploration of nature through to recognised learning actions:

1. *Explore*: iSpot is free and easy to use; participants explore species identified so far and see what others are spotting.
2. *Identify*: Once participants seek to identify species, they register, join the community, add observations and get help.
3. *Contribute*: iSpot motivates and encourages those who contribute. A multi-dimensional reputation system awards badges based on species groups and social interaction.
4. *Personalise*: The individual inquiry experience can be personalised by taking part in citizen science challenges, designing projects and building filters.
5. *Recognition*: Participants can receive recognition for learning; both informal and formal learning are supported. Quizzes build and test knowledge as skills increase; free online learning resources and structured courses are also available (Figure 6.2).

Exploring nature

Exploring nature, the first step of iSpot's learning methodology, is demonstrated by analysis of the site's "participatory learning" approach which highlighted how the learner as "active participant" takes part in "authentic, open-ended creative activities, developing their interest and passion" (Clow & Makriyannis, 2011, p. 35). The core aim of iSpot is to encourage and support people as they learn about and identify wildlife. It seeks to:

- lower barriers to identification with free, open accessible web and mobile software
- be open to all
- create a social network around crowdsourcing biodiversity
- connect beginners with experts
- create a new generation of naturalists.

As an online community, iSpot has "levels of social participation" which play a role in the learning experience, i.e. reading, contributing, collaborating and leading (Clow & Makriyannis, 2011, p. 35) in a way that aligns with established models of community engagement and social participation (Preece & Shneiderman, 2009). Many begin by simply exploring the site, searching, browsing and viewing observations and learning through interaction with the site just from browsing without having registered, which can be a valuable experience. A study of participatory activities from 50 sites highlighted "browsing" alongside "gathering and sharing content" as the first of four methods of connecting, participating and collaborating around a common objective (Clow & Makriyannis, 2011, p. 35).

Evidence of just how participants explore the site can be drawn from iSpot user analytics tracked (via Google Analytics) over the past 8½ years. Web analytics, as an evaluation technique, was devised to get more value from understanding how a site is used and the most valuable metrics are hits, page views and session information (Phippen, 2004). A study of the possible use of web analytics to evaluate "behaviour and usage" of a selected virtual community notes the value of "analytical methodology in the evaluation of a socially focussed web site" (Phippen, 2004, p. 183). Up to mid-September 2016, iSpot served just over 3.8 million user sessions (each period of time someone engages with the website) to 1.63 million users who had at least one session over the timeframe. Each viewed an average of nine pages per session, achieving a total of 33 million page views. The average session duration of 8–10 minutes further suggests that learner engagement is taking place. Data tracked over the lifetime of the website so far show consistent maintenance of a healthy new versus returning visitor ratio: 43% new/57 % returning. A review of visitor patterns suggests that viewing habits are aligned with purposeful browsing; other than the front page, iSpot's browse observation search was the second highest page viewed (http://www.ispotnature.org/browse_observations).

Public engagement, outreach, media and communications messages and activities also encourage people to learn from exploring iSpot, taking their interest in the natural world further. Publicity materials support public-facing initiatives across the UK and OU/BBC radio and TV programmes have taken iSpot into millions of households, seeking to inspire viewers to get outdoors and explore nature. Stories are also shared about interesting discoveries, such as the story of 6-year-old Katie finding a rare moth, the Euonymus leaf notcher (*Pryeria sinica*), which had not been recorded in Europe before (http://www.ispotnature.org/node/7407). The story reached an estimated audience of over 3.5 million through the media, resulting in 7,000 user sessions (Google Analytics) to iSpot during October 2009 alone (Ansine, 2013).

Identifying wildlife

Being able to identify species accurately is crucial and iSpot supports identification, the second step of the model (Figure 6.2), by providing participants with options to select the species of interest and giving them control of when and how to participate. Inquiry is core to this informal learning process. Informal learning here is any activity "involving the pursuit of understanding, knowledge or skill" that occurs outside the classroom (Livingstone, 1999; p. 2), a type of learning which is intentional and self-directed occurring "without direct reliance on a teacher/mentor and an externally organized curriculum" (Livingstone, 2012, p. 49). Informal learning, demonstrated by iSpot, gives learners options to choose what they do, the direction of learning and the time and effort utilised (Braund and Reiss, 2004).

On iSpot this choice is initiated from the help received to identify a species through adding an observation from the simple task of an individual taking a photo of a plant, animal or organism, posting it and selecting the group it belongs to (one of eight: amphibians and reptiles, birds, fish, fungi, invertebrates, mammals, other organisms, plants). The geolocation and date, entered or picked up from EXIF data, indicate where and when it was found; the potential name of the species can be suggested, and then checked automatically against the UK or region-specific species dictionaries or the global Catalogue of Life. Participants can also add their level of certainty of the name offered, i.e. "I'm as sure as I can be", "It's likely to be this but I can't be certain" or "It might be this". Other comments can be included, such as distinguishing features. Identification then takes place with the assistance of the community who can support the determination of the ID by clicking "agree" or posting alternatives if not.

Learning, as part of the process of identification, is demonstrated by this example of an iSpot identification sequence in Figure 6.3 (http://www.ispotnature.org/node/31205). A photo of a non-obvious species of damselfly (an immature female not showing its mature colours) is cautiously identified by the original observer, who suggests what it might be. This ID is corrected by an expert (a British Dragonfly Society representative) who provides a very helpful explanation of the identification features in the comments section. Agreements from other users add further validity to the identification. The process that occurs from upload through to identification can be interpreted as the individual controlling or framing the inquiry, empowered by the community. "iSpot seeks to engineer social connections in the threefold interests of biodiversity science, learning and conservation. That anyone can now get an identification of almost any organism within minutes or hours, entirely free, is potentially revolutionary" (Silvertown et al., 2015, p. 142).

Analysis of the impact of iSpot's identification process is relevant here. Participants, at the beginning of their iSpot learning experience, were able to provide IDs for less than 40% of their first observations but by their 50th observation had an increased percentage of correct IDs, correctly identifying over 60% themselves. Learning, it is surmised, is likely to be part of this (Clow & Makriyannis, 2011; Scanlon et al., 2014; Silvertown et al., 2015). Trends also indicate that participants are using what they

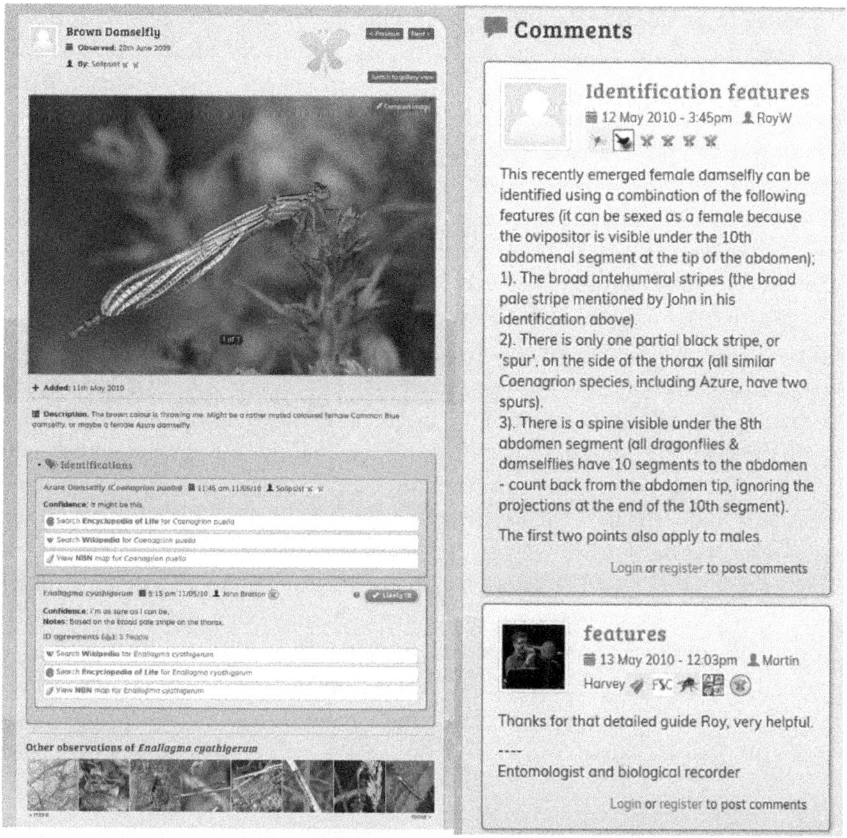

FIGURE 6.3 Learning from the process of identifying an observation.

have learnt on iSpot to help each other and therefore becoming less reliant on help from experts (Silvertown et al., 2015).

Contributing observations

How participants use and contribute to iSpot, the third step of the learning model, can be considered in the context of three main models of public involvement in citizen science projects (Bonney et al., 2009a; Roy et al., 2012; Shirk et al., 2012): contributory projects defined by scientists with the public predominantly contributing data; collaborative projects, initially designed by scientists with the public contributing data and helping to refine, design, analyse data and/or disseminate findings; and co-created projects which are designed collaboratively by scientists and the public (Bonney et al., 2009a). iSpot fits within this third category: co-created citizen science with content almost entirely contributed by the diverse community (Roy et al., 2012).

iSpot can be described as a "crowd learning" hub, "harnessing the knowledge and expertise of many . . . it enables learners to gain information related to what they want to know, at the time when they want to know it" (Sharples et al., 2013, p. 20). Contributing participants quickly learn to spot, name and identify various species and varieties – turning what may begin as just a casual interest into a lifelong learning journey. Up to September 2016, iSpot had crowdsourced the identification of 40,000 taxa, with earlier analysis suggesting that >80% of these were at species level (Silvertown et al., 2015). Up to early September 2016 nearly 60,000 registered participants had posted just over 653,000 observations from 174 countries, with 786,184 identifications offered and over 1.8 million agreements to these identifications. iSpot crowdsources identification from photographs and 1.25 million were uploaded over this timeline through the efforts of the active online community.

iSpot rewards those who contribute by giving social points and scores for activity on the site in the form of badges (Figure 6.3). This innovative reputation system is a core feature behind how the site works. Participants pose species queries, contribute and learn through a system that motivates and rewards for interacting with others on the site (Silvertown et al., 2015). iSpot's role can be described as supporting inquiry-based learning, helping participants make science "personally meaningful and relevant to their everyday lives" (Anastopoulou et al., 2012, p. 251). Participants gain social points (stars) and scores for each of the species groups represented (Figure 6.4). There is a social level and eight species-related groups: birds, fish, amphibians and reptiles, invertebrates, mammals, plants, fungi and other organisms. Points (shown by an icon representing each group) are awarded based

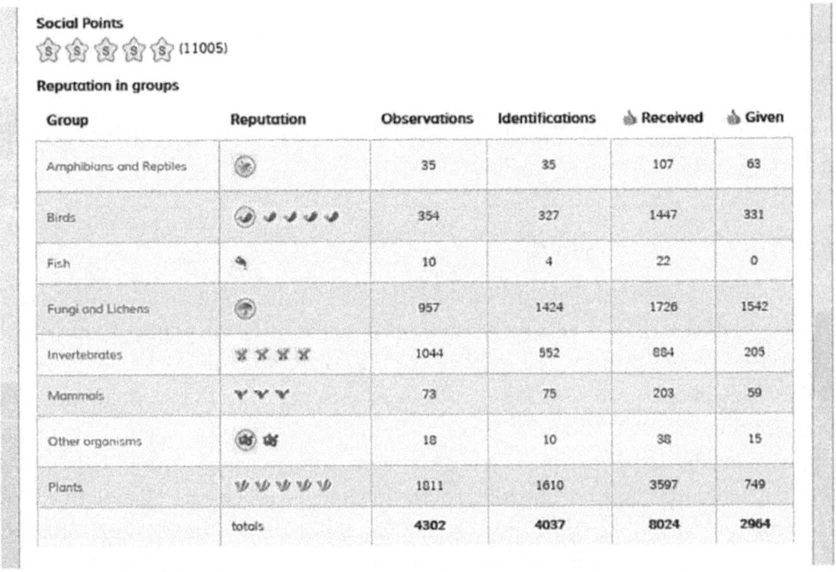

Social Points
⭐⭐⭐⭐⭐ (11005)

Reputation in groups

Group	Reputation	Observations	Identifications	👍 Received	👍 Given
Amphibians and Reptiles		35	35	107	63
Birds		354	327	1447	331
Fish		10	4	22	0
Fungi and Lichens		957	1424	1726	1542
Invertebrates		1044	552	884	205
Mammals		73	75	203	59
Other organisms		18	10	38	15
Plants		1811	1610	3597	749
	totals	4302	4037	8024	2964

FIGURE 6.4 The iSpot reputation system – user profile.

on "the weighted agreements given by other participants for identifications" (Silvertown et al., 2015, p. 133). Reputation points are therefore earned when one proposes an ID which is then agreed with by others, "weighted by the agreers' own reputation scores for that taxon" (Silvertown et al., 2015, p. 125).

Observations posted are also biological records (Roy et al., 2012) and as such the site has become an integral part of the natural history community in the UK as well as other parts of the world. Representatives from various biological recording groups, schemes and societies join amateurs and provide expertise in correct identifications (Silvertown et al., 2015), enhancing the scope for learning as participants engage with and learn from representatives with specialist knowledge of the taxa/species represented. These relationships are beneficial for all: groups can request iSpot data; representatives are badged with an icon linked directly to organisational websites.

Personalising experience

iSpot stores location information as it collects observations, and this capacity to localise data makes it well-suited for inquiry-based learning as this process, step four of the learning model, gives the participant more "control over the learning process" (Jones et al., 2013, p. 22). Participants can learn through personalising their own citizen science challenges facilitated through functionality that creates filters to view the site the way an individual, group or organisation would like to. A project can be set to filter groups of observations for an area, i.e. single site or region, by taxonomic rank, for example by family, order or a single species; or by a selected tag, habitat or time period. It can be filtered to a combination of any or all of these categories and viewed as a map, picture gallery or summary description. The iSpot projects function was introduced in 2014, and up to mid-September 2016, nearly 3,000 projects were added. Most have been developed by iSpot participants based on their particular interest, i.e. self-directed, while some have been developed by the iSpot project team to support learning for an OU course (see the course discussion later) or based on a request from an organisation.

Personalisation experiences – iSpot projects in the UK and Ireland

iSpot project filters are able to capture new observations posted as well as group together historic observations, providing a useful structure for learning and making it easier to access and pick up relevant trends and other information, thereby providing a useful structure for observing and learning. Preliminary analysis of a subset of projects from within the UK and Ireland iSpot community (a total of 290 projects) indicates how some participants chose to filter information, choosing what they wanted to explore further, with certain learning patterns emerging. Of the projects analysed, most (147) were filtered to "area" only. "Area" was often defined geographically to the UK or a subset, e.g. Scotland or Ireland. However, many narrowed this down, specifying a home garden or allotment. Others localised to a nature reserve, park, school or university grounds. Some are grouped together by "area and taxonomy", such as a project set up to bring together plants in South Hampshire (http://www.ispotnature.org/projects/vc11_plants). Of the 290 projects reviewed, 40 were defined to "area, taxonomy and tag". An example is a project defined with specific tags to collate records of plant galls on iSpot within the UK and Ireland (http://www.ispotnature.org/projects/plant-galls).

Project themes/topics also varied based on how participants chose to define their frame of inquiry, i.e. what they wanted to learn about. The 290 projects analysed were created by 146 participants, and from these eight developed five or more projects each, of varied interests. While the majority of projects had a general focus on wildlife, invertebrates had the highest number of projects categorised by taxa or species (over 60), followed by plants (over 30), then fungi and lichens (Figure 6.5). There are other filters, but these were less frequently used and are not analysed here.

The purpose of projects can also vary, such as learning from observations in a garden, school or university; projects are used to support classroom learning and community-based initiatives engaging the public. Filters framing the level of inquiry also vary; for example, many incorporate historical and current data, while others are tagged to a set timeline. The Glastonbury Abbey BioBlitz 2015 project (http://www.ispotnature.org/projects/glastonbury-abbey-bioblitz-2015) is described as a record of "a 24-hour continuous race to record as many different species as possible from the grounds of the historic Abbey with the help of naturalists, families and friends". Almost 450 observations were posted on iSpot and recorded in the project from the event. The project was set up to capture records

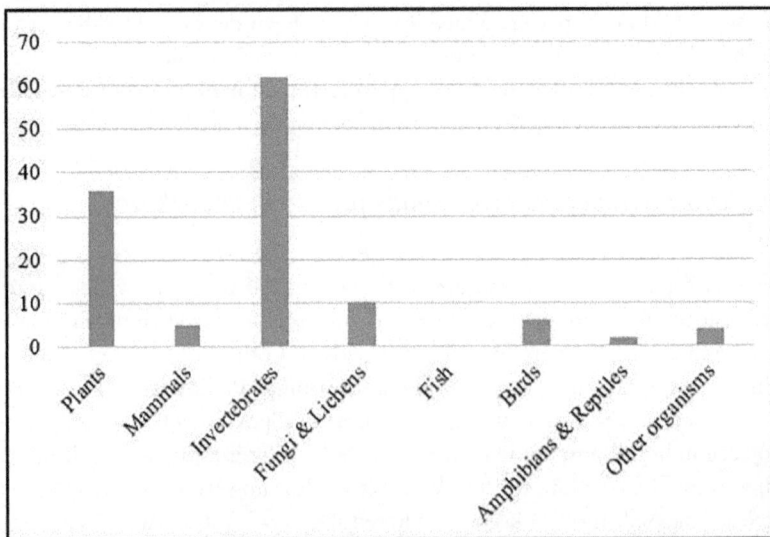

FIGURE 6.5 The iSpot project themes and topics.

from an annual BioBlitz event which began in 2011 as part of a pilot integrating the use of iSpot in the community (Scanlon et al., 2014). Feedback from the evaluation of the first year's activities showed evidence of participant engagement and learning which have continued with the integration of projects.

Receive recognition for learning with iSpot

While the complete five-step model for iSpot supports a learning process, the final step brings out more recognised learning activities. In these, participants are more likely to see themselves in the role of learners. Two examples illustrate how such learning takes place: first, informal learning supported through an automated iSpot quiz; and second, the structured course *Introduction to Ecosystems*.

Informal learning: the iSpot quiz

The iSpot quiz was developed and integrated in 2013 to understand better and assess how the iSpot community learn from the site. As noted, iSpot provides opportunities for informal learning, and the quiz provides a framework for self-assessing this. The quiz gives learners options to choose their own inquiry: participants select one of the main groups of organisms on iSpot – amphibians and reptiles, birds, fish, fungi and lichens, invertebrates, mammals and plants – and choose from five levels of difficulty. Each quiz has ten questions and there are three question types:

1. select image: where a species name is given and the corresponding image has to be selected from four options
2. select name: where an image is given and the species name has to be selected from four options
3. identify image: where an image is given and the species name has to be input as text (with the help of an autocomplete).

The quiz can be taken either as a logged-in participant (i.e. registered) or not. Questions are based on a random selection of the observations in each of the main areas, i.e. British Isles, Southern Africa, and the rest of the world. The quiz uses images from iSpot, choosing observations where the iSpot reputation system has allocated the species identification to a level of "likely".

Themes participants choose to assess themselves on/learn about

Within 12 months of development, initial trends saw one or more quizzes taken by an average of 50 participants per week (Scanlon et al., 2014). Recent analysis indicates a total of 35,832 quizzes taken between 1 August 2013 and 1 September 2016, by both registered and unregistered participants, in approximately equal proportions. From this, Table 6.1 shows the number of quizzes taken, demonstrating

TABLE 6.1 Number of quizzes taken and unique quizzes created in each group of organisms at each level of difficulty

Group of organisms	Difficulty level											
	Easy				Intermediate		Expert				Total quizzes taken	Total unique quizzes created
	Level 1		Level 2		Level 3		Level 4		Level 5			
	Quizzes taken	Unique quizzes created	Quizzes taken	Unique quizzes created	Quizzes taken	Unique quizzes created	Quizzes taken	Unique quizzes created	Quizzes taken	Unique quizzes created		
Amphibians and reptiles	1,100	34	411	20	326	30	129	15	344	24	2,310	123
Birds	2,818	100	1,946	61	1,814	54	1,275	47	3,123	206	10,976	468
Fish	639	19	254	13	204	18	85	11	187	17	1,369	78
Fungi and lichens	803	30	381	71	325	74	167	37	188	36	1,864	248
Invertebrates	2,108	78	1,045	98	1,140	211	425	89	1,137	569	5,855	1045
Mammals	1,728	36	950	23	845	31	521	27	1,092	75	5,136	192
Plants	2,996	150	1,816	61	1,555	77	665	63	1,290	133	8,322	484
Grand total	**12,192**	**447**	**6,803**	**347**	**6,209**	**495**	**3,267**	**289**	**7,361**	**1060**	**35,832**	**2638**

participants' interest, i.e. what they were interested in learning and therefore chose to assess themselves on. New quizzes are generated as required to ensure each participant never takes an individual quiz more than once. Each individual quiz (i.e. a particular set of questions using a particular set of observations) is referred to as a unique quiz. Each unique quiz is taken 100 times, i.e. by 100 different participants, then no longer used (retired). Using unique quizzes is the chosen method in comparable scenarios. Williams and Greenberg (2004), in a teaching and testing context, developed a system for generating a very large number of unique quizzes to enable thousands of students to do practice quizzes, and receive the answers, before doing their assessment, which should not repeat the same questions. Their questions were mathematically based, which made them relatively easy to generate. In the context of iSpot, achieving the large database of correctly identified images required for testing species identification would be extremely difficult and time consuming without the help of the thousands of iSpot participants.

The most popular quizzes were "expert" (level 5) bird quizzes (Table 6.1), reflecting an interest in birds as the most popular group of organisms among iSpot participants. This suggests a curiosity in testing their knowledge and learning more about this group and possibly an appetite for teaching resources in this subject area. The second highest were the "easy" (level 1) plant quizzes; while fish quizzes were done the fewest times. Registered participants generally take a few quizzes over a short period of time but a small number of people take a large number of quizzes: three participants took 200–300 quizzes, one 356 quizzes and another 593 quizzes. The highest number of quizzes taken by participants were on invertebrates. The impact of this considerably boosted the total number of invertebrate quizzes overall that the system had to generated to ensure that each participant did not take an individual quiz more than once.

Tracing iSpot participants' learning journies through time would require that they take a quiz on the same group of organisms at the same level of difficulty on several occasions over an extended period of time. However, almost none of the participants follow this pattern, but despite this ad hoc trend, the pattern of usage (large numbers of quizzes taken in specific subject areas) demonstrates a desire to learn more and assess that learning also.

Testing across a range of species

Users can test themselves over a very wide range of species representing all of the commonly found groups of organisms in UK. Table 6.2 shows the numbers of taxa that have appeared in the British Isles version of the quiz, with some taxonomic groups showing greater diversity than others. The quiz chooses observations at random, which means that, for example, within invertebrates, harlequin ladybird (*Harmonia axyridis*), the most frequently observed species, appeared many times.

But there are likely to be some rarely recorded taxa on iSpot that have yet to appear in the quiz. The plants group currently has the most species in the quiz, even though there are over twice as many invertebrates in the UK species dictionary; clearly many of the invertebrates are rare or difficult to identify and so have not yet

TABLE 6.2 Number of taxa within each group of organisms in the British Isles version of the iSpot quiz

Group of organisms	Number of species
Amphibians and reptiles	32
Birds	506
Fish	137
Fungi and lichens	507
Invertebrates	1,519
Mammals	87
Plants	1,973
Total	**4,745**

made it into the quiz. In Table 6.2 all of the common and several introduced species are represented in the amphibian and reptiles group, even though only 32 taxa have been used in the quiz. It must be noted that this is representative, as Britain has very few amphibian and reptile species. The group with the lowest proportion of species shown in the quiz compared to the total UK inventory is fungi and lichens, but there are over 500 species represented, including all of the commonly recorded groups of fungi. iSpot uses the standard UK species inventory from the Natural History Museum (http://www.nhm.ac.uk/our-science/data/uk-species.html) and this contains some non-native species.

Following on from the discussion around whether participants self-assess, the plants quiz in Table 6.3 shows the quiz difficulty level (more difficult to right), and iSpot reputation increasing down the table. The reputation categories chosen reflect the one- to five-star rating and knowledgeable/expert status, as shown on iSpot, with the one-star rating split further into reputation levels zero and one. The body of the table shows the frequency with which participants, with a particular reputation, chose quizzes of a particular difficulty level. Participants' reputation is indicated at the time they chose the particular quiz.

Table 6.3 suggests that people with a lower reputation prefer the easiest quizzes, whereas those with a four-star level of reputation tend to do the most difficult quizzes. It is particularly interesting that those with a five-star earned reputation or

TABLE 6.3 Participation in iSpot plant quizzes by iSpot reputation and quiz difficulty level

Reputation points	Reputation stars/expert status	Difficulty level				
		Level 1	Level 2	Level 3	Level 4	Level 5
0	*	810	398	337	135	172
1	*	66	70	40	4	7
2–9	**	216	159	37	20	57
10–74	***	99	115	144	22	48
75–499	****	148	143	151	116	194
500	*****/Knowledgeable	26	21	38	38	149
1,000	Expert	12	1	0	1	11

knowledgeable status mostly try the most difficult quizzes, perhaps to confirm that they are good at identifying plants. However, there are few data from full expert status participants; there are very few such participants and they may be very busy. In further analysis, most of the small number of participants who achieved 9 or 10 out of 10 at the most difficult level of the quiz had a zero-level reputation, suggesting these participants clearly had a considerable level of expertise but are not contributing iSpot identifications (if they were, then their iSpot reputation would not be zero).

In general, this analysis shows a large number of quizzes taken, demonstrating a considerable appetite for self-assessed learning. Most quizzes were done by those with zero reputation; from this we can suggest that many may be more interested in doing the quizzes rather than submitting observations (Table 6.3). Unfortunately, however, participants do not repeat quizzes over time as would happen in a conventional learning context. As noted, a wide range of difficulty levels and groups of organisms were selected, although birds were the most popular. Those taking part choose quizzes based on their ability; those with lower reputation take the easier quizzes. Those with high reputation took the more difficult quizzes and may complete them more quickly, demonstrating a considerable range of abilities on iSpot. Those taking the most quizzes tend to specialise in a particular group of organisms. The large numbers of observations posted by participants covering all aspects of biodiversity in UK allows the system to generate an almost unlimited number of unique quizzes that can test anyone from complete beginner to the keenest biodiversity recorder. Members of the iSpot community are exploring the iSpot database through the quiz to further their understanding of UK biodiversity through inquiry learning.

Recognised formal learning: Introduction to Ecosystems

MOOCs demonstrate changes in thinking of online learning, but although they are able to reach large numbers, this growth also raises questions around how "effectively they support learning" (McAndrew & Scanlon, 2013, p. 1). The MOOC *Introduction to Ecosystems*, offered by the OU on the FutureLearn platform, incorporates a practical element designed to encourage learners to take on the role of citizen scientists using iSpot and this integration, it can be suggested, meets this challenge: "The emergence of 'citizen inquiry' activities is promising, leading to ideas of crowd learning, combining elements of inquiry learning and cyberscience. The challenges are to make such opportunities for informal learning bring lasting benefits" (McAndrew & Scanlon, 2013, p. 2).

iSpot facilitates citizen inquiry through species identification, building an informal to formal learning journey around biodiversity. Informal learning, as defined earlier, is self-directed, occurring outside the classroom (Livingstone, 2012). The integrated tools and features such as iSpot's badging reputation system offer informal accreditation by acknowledging and rewarding achievement through progression towards goals (Sharples et al., 2013). This presents an individualised record of one's activity, learning progression and personal motivation and is an important part of iSpot's informal to formal learning journey. The integration of citizen science opportunities using iSpot within the more structured learning of this course can be described as contributing to what has been referred to as "semi-formal" learning, a term adapted to define outside-the-classroom learning which crosses over, sharing characteristics of informal and formal learning (Jones et al., 2013, p. 22). This is "associated with high motivation" (Jones et al., 2013, p. 21) and the ability of learners to control this and make it relevant, supported by available technology.

Inquiry learning activities and tasks are a core part of the MOOC and mapped into the course learning outcomes, contributing to the five key attributes or aims each learner should associate with studying the course:

1. personal: gives a feeling of addressing the personal interests of the learner
2. dynamic: exciting and varied materials and experiences
3. current: right up to date and dealing with the latest issues
4. authentic: provides contact with the research scientists whose work is featured
5. thought provoking: encourages reflection and discussion (adapted from Robinson & Ash, 2014, p. 132).

Introduction to Ecosystems is a 6-week course and each week has a number of steps guiding learning, each of which is media-led (images, diagrams, audio, video, web link, etc.). In week 4 students carry out an observational exercise and are instructed to use iSpot to help with identifications. Each learner is asked to post a minimum of four observations of organisms from a local habitat to iSpot, identifying them with help from the online community. This exercise is designed to motivate and "promote active learning" by encouraging learners to participate in activities interacting with "the natural world and their fellow learners" (Robinson & Ash, 2014, p. 133). It also encourages engagement with nature after the formal course has ended. On finishing the course, participants are encouraged to continue contributing to iSpot and are directed to other OU learning options.

The extent to which iSpot supports inquiry learning for students in a structured course is reviewed in this section of the chapter. Analysis is based on learner activity during the first course presentation, November 2013 to January 2014, and based on:

- tracking of iSpot-registered users and other usage data throughout the course presentation
- trends in the use of the website through Google Analytics-captured data, including:
  - o sessions and visits by course week
  - o overall visitors across the full presentation
  - o page views
  - o average visit duration

- registration information from how participants "heard about" iSpot (selecting options *FutureLearn* and *OU Course*)
- use of the observation tag *#FLeco13*.

Associated with this activity, iSpot online sessions and registrations grew over the timeline of the course. Between November 2013 and January 2014 iSpot-registered participants increased by 3,626 (approximately 12%); this is estimated as over a fifth of those registered on the course (Robinson & Ash, 2014). iSpot activity also increased, with the number of observations, identifications and images posted each increasing by 5%. General trends indicate that the rate of users grew over the time-line of the course; at the same time learners were engaging with the site between an average of 7 and almost 13 minutes per session. Data collated indicate that when registering on iSpot some new participants indicated they "heard about" iSpot via FutureLearn and a number selected the option "OU Course". It can be estimated that over 2,000 registered on iSpot linked with this course at that time.

iSpot supports learning as part of set coursework activity and, to collate this, learners are asked to tag their observations using "#FLeco13" (updated each course year). This activity is filtered into an iSpot project to connect and collate observations made on the course as well as create an easily accessible way to group students. Over the timeline of this first presentation, approximately 900 observations were recorded and posted on iSpot by learners with this tag. Comments from learners, such as those noted below, provide further evidence of impact and individual learning journeys as they progressed through course activities assisted by the iSpot community.

- Learners are supported and encouraged by the community to continue to grow their interest: "I'll have a go and take a better photo – good excuse to visit again!" (http://www.ispotnature.org/node/388573?nav=parent_ob)
- "So pleased to have some help with getting started." (http://www.ispotnature.org/node/386550)

A learner is encouraged and commended for getting a photo of the "elusive" water rail *Rallus aquaticus* (http://www.ispotnature.org/node/387263), while another interacts with a more expert iSpot user and is guided on the intricacies of getting an ID: "You need close ups or a good description to get down to species level. Nice first post" (http://www.ispotnature.org/node/387392).

A review of the MOOC concludes that a large number of learners signed up for and completed the course and the "pedagogical model", which includes iSpot, contributed to "motivated engagement and discussion" (Robinson & Ash, 2014, p. 135). In terms of more structured teaching and learning, iSpot has also been integrated as a carefully designed route supporting formal science learning, includ-ing certificate level, undergraduate and masters modules and courses. From 2009 to 2012 iSpot was a core part of the learning pathway in the OU introductory level course *S159 Neighbourhood Nature,* which combined both theory and practice and used iSpot to support students with fieldwork activities. Students devised and con-ducted a small field study and wrote about this for an assessment at the end of the module. During their studies, students learned how to make observations and used iSpot to record these. Course reviews and student comments indicate that many found it invaluable to their learning experience (Ansine, 2013; Woods et al., 2016).

Conclusion: Citizen inquiry in practice – the iSpot experience

There is a link between science education, learning and how the public gain their understanding of science and citizen science plays a role. Science education is a requirement for developing an "informed citizenry" (Jenkins, 2004) and, as learning occurs in a social context, effective science education helps make connections between science experienced in a classroom setting and everyday life (Jegede & Aikenhead, 2004). Citizen science, as demonstrated by iSpot, can be described as playing a key societal role, by offering accessible science that relates to the concerns, interests and activities of citizens as part of their daily lives (Jenkins, 2004).

iSpot can be described as providing motivating links between informal and formal learning, offering a pioneering approach through a five-step model under the themes: explore, identify, contribute, personalise and recognition. iSpot provides an environment in which learners are an active participants, engaging in authentic, open-ended creative activities, developing their interest and passion. As outlined through the discussion above, this cycle of learning (Figure 6.2) is being delivered through an "ecosystem of activity specifically designed to support and encourage learning" (Clow & Makriyannis, 2011, p. 35); it can be concluded this demonstrates citizen inquiry in action.

The inquiry learning process, we suggest, occurs within a supportive online community made up of participants of different ages, abilities and experience – the general public, whether new to wildlife identification, or others more experienced. It begins from the simple process of browsing the hundreds of thousands of observations of a wide range of species posted on the site; as noted, Google Analytics data show engagement through exploration lasting approximately 8–10 minutes per visit. Participants start to frame their own inquiry posing identification questions, crowdsourcing help, sharing and learning as they do so. Through crowdlearning (Sharples et al., 2013) contribution is rewarded by badges in the managed reputation system. Participants are motivated to continue, which is itself informal accreditation, acknowledging achievement through progression towards goals while presenting an individualised record of their activity. This learning progression with personal motivation is significant in contributing to iSpot's informal to formal learning journey.

Inquiry learning is further personalised with iSpot projects, which enable participants to "exchange knowledge and methods", collaborating with other iSpot participants, and this enhances their investigation (Aristeidou et al., 2013). The patterns highlighted in the analysis of projects in the UK and Ireland demonstrate how, through citizen inquiry, participants are choosing to learn, with a tool that allows them to "demonstrate control over the learning process allowing the learner to decide how to carry out the inquiry" (Jones et al., 2013). Also, whether the project is set up by the individual or to facilitate course activities, this process of filtering data collections to new observations posted, to older historical observations or both, facilitates citizen inquiry though combined access to "knowledge sharing and peer review" (Aristeidou et al., 2013).

Receiving recognition, the final step of iSpot's inquiry learning methodology, enables participants to see themselves in the role of a learner in a direct way. The introduction of the iSpot quiz combined fieldwork and the knowledge of many to build a system that tests species identification skills. The same framework could also be used to generate quizzes and help learning through contributions from across a diverse range of other subject areas, using the crowdsourcing framework to collect data and facilitate correct identification; adapting the iSpot model for learning. The example of the MOOC highlights the impact of iSpot when used in a more structured learning environment, and importantly, how this can be demonstrated from the context of the leaners themselves.

Importantly, the steps (represented as a cycle in Figure 6.2) integrate and overlap, achieving the overall goal of facilitating learning. As discussed, iSpot projects are also set up and built into courses and facilitate interaction between learners as well as collate activity by year. Learners are directed to custom-made pages with information to support their activities on the site (http://www.ispotnature.org/node/378009). The first stage of learning by exploring nature with iSpot can be accessed at any time, so beginning participants may be motivated to contribute through the rewards-based system, use the informal learning via the quiz to assess their growing knowledge in a particular species group or be introduced to the idea of engaging with iSpot by a task within more structured learning such as the *Introduction to Ecosystems* MOOC.

This chapter has shown both how citizen inquiry leads to learning and how a five-step methodology helps to develop and refine the role of learning in citizen science. The model values the participation of a wide range of learners from those who come to explore, to those that see the site as part of their formal learning experience. iSpot also brings benefits to the scientists and experts involved, giving them routes to extend public understanding while gaining new sources of validated data from observations posted. It is further concluded that www.iSpotnature.org as a citizen science platform does and can continue to play an important role enhancing scientific literacy and providing a framework which contributes to a journey from informal to formal learning through citizen inquiry.

Acknowledgements

We would like to thank the iSpot project team in the Faculty of Science, Technology, Engineering and Mathematics and the Institute of Educational Technology for their hard work and the iSpotnature.org community of thousands for their contributions, without which this work would not be possible. We also acknowledge funding from the Big Lottery Fund for England (through OPAL: www.opalexplorenature.org), British Ecological Society, Garfield Weston Foundation, Wolfson Foundation (through the OpenScience Laboratory: www.opensciencelab.ac.uk), British Council, South African National Biodiversity Institute and the OU.

References

Anastopoulou, S., Sharples, M., Ainsworth, S., Crook, C., O'Malley, C., & Wright, M. (2012). Creating personal meaning through technology-supported science inquiry learning across formal and informal settings. *International Journal of Science Education, 34*(2), 251–273.

Ansine, J. (2013). Reaching the public through iSpot: Your place to share nature. Case Study 8.5. In Bowater, L., & Yeoman, K. (Eds.), *Science Communication: A Practical Guide for Scientists*. Oxford: Wiley Blackwell.

Aristeidou, M., Scanlon, E., & Sharples, M. (2013). A design-based study of Citizen Inquiry for geology. *EC-TEL 2013 Eighth European Conference on Technology Enhanced Learning*, pp. 7–13. Retrieved on September 5, 2016 from: http://oro.open.ac.uk/39220/1/__userdata_documents2_ma7262_Desktop_Aristeidou_Scanlon_Sharples_DC.pdf.

Bonney, R., Cooper, C. B., Dickinson, J., Kelling, S., Phillips, T., Rosenberg, K. V., & Shirk, J. (2009a). Citizen Science: A developing tool for expanding science knowledge and scientific literacy. *Bioscience, 59*(11), 977–984. https://doi.org/10.1525/bio.2009.59.11.9.

Bonney, R., Ballard, H., Jordan, R., McCallie, E., Phillips, T., Shirk, J., & Wilderman, C. C. (2009b). *Public Participation in Scientific Research: Defining the Field and Assessing its Potential for Informal Science Education*. A CAISE Inquiry Group Report, Center for Advancement of Informal Science Education, Washington. Retrieved September 5, 2016 from: http://www.informalscience.org/sites/default/files/PublicParticipationinScientificResearch.pdf.

Braund, M., & Reiss, M. (Eds.) (2004). The nature of learning science outside the classroom. *Learning Science Outside the Classroom*. London: RoutledgeFarmer.

Chinn, C. A., & Hmelo-Silver, C. E. (2002). Authentic inquiry: Introduction to the special section. *Science Education, 86*(2), 171–174.

Clow, D., & Makriyannis, E. (2011). iSpot analysed: Participatory learning and reputation. *Proceedings of the 1st International Conference on Learning Analytics and Knowledge* (pp. 34–43). ACM doi:10.1145/2090116.2090121.

Jegede, O. J., & Aikenhead, G. S. (2004). Transcending cultural borders: Implications for science teaching. In Scanlon, E., Murphy, P., Thomas, J., & Whitelegg, E. (Eds.), *Reconsidering Science Learning*. Oxford: The Open University, Routledge.

Jenkins, E. W. (2004). School science citizenship and the public understanding of science. In Scanlon, E., Murphy, P., Thomas, J., & Whitelegg, E. (Eds.), *Reconsidering Science Learning*. Oxford: The Open University, Routledge.

Jones, A. C., Scanlon, E., & Clough, G. (2013). Mobile learning: Two case studies of supporting inquiry learning in informal and semiformal settings. *Computers & Education, 61*, 21–32.

Jordan, J., Crall, A., Gray, S., Phillips, T., & Mellor, D. (2015). Citizen Science as a distinct field of inquiry. *BioScience, 65*(2), 208–211. doi: 10.1093/biosci/biu217.

Livingstone, D. W. (1999). *Exploring the icebergs of adult learning: Findings of the first Canadian survey of informal learning practices*. WALL Working Paper No. 10 1999. Centre for the Study of Education and Work, Department of Sociology and Equity Studies in Education and Ontario Institute for Studies in Education, University of Toronto. Retrieved September 19, 2016 from https://tspace.library.utoronto.ca/retrieve/4451/10exploring.pdf.

Livingstone, D. W. (2012). Probing the icebergs of adult learning: Comparative findings and implications of the 1998, 2004 and 2010 Canadian surveys of formal and informal learning practices. *The Canadian Journal for the Study of Adult Education (Online), 25*(1), 47–71. Retrieved on September 19, 2016 from http://cjsae.library.dal.ca/index.php/cjsae/article/view/112, 4.

McAndrew, P., & Scanlon, E. (2013). Open learning at a distance: Lessons for struggling MOOCs. *Science, 342*, 1450–1451.

Miller-Rushing, A., Primack, R., & Bonney, R. (2012). The history of public participation in ecological research. *Frontiers in Ecology and the Environment, 8*(6), 285–290.

Newman, G., Wiggins, A., Crall, A., Graham, E., Newman, S., & Crowston, K. (2012). The future of citizen science: Emerging technologies and shifting paradigms. *Frontiers in Ecology and the Environment, 10*(6), 298–304.

Phippen, A. D. (2004). An evaluative methodology for virtual communities using web analytics. *Campus-Wide Information Systems, 21*(5), 179–184.

Preece, J., & Shneiderman, B. (2009). The reader-to-leader framework: Motivating technology-mediated social participation. *AIS Transactions on Human-Computer Interaction, 1*(1), 13–32.

Robinson, D., & Ash, P. (2014). *Developing a pedagogical model for a massive open online course (MOOC).* Proceedings of the Frontiers in Mathematics and Science Education Research Conference, 1–3 May 2014, North Cyprus. Retrieved August 5, 2016, from: http://scimath.net/fiser2014/presentations/David%20Robinson.pdf.

Roy, H. E., Pocock, M. J. O., Preston, C. D., Roy, D. B., Savage, J., Tweddle, J. C., & Robinson, L. D. (2012). *Understanding citizen science and environmental monitoring.* UK Environmental Observation Framework, NERC Centre for Ecology & Hydrology. Retrieved August 5, 2016, from: http://nora.nerc.ac.uk/20679/.

Scanlon, E., Woods, W., & Clow, D. (2014). Informal participation in science in the UK: Identification, location and mobility with iSpot. *Educational Technology & Society, 17*, 58–71.

Sharples, M., McAndrew, P., Weller, M., Ferguson, R., FitzGerald, E., Hirst, T., & Gaved, M. (2013). Innovating pedagogy 2013. *Open University Innovation Report 12.* Retrieved September 19, 2016 from: http://www.open.ac.uk/iet/main/sites/www.open.ac.uk.iet.main/files/files/ecms/web-content/Innovating_Pedagogy_report_2013.pdf.

Shirk, J. L., Ballard, H., Wilderman, C. C., Phillips, T., Wiggins, A., Jordan, R., McCallie, E., Minarchek, M., Lewenstein, B. V., Krasny, M. E., & Bonney, R. (2012). Public participation in scientific research: A framework for deliberate design. *Ecology & Society, 17*(2), 29. Retrieved August 5, 2016, from: http://www.ecologyandsociety.org/vol17/iss2/art29/ doi: http://dx.doi.org/10.5751/ES-04705-170229.

Silvertown, J. (2009). A new dawn for citizen science. *Trends in Ecology and Evolution, 24*(9), 467–471.

Silvertown, J., Harvey, M., Greenwood, R., Dodd, M., Rosewell, J., Rebelo, T., Ansine, J., & McConway, K. (2015). Crowdsourcing the identification of organisms: A case-study of iSpot. *ZooKeys,* (480), 125–146. doi: 10.3897/zookeys.480.8803. http://zookeys.pensoft.net.

Tewksbury, J. J., Anderson, J. G. T., Bakker, J. D., Billo, T. J., Dunwiddie, P. W., Groom, M. J., Hampton, S. E., Herman, S. G., Levey, D. J., Machnicki, N. J., del Rio C. M., Power, M. E., Rowell, K., Salomon, A. K., Stacey, L., Trombulak, S. C., & Wheeler, T. A. (2014) Natural history's place in science and society. *Bioscience, 64*, 300–310. doi:10.1093/biosci/biu032.

Williams, M., & Greenberg, W. (2004) A high volume test engine and pedagogy for computer emporium instruction. Retrieved on June 1, 2017: https://www.researchgate.net/publication/237545029_A_HIGH_VOLUME_TEST_ENGINE_AND_PEDAGOGY_FOR_COMPUTER_EMPORIUM_INSTRUCTION?enrichId=rgreq-eb9f446bd407e2d9ebeb89e176fca1d4-XXX&enrichSource=Y292ZXJQYWdlOzIzNzU0NTAyOTtBUzoxNzU3NDcyMTgwMjY0OTZAMTQxODkxMjgxMDU4NQ%3D%3D&el=1_x_2&_esc=publicationCoverPdf.

Woods, W., McLeod, K., & Ansine, J. (2016). Supporting mobile learning and citizen science through iSpot. In H. Crompton & J. Traxler (Eds.), *Mobile Learning and STEM – Case Studies in Practice.* New York: Routledge.

7

GEOCACHING

Inquiry learning with a sense of adventure

Gill Clough

Introduction

The focus of this book is citizen inquiry – the mass participation of members of the public in inquiry-led investigations. The different chapters describe a range of citizen science projects designed to encourage and support participation in formal citizen science inquiries. This chapter explores informal citizen inquiry through the activity Geocaching. Geocaching is a worldwide phenomenon (over 2.8 million Geocachers as of September 2016) that has triggered mass participation in both the creation of and contribution to inquiries. This study unpicks how concepts such as adventure and excitement contribute to mass participation in informal inquiry-led investigations. These findings can be used to help generate engagement in formal citizen science inquiries.

The focus of this chapter is a PhD study of Geocaching conducted in 2007 (Clough, 2009). Geocaching is a leisure activity which fosters citizen inquiry and informal learning through the creation of location-based challenges that are devised by members of the community, then accessed and downloaded via the community website. The study collected data from 659 Geocaching community members to reveal how they were using new technologies to create location-based learning opportunities for each other. It also looked at the key motivators for taking part, both as a creator and as a consumer of citizen inquiries. The findings from this study provide insights into the increasing popularity of citizen inquiry and citizen science projects. The next section describes the historical antecedents of Geocaching and citizen inquiry with a focus on citizen-led informal learning and knowledge.

Inquiry learning in its historical context

The key role played by web-based and mobile technologies in citizen inquiry might suggest that citizen inquiry is a relatively recent phenomenon. However, mass public participation in citizen inquiries has a tradition that dates back to the early 20th century, before such technologies were available.

Mass participation in the collaborative creation of knowledge through data collection has a long history in the UK. The earliest recorded was the 1909 bird-ringing system launched by Witherby, which still continues today (Greenwood, 2005). This was followed, in 1928, by a British bird survey of herons, instigated by an amateur ornithologist Max Nicholson. He chose an easy-to-identify species which nest in large colonies and are therefore quite easy to find as his participants were all amateur bird watchers. By 1933 the potential of large-scale co-creation of data was becoming evident.

Nicholson and fellow bird enthusiasts created the British Trust for Ornithology (BTO) in 1933 with the aim of building up a national centre of ornithological knowledge. In 1933 another social research organisation was set up, called the Mass Observation Project. The data created using this method were subtly different to that created by the BTO. Instead of collecting observations of bird sightings, this project collected participants' personal observations on daily life. The aim of this activity was to produce a "new kind of popular and participatory social science which they called anthropology at home" (Sheridan, 2005). People were sent "directives" about three times a year; these directives were simply suggestions as to what they might write about, such as topics of interest and current affairs. Over the period between 1939 and 1945, over 500 people sent their diaries into the Mass Observation Project and over 3,000 people responded to directives.

But what motivated people to take part? There was no payment and no direct credit attributed to the contributors. Sheridan (2005) suggests that part of the attraction was in the quest for information with the goal of expressing that data in simple terms so that all observers could understand and thus transform their environment. But does data collection as an activity trigger informal learning, either intentional or unintentional? If it does, what is the role of technology in supporting this learning? Moving forward in time, the rise of the internet, with mobile technologies and the ability to connect with others to form a distributed community of inquiry, extended and augmented the ways in which people could contribute, creating a new form of membership, that of online community.

The phenomenon of online community was identified in the 1990s (Rheingold, 2000) and the potential of online community membership as a catalyst for learning and cognitive change was recognised (Cuthell, 2002; Fischer & Scharff, 1998; Looi, 2001; Preece, 2001). High levels of engagement and motivation were apparent in online communities, deriving from the common purpose and shared enterprise of their members (Conrad, 2002), elements which formal educators have sought to identify and create in online courses (Brown, 2001; Cocea, 2006; Miltiadou & Savenye, 2003).

Many communities that originated as online communities evolved to incorporate some form of face-to-face contact between their members. For example, members of the Whole Earth 'Lectronic Link (WELL: Rheingold, 2000) community came together for picnics and funerals (Rheingold, 2000) and some of these meetings became integrated as regular community practices (annual WELL summer picnic). Jones and Preece (2006) suggested the term "blended community" to refer to this type of community in which face-to-face contact became commonplace. However, although face-to-face encounters between online community members took place, they were not fundamental to the operation of these communities, and the precise geographical location of such encounters was not critical. GPS technology identifies location with precision, and the powerful functions available with mobile devices combined with Web 2.0 technologies support the creation and maintenance of associations between a particular location and information relevant to that location. Therefore, it became possible for a community to use location in a different way. Instead of viewing location as simply a spot for individuals to meet up, it was possible to look at location more creatively, as a focus for learning activities and knowledge construction. The Geocaching community has realised this potential.

The Geocaching website www.geocaching.com and associated web forums act as a repository for the collective resources and knowledge of the Geocaching community and provide an online record of the interactions that members have with each other, with the website and forums and, through their collective narratives of place, of their experiences of the physical locations in which the Geocaches are hidden. There are other caching websites, e.g. Terracaching and Navicaching, but Geocaching is the most popular.

The Geocaching community as inquiry learners

Geocaching is essentially a form of GPS-guided treasure hunt in which participants hide Geocaches and provide their GPS coordinates to others via the web so that they can find the Geocaches using GPS devices to guide them to the general location. Like many internet-based communities, Geocachers adopt a pseudonym, or Geocaching ID, under which they conduct their Geocaching activities. All posts they make to the Geocaching web forums, all Geocaches they hide, find and log are linked to their Geocaching ID. Once chosen, this ID cannot be changed without losing the link to all recorded Geocaching activities – their personal Geocaching history, in effect.

There are many different types of Geocache. The standard traditional cache consists of a container hidden somewhere in the landscape, with the GPS coordinates published on the website. The container holds a paper log book, which Geocachers sign to prove that they have found the cache, together with trinkets and "swaps". Once a cacher has found and logged a Geocache by signing the logbook, that person can then claim the find by logging it on the website. Each Geocacher's ID lists the number of Geocache finds they have made as well as the number of Geocaches they have hidden for others to find.

EarthCaches are a particular type of virtual Geocache in which some form of inquiry is necessary in order to be able to log the cache, and where the focus is on creating a learning experience. An earthcache has no physical container – instead the GPS coordinates lead to a location where the Geocacher has to conduct an inquiry, guided by the instructions in the Geocache description on the website. The Geocacher, having completed the inquiry, then emails the answer to the cache creator via the Geocaching website, logging the find once the cache creator confirms that the inquiry has been conducted correctly. For example, one EarthCache in the USA asks cachers to take the temperature of a stream at the bottom of a hill, then hike to the source of the stream partway up the hill (using the GPS as a guide), take the temperature there and then, by observing the surroundings and conducting inquiries, suggest reasons for the difference in temperature between the higher and lower areas of the stream.

Methodology

Because the Geocaching community is distributed worldwide, the internet was selected as the main research method. A variety of methodological approaches to researching using the internet have been proposed by internet researchers. Fernback (1999) adopted a cultural metaphor to refer to computer-mediated communication as a "place", describing a series of perspectives on online community which, "in addition to focusing on locale as a central concept in its definition, also encompass the notion of inter-dependency in community life, whether based on commonality of location, interest, values, economic livelihood, behaviours or roles" (Fernback, 1999, p. 209).

This view of virtual spaces as "independent realities" where people can meet up and interact is enacted through use of the term "cyberspace", reflecting "a tendency to view online forums and interaction as existing in an independent reality, separate from off-line environments, bodies, and concerns" (Kendall, 1999, p. 60). Kendall (1999) recommended participant observation, whereby the researcher spends time with participants as a way of "getting to know the particular norms and understandings of the group" (Kendall, 1999, p. 70). She described spending many months on the forums observing the conversations before participating more actively. However, this approach was not best suited to researching/studying an online community such as Geocachers, as they may spend more time engaged in practical, location-based Geocaching activities than they do on the web forums. Indeed, it is possible to be an active member of the Geocaching community without ever visiting the online forums.

Hine (2005) approaches the question of internet research methodology from two perspectives. The first perspective looks at the "research encounter, and research as a form of interaction" and discusses the rationale behind online surveys and online interviews, and whether or not these need to be supported by face-to-face interactions.

Hine's second perspective takes the approach that the internet is a valid site for social research, and discusses virtual ethnography as an online research method. "The success of ethnographers in claiming the internet as a field site attests to acceptance that the internet is a form of social space" (Hine, 2005, p. 109).

The Geocaching study presented in this chapter combined these methodological approaches to online research, taking the perspective of the "research encounter as a form of interaction", using an online survey and online interviews to collect data, and viewing the internet as "a form of social space", collecting data from the collected narratives and traces created there by its inhabitants. In addition to this, and in order to answer the three main questions, detailed qualitative and quantitative data were needed about Geocaching activities in physical locations, and any learning opportunities encountered whilst there.

The research questions (RQs) are as follows:

- RQ1: What motivates people to take part in a collaborative endeavour such as Geocaching?
- RQ2: Does Geocaching as an activity trigger informal learning, either intentional or unintentional?
- RQ3: If it does, does technology facilitate or otherwise support this learning?

Methods

The Geocaching study used the internet as both a data source and as a way of locating and recruiting participants from the worldwide Geocaching community. It employed three methods of data collection:

1. web survey – an online questionnaire providing self-reported data on the target research areas of mobile and Web 2.0 technology use and informal learning
2. Geocaching community resources and outputs from the Geocaching website and forums – providing evidence to support the findings
3. case study interviews of participants selected from the web survey respondents – conducted by telephone or email to real-world examples to illustrate the findings.

Web survey

Web surveys have been successfully used to research Geocaching in the past. Chavez et al. (2004) contacted a regional Geocaching association in order to identify a sample of 221 Geocachers who had either placed or found a Geocache in one of three county park systems in the study area (Anoka, Ramsey and Washington counties). These participants were invited, electronically, to participate in a web survey. This research targeted a specific geographical area, and obtained 133 participants, a response rate of 60%. However, the Geocaching study described in this chapter needed to collect data from a more widely distributed sample of Geocachers, so targeting a regional Geocaching association was not the best method.

It was decided therefore to draw on an approach used by Clough et al. (2008) that would help obtain data from a sample that was representative of Geocachers as a whole, rather than of a single geographically linked group. To explain, Clough et al. (2008) used a similar web-based approach to recruit participants for research into PDA and smartphone uses in informal learning, posting an invitation to participate in a web survey in a number of PDA and smartphone web forums. The invitation contained a link to an online web survey about PDA and smartphone usage, thus participants were self-selecting forum users. This approach generated over 200 responses. Publishing a questionnaire on the web makes it accessible from anywhere in the world, at any time of day, regardless of time zones, thus reaching a worldwide audience.

Geocaching website and forums

The Geocaching.com website is the focal point for Geocaching activities, and its web forum, Groundspeak, offers a vehicle for community discussions. In 2007, when this study was undertaken, there were 40,284 account holders registered with the main Geocaching.com website and 489,646 active caches worldwide. By the time of writing, in September 2016, the number of Geocachers had increased to over 2.8 million, with over 3 million active caches worldwide.

The web survey, posted on the Geocaching forum, Groundspeak, was the main method for data collection, and generated 659 responses. The survey collected demographic information, quantitative data on Geocaching activities and informal learning experiences together with qualitative detail on individual experiences, e.g. free-text questions such as "Why did you start Geocaching?", and quantitative questions such as "Did you hope that Geocachers seeking and finding your EarthCache would learn something as a result? Yes/No", followed by a free-text question asking for more detail from respondents who selected yes. This generated a rich data set covering many aspects of informal learning through online community membership.

The survey contained 52 questions:

- 25 radio button (click on one)
- three check-box (click on all that apply)
- 20 free-text (type as much as you want)
- four optional follow-up (email address, name, website, Geocaching ID).

Online questionnaires are not typically associated with qualitative data collection (Thomas, 2004), and the choice to include 20 free-text questions ran the risk that participants might give up because it required too much effort. However, the high response to the Clough et al. (2008) web survey suggested that enthusiasts would be likely to take the time needed to reply to a long web survey. The responses to the free-text questions in the Geocaching survey generated over 107,000 words, which confirmed that enthusiasts will reply at length about something they are passionate about.

Case study interviews

From the survey responses, five Geocacher IDs were selected as individual cases for follow-up interviews either by email or by phone. These case studies were chosen because they Geocached in the same geographical location and had therefore hidden and found each other's Geocaches. This connected them together through shared yet asynchronous experiences of the physical locations in which their Geocaches were hidden. These shared experiences left a persistent virtual record in the form of the Geocache webpage description and cumulative find logs. These virtual records were also used to provide examples of the findings from the survey and interviews.

Findings

The (web survey) question "Why did you start Geocaching?" sought insights into what motivated people to join the online community of Geocachers. The question was structured as a free-text question in order to capture the full range of possible responses rather than constraining the choices to a selection chosen by the researcher. Of the 659 participants who completed the web survey, 631 answered this question.

Figure 7.1 displays the codes identified as a bar chart together with the percentage of responses for each.

Because the data was free text, participants would often cite three or four reasons for getting into Geocaching. For example:

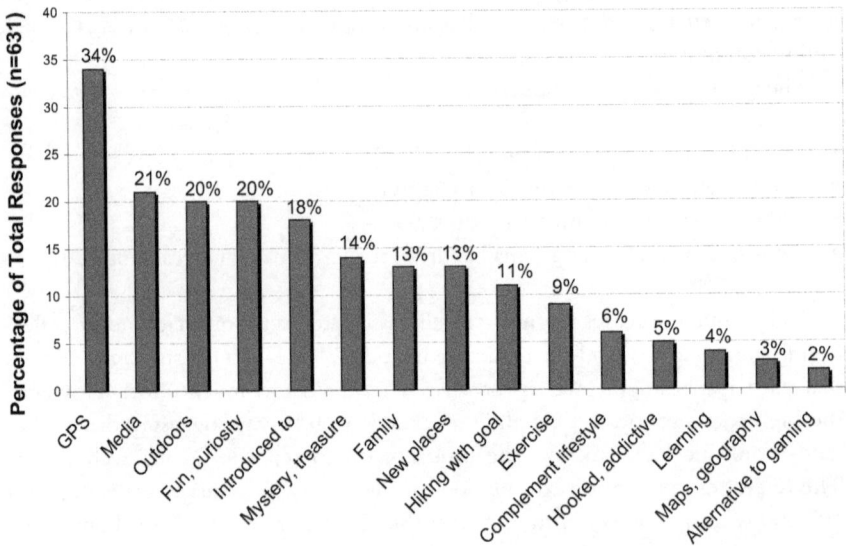

FIGURE 7. 1 Motivations for Geocaching.

> We like to hike and do other outdoor activities, and my husband likes gadgets, so we thought it would be a fun combination for our family.
>
> *(survey response 53)*

To ensure coding reliability, 25 of the responses were independently coded and compared. This resulted in a 92% match.

The remainder of this section describes the motivations in more depth (Table 7.1).

Technology-related motivations

GPS devices are fundamental to the activity Geocaching. Therefore, it is unsurprising that by far the highest percentage of responses (34%) gave GPS devices as one of the reasons they started Geocaching. The GPS device may have been received as a gift or purchased on a whim, and the recipient was looking for something to do with it:

> I was given a Garmin GPS by our central office in the Dept. of Health to plot out concentrations of wastewater problems within the county. . . . Now I'm on the Garmin website trying to find out how to even turn the blasted thing on! They had a link to this thing called "Geocaching".
>
> *(survey response 320)*

Alternatively, the GPS was already a familiar object used for another activity:

> Already owned a GPS, used for boating navigation. Geocaching was mentioned on a boating forum that I visited regularly, and I thought it would be a good alternative use for my GPS.
>
> *(survey response 222)*

These findings suggest that people may turn to the online Geocaching community as a way to learn how to use their technology, or to find additional ways of using it. The decision to look to an online community as a resource for learning about their GPS technology supports the principle that knowledge is socially constructed and that learning may be achieved through collaboration with others (Jonassen, 1995; Jonassen et al., 2003; Lundin & Magnusson, 2003; Sharples et al., 2007).

The role of the internet

The quotes in the preceding section highlight an important role played by the internet in enabling people to find out about Geocaching. Internet references include using an *online blog*, following a link out from the *Garmin website*, using *Google* and finding out through a *web forum* dedicated to boats. Indeed, 21% (*n* = 631) of Geocachers described finding out about Geocaching through some form of media and of these, 56% specifically mentioned internet searches:

TABLE 7.1 Motivations for Geocaching (*n* = 631)

Reason		Exemplar terms	Interest in Geocaching triggered by:
Technology-related motivations			
Owning or acquiring a GPS device	34%	bought gps gpsr technology gift whim	Looking for something to do with a GPS device
Communications media	21%	article heard website read com internet magazine site	Reading about or seeing a TV programme, or following a webpage link
Location-related motivations			
Getting outdoors	20%	outdoors outside places nature	Wishing to spend more time outside, with nature
Visiting new places, exploring surroundings	13%	area places visit home house local explore	Discovering new places, either near home location or further away
Mystery, treasure hunt, adventure, puzzles, excitement, challenge	14%	hunt treasure game	Looking for the thrill of the treasure hunt, of seeking something, adventure
Complementing existing activities			
Walking and hiking with a goal	11%	walking hiking purpose reason goal	Setting a goal for walks
Complement existing hobby, lifestyle or work	6%	hobby work combination	Using Geocaching to enhance existing activity, e.g. travelling long distances for work by car, looking up caches en route to take breaks from driving
Developed out of interest in maps or geography	3%	maps geography	Adopting Geocaching as a way to deepen enjoyment of an interest in the landscape
Social motivations			
Introduced by another	18%	heard friend told introduced	Experiencing encouragement from somebody who already knew about Geocaching
Spending time as a family, with children	13%	family husband wife kids together	Wanting activities suitable for children that would get the family outside together
Learning			
Learning	4%	learn	Learning new things
Health-related motivations			
Health or exercise	9%	exercise	Undertaking activity to get fitter, or as part of a programme of recovery after illness

Alternative to 3D gaming/stressful period/work/ computer	2% game work	Providing a valid and valuable alternative to an activity considered unhealthy
Fun and interest		
Fun or interesting, intrigued/curiosity	20% fun interesting looked thought enjoy idea intrigued curiosity	Feeling intrigued by the idea, thinking it sounded like fun
Addictive, craving, hooked	5% hooked addicted	Experiencing great pleasure from the activity of Geocaching

> I saw GPS receivers in a magazine and thought they looked like an interesting gadget so I googled them and came up with Geocaching.
>
> *(survey response 220)*

Although the internet was frequently used to provide a search engine to locate additional information about Geocaching by those who had encountered the term elsewhere, the hyperlinking nature of the internet also played a role.

> I followed a link in the signature of a post on a totally unrelated web forum, discovered that there were many caches in my area and started seeking them out. This was very recently, I've only been Geocaching for a few weeks.
>
> *(survey response 327)*

This fundamental interconnectedness of the internet assigned it a quasi-intelligent role in bringing Geocaching to the attention of people who were likely to be interested in it.

Location-related motivations

Geocaching is an outdoor activity. It therefore attracts people who want to do things outside. However, the responses to the web survey revealed that people have differing perspectives on why they wanted to engage with their surroundings.

Getting outdoors and experience locations

One of the major factors driving people to go Geocaching was a wish to get outside and experience locations:

> It was a way to get out of the house and on to the trails, goal oriented exploring of our world.
>
> *(survey response 49)*

In addition to the 20% who started Geocaching in order to get outdoors, appreciation of location recurred throughout the other free-text responses to the web survey. A desire to get outside and engage with nature, history and the physical environment was cited as one of the main factors that attracted people to Geocaching.

Mystery, discovery and challenge

Geocaching is, essentially, a form of treasure hunt assisted by GPS technology, i.e. where GPS technology is used in order to locate the treasure. This idea of challenge, adventure and puzzle solving was an important motivational factor for 14% of the web survey respondents:

> It is similar to hunting, or fishing, or any activity that gets you looking or searching for an object, place, or answer, I love the hunt.
>
> *(survey response 570)*

The idea of an activity that presents a challenge or goal resurfaces in other responses (for example, Geocaching providing a goal that complements existing activities such as walking and hiking). This challenge plays a key motivational role in attracting people to Geocaching.

Discovering new places, exploring local surroundings

In their responses to the web survey 13% of participants expressed an interest in finding out more about locations. This might be a wish to discover locations that they had never seen:

> It took me to new and interesting places I would never have gone.
>
> *(survey response 20)*

Some wanted to engage more deeply with their home location:

> The exercise and being outdoors, initially, but after finding the first few caches, I realized how fun it was to explore the area in which I have lived for many, many years, but never really knew much about.
>
> *(survey response 8)*

Participants also started Geocaching in order to discover more about an area they had recently moved to or were visiting on holiday.

> It seemed like it would be fun. I was new to the area and it provided a way to find interesting spots and nice hikes etc. It is a good reason to exercise.
>
> *(survey response 103)*

Underlying the responses to many of the questions posed in the web survey was the attraction of being guided to hidden locations that the Geocachers would not otherwise have found.

> Great way to get outdoors, find places I didn't know existed, and combine my other interests of maps and computers.
>
> *(survey response 146)*

Inherent in these responses was also the cooperative, social construction of new information or knowledge about locations. Some of this new knowledge was provided by other members of the Geocaching community: the cache creator provided the Geocache description and the GPS coordinates to guide others to that location, other Geocachers contributed their experiences and photos to the narrative through their find logs. The rest of the new knowledge about the location was created experientially by the Geocacher through interactions with the physical location, and mediated by the artifacts (i.e. GPS device, connected mobile technology, maps, cache descriptions) taken along during the hunt.

Walking and hiking with a goal

As described previously, Geocaching complements many lifestyles and hobbies. One leisure pursuit that was mentioned explicitly by 13% of participants was walking or hiking. Geocaching provides an extra level of enjoyment to a walk or a hike by providing an additional objective.

> Caching seemed like a fun way to spend time outdoors, and we liked the fact that it gives you a *purpose*, rather than just wandering aimlessly along featureless trails.

Complement existing hobby, lifestyle or work

Geocaching is an activity with a wide appeal, as the responses to this question suggest. Six per cent of participants went into detail about ways in which Geocaching fitted in with their lifestyle. Often, this was because they already followed an active lifestyle engaged in outdoor pursuits:

> Had a GPS. Like hiking, travelling, and visiting historic sites. This satisfies many of my interests at the same time.
>
> *(survey response 556)*

Alternatively, they already travelled for work, and Geocaching gave them a way of adding interest to their trips, or simply getting out of the car for some exercise and excitement.

> I travelled extensively for business and it gave me an opportunity to learn more about the areas I visited, plus it gave me a hobby I could do anywhere.
>
> *(survey response 71)*

The blended nature of Geocaching, combining online social technologies, mobile technologies, the challenge of the hunt and physical outdoor activities, gives it a broad appeal.

> The appeal of a clandestine outdoors hunt for objects using a GPS from information available on the internet combined my love of internet/computing, tech. gadgets, and the outdoors. *Perfect!*
>
> *(survey response 94)*

Three per cent of participants were already interested in exploring locations using the pre-GPS techniques of map reading. For these participants, Geocaching provided a new perspective for a pre-existing interest.

> As a retired surveyor, I have always loved using maps and this gave me a good excuse to do so and to find places I would not otherwise be likely to visit. Also I love gadgets!
>
> *(survey response 140)*

The fact that Geocaching is something people do by choice and which complements their other hobbies or activities makes it easy to integrate into their everyday activities.

Social motivations

Web survey participants were also asked "How do you most often Geocache?", given the five options and invited to select all that applied. Multiple selections were permitted because the group dynamics of a cache hunt differ according to variables such as who is available on a particular day and what type of cache it is.

When asked "Have you made contact with other members of the Geocaching community?" 95% ($n = 659$) responded "yes". Of these, the majority, 89%, had used email, 77% had met in person and 49% had used the phone. Often, a family or group of friends will regularly cache together. Often the geocache logs will mention the collaborative nature of the hunt, pointing to several Geocachers getting together to hunt, socially, for a Geocache.

In addition to this informal organisation of group Geocaches, a community ethos is reinforced through the practices of the Geocaching community. A specific type of cache, called an "event cache", can be created. Geocachers may sign up to come to this event cache, or can just turn up on the day. Sometimes an event cache has a theme: cash in trash out (CITO) is a common theme which combines a love of the countryside with a group attempt to keep it clean and tidy. One of the overriding benefits of event caches is that Geocachers get to meet other Geocachers, whom they may have encountered only as a Geocaching ID in a cache log. When asked whether they had attended an organised Geocaching event, 72% ($n = 659$) of web survey respondents replied positively.

Introduced by a friend

Preece and Shneiderman (2009) suggest that people are more likely to join an online community if others they know are already members, and this finding was confirmed in the responses to the web survey, with 18% (*n* = 631) of Geocachers joining as a result of hearing about it from someone else.

> I was told about it by someone who had gone Geocaching with a relative and knew that I enjoyed hiking, biking, and the outdoors.
>
> *(survey response 64)*

The cooperative nature of the main activity of Geocaching resurfaces in many forms depending on what part the Geocacher is engaged in (i.e. seeking information on Geocaching, searching for a Geocache, hiding a Geocache).

Spending family time with children

Cooperation and community are two ideals that underpin the activity of Geocaching. Geocachers introduce their friends and family to the sport, and 13% (*n* = 631) gave spending time with their family as one of the reasons they started Geocaching.

> Thought it would be a good way to get all the family out together in the open air and maybe learn a little more about nature.
>
> *(survey response 208)*

In fact, 31% of web survey respondents (*n* = 659) reported that their Geocaching ID referred to a group rather than to an individual.

Contributing to the Geocaching community

Each time a Geocacher seeks a Geocache and logs the find on the Geocaching website, that person is effectively participating in the community by contributing to the narrative of place that develops around each Geocache location. Geocachers generally hide caches near their home location so that they can easily access them to maintain them. This means that Geocachers hiding and seeking caches near their homes will recognise each other's IDs. Over time a small-scale community network can build up around a set of locations. This sense of community grows over time and was mentioned by participants in the web survey. For example:

> Was attracted to the avocation for learning more about my GPSr but stayed for the Geocaching community.
>
> *(survey response 501)*

> Came for the caches, stayed for the Geocachers.
>
> *(survey response 501)*

This growing sense of community was evident in many of the responses to the web survey.

Learning goals

Relatively few participants, 4% ($n = 631$), specifically mentioned learning as one of the reasons they started Geocaching. However, when asked in subsequent questions about whether or not they felt they had learned as a result of Geocaching, 89% ($n = 659$) reported that they had. This suggests that informal learning is not a primary motivating factor that drives people to join a community such as the Geocachers, but that it occurs over time as they engage in community activities.

Learning about locations

> To learn more about my surroundings and to get outside. More recently to learn quite a bit of history about the area since being relocated.
>
> *(survey response 148)*

Learning about nature

Thought it would be a good way to get all the family out together in the open air and maybe learn a little more about nature.

(survey response 208)

Learning about GPS technology

> As a way to learn how to use all the features of our GPS, and also to keep my wife from getting lost.
>
> *(survey response 261)*

Learning about geology and the Earth

As might be expected, in their responses to the web survey, 100% of Geocachers who had hidden an EarthCache had a learning aim in mind for those who found the cache. An EarthCache has no physical container, requiring the Geocacher hunting the cache to perform some inquiry related to the landscape in order to log the cache.

The following quote from a Geocacher who has hidden EarthCaches is typical:

> I wanted to encourage people to visit the coast of Suffolk and two of the places I found most interesting myself were because of the geology. I thought other people may want to visit too so I created the earth caches. With the learning activities I tried to create something quite simple but fun to do so that people wouldn't be put off visiting the areas.
>
> *(survey response 157)*

Only 5% ($n = 659$) of survey respondents had created an EarthCache, and of these, 85% ($n = 34$) felt that they had learned something in the process. All 34 survey respondents who had created an EarthCache hoped that people seeking their EarthCaches would learn as a result. Over half, 52% (n = 659), of web survey participants had searched for an EarthCache and of these 74% (n = 345) felt that they had learned something as they found and logged the EarthCache. For example:

> An excellent example of a rounded glacial valley with sarsen stones deposited by the retreating glacier, we were able to refer back to the *Ice Age* movie and help the children envisage what really happens. The size of the deposited stones was quite amazing.
>
> *(case study interviewee – Lydford Locators)*

The Lydford Locators also found Burrington Coombe EarthCache and used it to illustrate the way acidic water reacts with limestone rock, cutting through the stone to create the gorge with its complex cave systems under the ground. Inspired by these EarthCaches, the Lydford Locators set an EarthCache of their own in Leigh Delamere quarry. This EarthCache described the interesting strata in which ancient seashell fossils are exposed. It was mentioned in the interview that they chose this site because they felt that a service station was an incongruous, strange place to find an old quarry, and because the seashell fossils demonstrated that this area had once been under the sea.

Another case study interviewee, Wombles, enjoyed EarthCaching because it led him to interesting areas that he would not otherwise have come across. Geocaching has also led him to visit a variety of educational sites. For example:

> I was previously unaware of a site of major national importance just miles from my home: Fyfield Down at Avebury which has thousands of glacial stones but is off the beaten track.
>
> *(case study interviewee – Wombles)*

Wombles reported that EarthCaches have helped engage his children with geology. As a family, they went looking for the Charmouth EarthCache and the children found a fossilised ammonite in a rock, which "they [the children] thought was absolutely wonderful". They went on to say that, since this discovery/exploration/experience, the children have taken an interest in fossils.

Health-related motivations

Geocaching is self-evidently an outdoor activity that involves walking to find the cache. Therefore, it is reasonable to suppose that one of the reasons people may be attracted to it is for the exercise it offers. The word *exercise* was one of the more frequently occurring words in the tag crowd, appearing a total of 42 times in the responses, as typified by this respondent who started Geocaching in order to "Get exercise and see new places".

Geocaching could be used as a means to achieve a health-related goal:

> I also wanted something to get me fitter (I'm overweight) and this was a perfect choice
>
> *(survey response 195)*

Notably the data pointing to the anticipated health benefits were more diverse than simply exercising to get fitter.

Therapeutic effects

Geocaching was cited as a complementary therapy for a pre-existing illness. For example:

> I have now been diagnosed with MS [multiple sclerosis] but I feel sure that the regular gentle exercise helps to slow down the progression of the disability.
>
> *(survey response 211)*

Others referred to Geocaching as a way of reaching a sense of peace and calmness in order to counteract panic or anxiety.

> I was on a medication with very high anxiety as a side effect. I needed an outlet and walking initially fit the bill. Once I found out about caching and the many areas it would take me I became engrossed in regular caching walks. Caching literally helped me keep my sanity.
>
> *(survey response 251)*

Both the above quotes suggest that these benefits became apparent over time. In the first, the participant found that the regular exercise of Geocaching helped alleviate the symptoms of their medical condition. In the second, the participant initially went walking in order to combat anxiety attacks, and subsequently found that Geocaching provided the impetus he needed to continue going out.

This sense of benefits from Geocaching developing over time was a frequently occurring theme in responses.

Alternative to 3D gaming/stressful period/work/computer

Not all the health benefits described involved moving toward a specific health or exercise goal. An alternative approach framed Geocaching as a way to escape from an activity perceived as damaging to health. For example, Geocaching was a way to avoid spending too long in front of a computer or at work:

> Needed motivation to get more exercise and fresh air. Spent too much time with my computer.
>
> *(survey response 513)*

In some cases, computer or video games were identified specifically as something to be avoided:

> I was an online gamer playing *Dark Age of Camelot* (a MMORPG – massively multi online role-playing game) every day from 2–16 hours. Most days averaged 4–8 hours. . . . I went out and found my first Geocache. It had been placed by the neighbor who told me about the hobby. I never gamed again. I went from an indoor game slave to an outdoor cache seeker. My leisure activities went from mousing around the virtual world to hiking in the real world. Geocaching saved me.
>
> *(survey response 57)*

The health and exercise category is small – only 9% ($n = 631$) – but nevertheless significant because it represents a personal, and sometimes unexpected, benefit of Geocaching that makes a measurable difference to the individual (i.e. in the form of weight loss, improved fitness, recovery from illness or slow-down of disease progression).

Fun and intrigue

One overriding theme that emerged from the responses was the fact that Geocaching sounded "fun", "interesting" or "intriguing". Regardless of whether the primary reason for joining was to find more uses for a GPS device, do more exercise, find a family-friendly activity or simply engage with nature, 20% ($n = 631$) mentioned that Geocaching "sounded like fun".

> Fun way to get my kids hiking. The "treasure hunting" aspect was fun.
>
> *(survey response 606)*

In describing the benefits of Geocaching participants often repeated the same terms. The idea of becoming "addicted" or "hooked" was mentioned as a positive by 5% of participants.

> I took a GPS class; we spent about 5 minutes figuring out how to use the GPS, then went Geocaching. I was immediately intrigued and hooked.
>
> *(survey response 467)*

Whatever their other reasons are, Geocachers need to enjoy the activity of Geocaching because there is no external driving force obliging them to do it.

Conclusions

This study provides rich insights into the reasons why people contribute to mass participation activities. In answer to RQ1, What motivates people to take part in a collaborative endeavour such as Geocaching? Geocachers provided a wide range of motivations in their free-text responses. Some of these reasons were connected to the practices of the Geocaching community such as a desire to experience location in a new way, a pre-existing interest in mobile GPS technology, walking or hiking or a wish to find things that are hidden from the gaze of others. Other reasons were more personal, situating Geocaching as a means of improving fitness, coping with health problems or simply getting away from the computer and spending time outside. Many of the reasons were interrelated, for example, getting outdoors in order to take exercise and spend time with the family, and all the responses reflected a high level of commitment and enthusiasm.

In answer to RQ2, Does Geocaching as an activity trigger informal learning, either intentional or unintentional?, a noteworthy finding was that very few (4%: $n = 631$) named learning as a specific reason for taking part, yet a majority (89%: $n = 659$) reported that they had learned something as a result. This suggests that joining a citizen-led activity such as Geocaching that integrates inquiries at different levels presents unanticipated learning opportunities that occur through participation.

RQ3 asked: Does technology facilitate or otherwise support this learning? Both mobile and social technologies emerged as important motivational and enabling features of Geocaching membership. Ownership of a GPS device could trigger an internet search for information on how to use it or for details of other activities that the device might support. The choice of an online community such as the Geocachers is the means through which to acquire new knowledge that makes use of the collaborative affordances of social technologies.

Participation in the cooperative, social construction of knowledge was not limited to those who were motivated to join the community by technology. Geocachers who wanted to discover new locations were presented with learning opportunities through their interactions with other members of the community and with location. These learning opportunities arose from reading cache descriptions and narratives, and from experiencing locations in a way that was informed by the knowledge and experiences of others through the descriptions and cache logs. The question "Why did you start Geocaching?" asked for a snapshot of motivations for joining the community. Yet, through the rich detail of their responses, Geocachers illustrated that motivation is not a one-off single occurrence but instead changes over time through engagement in community practices.

These changes over time were significant. Many of the responses highlighted changing understandings that took place as the Geocachers experienced locations:

> I started Geocaching for the exercise and being outdoors, initially, but after finding the first few caches, I realized how fun it was to explore the area in which I have lived for many, many years, but never really knew much about.
>
> *(survey response 8)*

These evolving understandings point to a temporal relationship between membership of the Geocaching community and informal learning, suggesting that this relationship develops over time through participation in the community activities.

This chapter highlights the important role played by mobile and social technologies in connecting people with each other through shared experiences of location and acting as catalysts for motivation to take part in a collective endeavour. Such motivations existed long before the emergence of our modern technologies. Although the findings highlight the role of technology, they also show that technology is not the only motivational factor. Other factors included taking part in a group endeavour, contributing to a mass data collection, engaging in activities that involve the whole family, providing learning opportunities for children, getting out in the countryside, enjoying the excitement of a challenge and experiencing the adventure of the hunt. These motivators predate our modern technologies, and are now complemented by the social and mobile technologies that support modern citizen science inquiries.

References

Brown, R. (2001). The process of community-building in distance learning classes. *Journal of Asynchronous Learning Networks, 5*(2), 18–35.

Chavez, D., Schneider, I., & Powell, T. (2004). *The Social-Psychology of a Technology Driven Outdoor Trend: Geocaching in the USA*. Paper presented at the Hawaii International Conference on Social Sciences, Honolulu, HI, June 16–19.

Clough, G. (2009). *Geolearners: Informal Learning with Mobile and Social Technologies*. PhD thesis. Milton Keynes: Open University.

Clough, G., Jones, A. C., McAndrew, P., & Scanlon, E. (2008). Informal learning with PDAs and smartphones. *Journal of Computer Assisted Learning, 24*(5), 359–371.

Cocea, M. (2006). Assessment of motivation in online learning environments. In *Adaptive Hypermedia and Adaptive Web-based Systems* (Vol. 4018, pp. 414–418). Berlin: Springer.

Conrad, D. (2002). Deep in the hearts of learners: Insights into the nature of online community. *Journal of Distance Education, 17*(1).

Cuthell, J. (2002). MirandaNet: A learning community – A community of learners. *Journal of Interactive Learning Research, 13*(1/2), 167–187.

Fernback, J. (1999). Is there a there there: Notes toward a definition of cybercommunity. In S. Jones (Ed.), *Doing Internet Research – Critical Issues and Methods for Examining the Net*. London: Sage Publications.

Fischer, G., & Scharff, E. (1998). Learning technologies in support of self-directed learning. *Journal of Interactive Media in Education, 98*(4).

Greenwood, J. J. D. (2005). Science with a team of thousands: The British Trust for Ornithology. In R. Finnegan (Ed.), *Participating in the Knowledge Society*. Basingstoke: Palgrave Macmillan.

Hine, C. (2005). *Virtual Methods: Issues in Social Research on the Internet*. New York: Berg.

Jonassen, D. (1995). Supporting communities of learners with technology: A vision for integrating technology with learning in schools. *Educational Technology, 35*(4), 60–63.

Jonassen, D. H., Howland, J. L., Moore, J. L., & Marra, R. M. (2003). *Learning to Solve Problems with Technology: A Constructivist Perspective*. Upper Saddle River, NJ: Merrill Prentice Hall.

Jones, A., & Preece, J. (2006). Online communities for teachers and lifelong learners: A framework for comparing similarities and identifying differences in communities of practice and communities of interest. *International Journal of Learning Technology, 2*(2/3), 112–137.

Kendall, L. (1999). Recontextualising "cyberspace". Methodological considerations for on-line research. In S. Jones (Ed.), *Doing Internet Research – Critical Issues and Methods for Examining the Net*. London: Sage Publications.

Looi, C. K. (2001). Enhancing learning ecology on the internet. *Journal of Computer Assisted Learning, 17*, 13–20.

Lundin, J., & Magnusson, M. (2003). Collaborative learning in mobile work. *Journal of Computer Assisted Learning, 19*(3), 273–283.

Miltiadou, M., & Savenye, W. (2003). Applying social cognitive constructs of motivation to enhance student success in online distance education. *Educational Technology Review, 11*(1), 78–95.

Preece, J. (2001). *On-line Communities: Designing Usability, Supporting Sociability*. New York: Wiley.

Preece, J., & Shneiderman, B. (2009). The reader-to-learner framework: Motivating technology-mediated social participation. *AIS Transactions on Human Computer Interaction., 1*(1).

Rheingold, H. (2000). *The Virtual Community: Homesteading on the Electronic Frontier,* revised edition. Cambridge, MA: MIT Press.

Sharples, M., Taylor, J., & Vavoula, G. (2007). A theory of learning for the mobile age. In R. Andrews & C. Haythornthwaite (Eds.), *The Handbook of Elearning Research* (pp. 221–247). London: Sage Publications.

Sheridan, D. (2005). Researching ourselves? The mass–observation project. In R. Finnegan (Ed.), *Participating in the Knowledge Society*. Basingstoke: Palgrave Macmillan.

Thomas, S. J. (2004). *Using Web and Paper Questionnnaires for Data-Based Decision Making*. Thousand Oaks, CA: Corwin Press.

8

TOWARDS CITIZEN INQUIRY

From class-based environmental projects to citizen science

Yurong He, Carol Boston, Jennifer Preece, Anne Bowser, Derek L. Hansen and Jennifer Hammock

Introduction

Citizen science can be considered as a type of vehicle for inquiry-based learning. Non-professionals can learn scientific research processes, gain scientific knowledge, and improve their attitudes towards science through participating in citizen science (Bonney et al., 2009; Brossard, Lewenstein, & Bonney, 2005). Citizen inquiry combines the strengths of citizen science and inquiry-based learning, which has been applied mostly in informal learning settings (Aristeidou, Scanlon, & Sharples, 2013; Herodotou, Villasclaras-Fernández, & Sharples, 2014).

However, citizen inquiry is also a suitable approach for more formal learning environments. Citizen science researchers and science instructors are making efforts to incorporate citizen science in semi-formal and formal learning settings and they are also adding inquiry-based learning elements (Cutraro, 2016).

Introducing citizen science to university students and preparing them to contribute data to citizen science projects is challenging for many instructors. Although a limited number of school educators are recruited into student–teacher–scientist partnership programs focused mainly on primary and secondary education (e.g., Finarelli, 1998), many university professors do not have such opportunities and resources. An alternative is that professors could make unilateral decisions to incorporate an existing citizen science project into their classrooms with limited or no direct support from the scientists themselves. Such educators might be considered to be special kinds of volunteer to the citizen science projects because they could be responsible for bringing many students along. So far there are limited empirical examples that could provide university professors with guidance for doing citizen inquiry in formal learning environments and that provide information about what level of student motivation and performance they should expect.

Therefore, in this study, we aimed to provide one such example by selecting a formal university-based class field environment in which to examine how to teach students about citizen science and help them gain experience with collecting and sharing observation data through a citizen science project. We also investigated different factors that might influence students' motivation to participate and the quality and quantity of their contribution, which are also linked to their learning outcomes.

In order to prevent the possibility that novice students would contribute poor-quality data to the detriment of an actual citizen science project, we developed a citizen science project called Tree and Bird Observation on Campus (TBOC) for this study. It was included as part of a 5-week unit on citizen science in a science, technology, and society colloquium offered to first-year university students in an honors program at an American university. A field experiment and an interview study were conducted to investigate how students' motivation and contribution were influenced by the three factors: feedback, the condition of working alone or together, and task difficulty.

What follows is an introduction to motivation theory and a rationale for exploring these particular factors in relation to students' motivation and contribution. Corresponding research questions and hypotheses are listed below. We then describe the procedure, materials, and results of the TBOC project. Finally, the results and implications of this study are discussed.

Background

Motivation theory

The Hierarchical Model of Intrinsic and Extrinsic Motivation (HMIEM) (Vallerand, 1997; Vallerand & Ratelle, 2002) provides a holistic understanding about how human behavior is motivated in education, sports, and other contexts (Vallerand, 2012). HMIEM addresses different levels of motivation. In this study, we focus on one level of motivation: situational motivation. *Situational motivation* refers to the influence of an individual's experiences engaging in a specific activity at a given moment in time. We aim to investigate the influence of various controllable factors on university students' motivation to participate in a particular citizen science project within the context of a university course.

Situational motivation is in turn composed of four subtypes of motivation: (1) *intrinsic motivation*, in which people engage in a certain activity for its own sake (Deci & Ryan, 1985; Ryan & Deci, 2000); (2) *identified regulation*, in which people identify with the importance and value of a certain behavior; (3) *external regulation*, in which people's behavior is regulated by external demands, rewards, or concerns about potential negative consequences; and (4) *amotivation*, in which people cannot connect the behavior with any purpose or expectations (Deci & Ryan, 1985; Ryan & Deci, 2000). The Situational Motivation Scale (SIMS) survey developed by Guay, Vallerand, and Blanchard (2000) was used to assess situational motivation in this study.

Different types of feedback

In citizen science, lack of feedback may discourage volunteers from continuing to contribute; feedback lets volunteers know that their efforts are appreciated, which keeps them from feeling peripheral to the scientific endeavor (Rotman et al., 2012). Some citizen science projects are aware of the importance of providing some level of feedback and attribution, at least in aggregate, to encourage volunteers to participate again, improve their skills of contributing better data, and deepen their understanding of the project (Devictor, Whittatker, & Beltrame, 2010; Rotman et al., 2012; Wal, Sharma, Mellish, Robinson, & Siddharthan, 2016). Nevertheless, the effect of aggregated feedback on improving individual contributions is limited because it is difficult for people to adjust their effort and strategies to match the task requirement if they do not know how they themselves are specifically doing (Locke & Latham, 2002).

In this study, we examined the effects of different types of instant and individualized feedback on students' motivation and contributions. We adapted the design of the studies conducted in the context of Wikipedia (Zhu, Kraut, Wang, & Kittur, 2011; Zhu, Zhang, He, Kraut, & Kittur, 2013). Zhu et al. (2011) identified four types of individualized feedback: positive feedback (e.g., acknowledging the work of a Wikipedia content contributor), negative feedback (e.g., criticizing a contributor who did not follow Wikipedia guidelines), directive feedback (i.e., providing directions, such as instructions and commands, to help contributors correct their errors), and social feedback (e.g., maintaining a social relationship and supporting group cohesion).

Positive and social feedback increased Wikipedia newcomers' motivation, while the negative and directive feedback increased their efforts (Zhu et al., 2013). Because there was no single type of feedback that increased newcomers' motivation and contribution, researchers proposed that one possible way to improve both is to combine multiple types of feedback. Based on Zhu et al.'s (2011, 2013) studies, we explored the effects of two types of feedback on contributors' motivation and contributions in the context of citizen science: positive-only feedback, and positive directive guidance feedback. We asked the following research question and proposed the hypotheses below:

Q1: What are the effects of receiving feedback on students' (a) motivation; and (b) contribution?

H1: Compared with receiving positive-only feedback, receiving feedback that is both positive and directive is associated with:

a. higher situational motivation;
b. larger quantity of contribution; and
c. higher quality of contribution.

Condition of working alone or together

In any given context, a person may or may not prefer the presence of others, and may choose to work alone or to work with others (Strough, Cheng, & Swenson, 2002), a decision which may in turn impact motivation and effectiveness (e.g., French,

Walker, & Shore, 2011; Patrick & Strough, 2004; Strough et al., 2002). Most citizen science projects provide clear, step-by-step instructions on how to contribute data. However, projects that rely on participants going into the field to collect data rarely note whether solo work or teamwork is more appropriate for the tasks, or whether independent or cooperative contributions are preferred. Previous research on citizen science has paid much more attention to the results of contributors' contributions than to ways in which they chose to contribute. However, when doing classroom activities, working alone and working together are very common choices for educators and students. But we know little about whether solo work or team work makes a difference here. Thus our question and hypotheses are:

Q2: What are the effects of working alone or together on students' (a) motivation; and (b) contribution?

H2: Compared to students who choose to work alone, those who choose to work together will have:

a. higher situational motivation;
b. larger quantity of contribution; and
c. higher quality of contribution.

Task difficulty

As citizen science projects are developed in multiple disciplines in numerous ways, the levels of complexity and difficulty of different citizen science tasks naturally differ (Nov, Arazy, & Anderson, 2010). In previous research on goal setting in psychology, task difficulty has long been found to be a factor influencing task performance (Locke, Shaw, Saari, & Latham, 1981), and a moderator of the effects of different goals on individual task performance (Locke & Latham, 2002). These results could apply to citizen science tasks with different difficulty levels.

People usually do more and better on easy tasks than on difficult ones. With more difficult tasks, higher-level skill and strategies are required, but individual skills and strategies vary considerably (Locke & Latham, 2002). It is difficult to control each individual's skills and strategies and measure their influences on task difficulty and other factors. We therefore decided to let all the students experience all levels of difficulty manipulated in this study. We could not measure motivation separately for tasks with different difficulties. Instead we focused on how task difficulty influenced students' task performance. Accordingly, we proposed a question and related hypotheses:

Q3: What are the effects of task difficulty on contribution quantity and quality?

H3a: Students' contributions are of higher *quantity* for an easy task than for a difficult task.

H3b: Students' contributions are of higher *quality* for an easy task than for a difficult task.

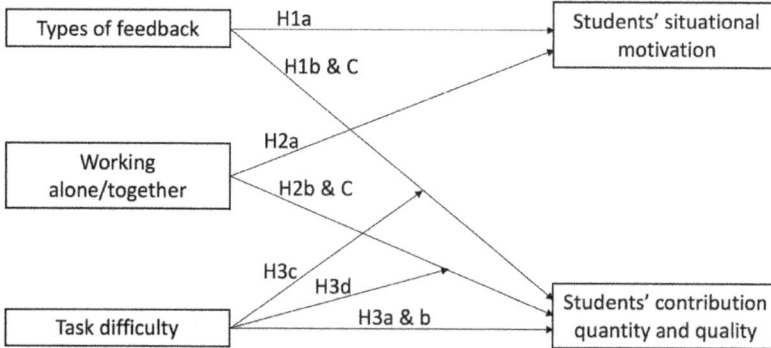

FIGURE 8.1 The relationships between hypotheses.

> H3c: Feedback is more influential on quantity and quality of contribution for easy tasks than for difficult tasks.

> H3d: Working alone or together has a greater influence on the quantity and quality of contribution for easy tasks than for difficult tasks.

Figure 8.1 summarizes the relationships of all the hypotheses.

Methodology

This study encompassed a field experiment based on a citizen science project followed by interviews to clarify experimental results. The study consisted of four phases: (1) preparing students by introducing citizen science to them; (2) engaging students in TBOC and completion of SIMS; (3) interviewing a subset of students; and (4) analyzing data associated with students' motivation, data quantity and quality, and the interview transcriptions.

Participants

A class of first-year students at a public university expecting to major in engineering or computer science were recruited as young adult citizen science project participants ($n = 74$). Seventy students (male = 54, female = 16; age=18~19 years) signed the Institutional Review Board (IRB) consent form indicating that they would allow researchers to use their TBOC data.[1] Sixty-seven of these 70 students (90%) contributed data for the TBOC project; 26 of them (39%) participated in follow-up interviews for extra credit.

Students were told the TBOC project needed their help in collecting observation data about trees and birds on the campus for solving scientific problems in this environment. Students were surveyed to collect baseline data about their knowledge of, and experience with, citizen science. Only 13 of 70 students (19%) had heard of citizen science, and no one had participated in observation data collection before.

Procedure

The first phase lasted two class periods. The students were introduced to a diverse collection of citizen science projects (Wiggins & Crowston, 2011). They were asked to explore different types of projects and become familiar with different data contribution tasks by themselves.

In the following two class sessions, students collected tree and bird data in two rounds of field observations (i.e., observations 1 and 2). Prior to undertaking the first field observation, the students received information about data collection procedures and materials. They were allowed to choose whether they wished to work alone or with a partner. The students who chose to work alone ($n = 29$) did so for both rounds of observation, while those working with a partner ($n = 19$ pairs) retained the same partners for both rounds of observation.

The students' task was the same in both rounds of observation: they went to one of five pre-determined locations on campus, completed and returned paper-based records, and took pictures using personal smartphones. They were encouraged to explore how to find the appropriate targets to observe and experiment with different ways of making their observations. All students were asked to fill out the situational motivation survey after they finished each round of outdoor data collection. Following observation 1 and before observation 2, the students received one of the two types of individualized feedback via email from the first author.

The face-to-face semi-structured interviews were conducted within 1 month of observation 2. The interviews lasted 20–45 minutes and addressed students' prior level of interest in trees and birds; students' reasons for, and feelings about, choosing to work alone or in pairs; and students' feelings about receiving feedback and how the feedback influenced their behavior in observation 2.

Materials

The data collection materials provided to students included a tree and bird observation sheet, a tree walk map with common/scientific names of trees and their location on campus, and a bird guide with the common name and colorful photos of birds commonly found on campus. The content in the tree and bird observation sheet required students to observe at least one tree and one bird on campus during each observation, complete the semi-open-ended and open-ended questions on the sheet by describing the tree's and bird's appearance and location and identifying them, then take at least one photo of the tree and one of the bird and send the photos to the first author using their smartphones.

The structure of the feedback email that students received was adapted from Zhu et al. (2013). The following components were included in the feedback email: [Social Opening] + [Base Message] + [Positive Component] + [Directive Component] + [Simplified Social Closing] + [Signature]. Note that students receiving positive-only feedback received email *without* the directive component. Table 8.1 shows examples of the two types of feedback.

TABLE 8.1 Examples of positive-only and positive corrective guidance for individual and pairs of students contributing observation sheets and photos

Feedback component		Positive-only feedback for an individual student who completed tree and bird sheet and took one tree photo	Positive corrective guidance feedback for a pair of students who completed tree and bird sheet and took one tree photo and one bird photo
Observation sheet	Social opening	Hello [the student's first name],	Hello [the students' first names],
	Base message	I reviewed your observation sheet. Thank you very much for your observation.	
	Positive component	The information you provided about the tree and bird seems clear and covers the important features of the tree and bird.	
	Directive component		It would be great if you would provide more details about the tree and bird when you fill out your observation sheet next time.
	Social closing and signature	My best [researcher's first name]	
Photo	Social opening	Hello [the student's first name],	Hello [the students' first names],
	Base message	Thank you very much for your photo(s).	
	Positive component	Your photo reflects the tree's appearance quite well, especially as this is a challenging task.	Your photos reflect the tree and bird's appearance quite well, especially as this is a challenging task.
	Directive component		It would be great if you would also make a few small improvements for your next observation, such as taking several more pictures reflecting different features of a tree (e.g., shape, leaves, flowers), or spending a little more time finding birds and trying to take better-quality bird photos (e.g., so the photo is clearer, the bird is not so far away and is more recognizable).
	Social closing and signature	My best, [researcher's first name]	

Note: Different types of feedback were given to both individual and paired students.

Field experiment design and measures

Independent variables (IV)

- The type of feedback (between-subject): The positive-only and positive directive guidance feedback were randomly sent to the students between the two rounds of field observation. Half the students who chose to work alone and in pairs received positive-only feedback, while the other half received positive directive guidance feedback.
- Working alone or together (between-subject): Students were allowed to choose their preferred way of working (i.e., work alone or in a pair). Given the limitation of the sample size, we restricted the number of students in each experimental condition in order to balance the two. Therefore a few ($n < 10$) who did not have a choice preference were distributed between the two groups to balance the student numbers.
- Task difficulty (within-subject): Collecting tree data is an easy task, while collecting bird data is a difficult task, given their mobility.

Dependent variables (DV)

- Motivation: We adopted the 16-item SIMS survey (Guay et al., 2000) to assess students' situational motivation to participate in each round of the field observation. SIMS measures four sub-motivations (intrinsic motivation, identified regulation, external regulation, amotivation) via a 7-point Likert scale (1 = not at all, 7 = exactly). Students were asked to fill out this survey after each round of observation. We calculated the change in motivation by comparing each participant's scores on four subscales in observation 2 and their corresponding scores in observation 1.
- Data quantity: The quantity of data was measured individually for observations 1 and 2 by counting the number of words on each completed tree and bird observation sheet and the number of tree and bird photos taken by each individual and pair of students. We calculated the change in data quantity by using each individual and pair's data quantity for observation sheets and photos in observation 2 minus their corresponding quantities in observation 1.
- Data quality: The quality of data was evaluated individually for observations 1 and 2. For the written observation records, two researchers assessed the quality as raters by counting the number of useful descriptive statements made on each tree and bird observation sheet separately. "Useful" meant that the description was directly related to the trees' and birds' appearance, location, or species. Participants were not otherwise instructed in what to observe, which allowed them to be guided by their own inquiry. The two raters independently coded and counted the useful descriptive statements (e.g., an adjective, a phrase, or a sentence) on the observation sheets. The Cohen's kappa value for tree and bird observation quality came in at 0.60 and 0.57 respectively, indicating that the two raters reached moderate agreement on written observation quality

(Fleiss, 1981). They then discussed the differences in their ratings and achieved agreement. We calculated the change in quality of the written observations by using the number of individuals' and pairs' useful descriptive observations for trees and for birds in observation 2 minus the corresponding counts in observation 1.

Since the quality of students' personal smartphone cameras influenced the quality of photos, we did not give an absolute quality grade for each photo. We instead evaluated the relative quality of photos by manually comparing the quality of photos taken by the same individual or pair between two activities and then deciding whether photos in one round of observation were better than, worse than, or about the same as for the other round. The information about order of the observations was removed, so that knowing the order would not bias the judges' decisions.

The photo quality evaluation criteria included (1) focus, (2) lighting, and (3) content. For tree photos, the content judgment reflected the extent to which different features were included (e.g., shape, leaves, flowers); for bird photos, the proportion of the bird's body in the photo was assessed. The Cohen's kappa value for the relative quality evaluation of tree and bird photos was 0.70 and 0.69 respectively, indicating that the two raters reached substantial agreement on photo quality (Fleiss, 1981). They discussed their differences to achieve agreement on the photos.

Analysis

Quantitative analysis strategy

We analyzed data from students who signed the IRB consent forms, participated in two rounds of observation, and submitted their observation sheets and motivation surveys for both activities. In the end, we had valid data for 52 students: 22 students who worked alone, 24 students who worked in 12 pairs, and another 6 students were also in the paired condition but had a partner who did not complete the motivation survey (i.e., there were a total of 18 pairs). Therefore, there were 40 complete data sets (22 individuals and 18 pairs). We used SPSS 20 to conduct the quantitative analysis.

To test the situational motivation, we used multivariate analysis of variance (MANOVA) to analyze: (1) the effects of working alone/together (alone = 0, pair = 1) for observation 1; and (2) the effects of working alone/together and type of feedback (positive only = 0, positive directive guidance = 1) for observation 2. We then used ordinal logistic models in generalized linear models (GLM) to analyze how the two independent variables were associated with the change in motivation between the two observations (lower motivation in observation 2 compared with observation 1 = 0; same = 1; higher motivation in observation 2 compared with observation 1 = 2).

To test the quality and quantity of contributions, task difficulty was also included in the independent variables along with working alone/together and type of feedback. Task difficulty is a within-subject variable: the quantity and quality of the same user's (or pair's) contribution were measured twice, once for the easy task, and again for the difficult task. Generalized estimating equations (GEE) were used to analyze the relationships among the three independent variables and the two dependent variables. As we were interested in exploring the moderator effect of task difficulty on the quantity and quality of students' contributions, we used effect coding for each independent variable: working alone/together (alone = −1, pair = 1); type of feedback (positive only = −1, positive directive guidance = 1), and task difficulty (difficult = −1, easy = 1). When analyzing the contribution quantity (i.e., word counts of observations and number of photos in each observation) and the change in quantity between observations 1 and 2 (i.e., fewer = 0; same = 1; more words/photos in observation 2 compared with observation 1 = 2), we chose to fit Poisson loglinear models and ordinal logistic models, respectively. When analyzing the contribution quality (i.e., number of useful descriptive statements, no absolute quality grade for photo in each observation) and quality change between observations 1 and 2 (i.e., worse = 0; same = 1; better quality in observation 2 compared with observation 1 = 2), we chose to fit Poisson loglinear and ordinal logistic models, respectively.

Because this study was exploratory, we not only fitted a model with main effect terms, but also models with both main effects and all interaction terms. For GLM, Akaike's information criterion (AIC) and Bayesian information criterion (BIC) were used as an indication of model goodness of fit. For GEE, the indication of model fit was the corrected quasi-likelihood under the independence model criterion (QICC). But the goodness-of-fit statistics are not available for the ordinal multinomial models.

Qualitative analysis strategy

We analyzed the interviews in an open coding approach inspired by Strauss and Corbin's (1997) grounded theory. The interview transcriptions were repeatedly reviewed until the underlying concepts and themes emerged from the data. Among 26 interviewees, 15 had received positive directive guidance feedback and 11 had received positive-only feedback; 14 had worked alone, and 12 had worked in a pair.

Descriptive results for motivation and contribution

Table 8.2 shows the means, standard deviations, reliabilities, and inter-correlations among the students' four sub-motivations to participate in the two rounds of observations of the TBOC project. Except for the mean of amotivation, the means of the other three sub-motivations increased slightly in observation 2. External regulation is the dominant sub-motivation because the task was a part of an assignment

TABLE 8.2 Means, standard deviations, reliabilities, and inter-correlations among four subscales

Measures	# of items	α	Mean	SD	Intrinsic motivation	Identified regulation	External regulation
Observation 1							
Intrinsic motivation	4	0.82	3.71	1.00	–		
Identified regulation	4	0.78	3.07	1.02	0.586**	–	
External regulation	4	0.78	5.12	1.10	−0.326*	−0.458**	–
Amotivation	4	0.78	3.62	1.14	−0.087	−0.012	0.395**
Observation 2							
Intrinsic motivation	4	0.80	3.78	0.89	–		
Identified regulation	4	0.79	3.24	0.98	0.745**	–	
External regulation	4	0.88	5.14	1.12	−0.262	−0.333*	–
Amotivation	4	0.86	3.50	1.21	−0.099	0.062	0.332*

$*p < 0.05; **p < 0.01$.

in a formal learning setting. Intrinsic motivation is positively related to identified regulation, but negatively related to external regulation. External motivation is positively related to amotivation.

For quantity of written observation and photo, the students used on average 26 words (SD = 8.23) to describe and took 0.93 photos (SD = 0.66) photos for tree and used on average 22.55 words (SD = 8.94) to describe and took 0.76 photos (SD = 1.54) for bird in observation 1. In observation 2, the students contributed on average more textual and photo data in observation 2 than observation 1: 28.05 words (SD = 10.20) and 1.63 photos (SD = 1.29) for tree and 27.95 words (SD = 13.80) and 1.03 photos (SD = 1.48) for bird.

For quality on the written observation, the students provided on average 9.8 (SD = 0.88) and 7.9 (SD = 2.34) useful descriptive statements to describe tree and bird respectively in observation 1. They provided more useful descriptive statements for observation 2 than observation 1: 9.95 (SD = 1.15) and 8.73 (SD = 1.57) useful descriptive statements for tree and bird respectively .

For quality of photo, a total of 26 individuals and pairs took photo(s) of trees during both rounds of observation, and only 12 individuals and pairs total took photo(s) of birds in both rounds. In observation 2, the numbers of students who took better, same, or worse photos for tree are 16, 8, and 2 respectively. For bird, the numbers of students who took better, same, or worse photos are 7, 1, and 4 respectively.

Motivation

In order to answer Q1a and Q2a, and test H1a and H2a about how working alone/ together and type of feedback could influence the students' situational motivation, we first ran a one-way MANOVA on the data we collected in observation 1.

The results show that the students who worked together had significantly higher identified regulation (e.g., "I engaged in this activity because I believe that this activity is important for me") than those who worked alone ($F_{1, 50}$=7.73, p< 0.05, η^2= 0.13, $\text{mean}_{\text{alone}}$ = 2.64, $\text{mean}_{\text{together}}$ = 3.38). We further checked the influence of working alone/together on every item in the other three subscales and found that the students who worked together had a significantly higher score on one item for intrinsic motivation (i.e., "I engaged in this activity because I think that this activity is interesting") than those who worked alone ($F_{1, 50}$=5.21, p< 0.05, η^2= 0.09, $\text{mean}_{\text{alone}}$ = 3.55, $\text{mean}_{\text{together}}$ = 4.27). These results support H2a, that working with others is related to higher motivation. We also ran a two-way MANOVA: working alone/together (alone vs. pair) × feedback (positive-only vs. positive directive guidance) on the data we collected in observation 2. No significant results were found.

For the change of subscale scores between two rounds of observation into three categories – the scores decrease, there is no change, or the scores increase in observation 2 compared with observation 1 – we fitted ordinal logistic models in GLMs to test the main effects of type of feedback and working alone/together (H1a and H2a). The results show that the type of feedback is related to higher scores on external regulation (Table 8.3, model 1). The positive directive guidance feedback helped maintain or increase students' external regulation 3.28 times more than positive-only feedback. When we further tested the interaction effect by adding the interaction terms (alone vs. pair), the significant results of the type of feedback disappeared (Table 8.3, model 2). According to AIC and BIC for model 1 and 2, smaller numbers indicate a better model. Thus model 1 is better fitted than model 2. These results confirmed that H1a is supported.

TABLE 8.3 Results of two generalized linear models for the change of external regulation between observations 1 and 2, depending on working alone/together and the type of feedback

Dependent variable	External regulation change between observation 1 and 2			
Predictors	Model 1		Model 2	
	B (S.E.)	Exp(B)	B (S.E.)	Exp(B)
Main effect				
Working alone/together	−1.00 (0.57)	0.37	−1.44 (0.82)	0.24
Type of feedback	1.19 (0.55)**	3.28	0.65 (0.90)	1.91
Interactions				
Working alone/together × Type of feedback			0.86 (1.13)	2.35
AIC	34.60		36.03	
BIC	42.41		45.79	

**p < 0.05.

AIC, Akaike's information criterion; BIC, Bayesian information criterion.

Contribution quantity and quality

GEE analysis results are presented for Q1b, Q2b, and Q3 as well as for the tests of H1b and c, H2b and c, and H3a, b, c, and d.

Observation sheet data quantity

Table 8.4 shows the regression analysis results when dependent variables are data quantity (i.e., the number of words) on the observation sheet. In column Observation 1, we see that when doing the easy task (i.e., observing trees), the students contributed 1.15 times the number of words they contributed for the difficult task (i.e., observing birds) in model 1. This result supports H3a. But this result is not robust and is no longer significant when we add the interaction terms (model 2). The goodness of fit for model 1 (QICC = 289.60) is smaller than that for model 2 (QICC = 291.37), indicating that model 1 is better than model 2.

In column Observation 2, after the students received feedback, we see that the students who received positive directive guidance feedback contributed 1.4 times the number of words compared with those who received positive-only feedback in model 1. These results support H1b. The goodness of fit for model 2 (QICC = 314.14) is smaller than that for model 1 (QICC = 317.29), indicating that model 2 with interaction terms is better.

In column Change between observations 1 and 2, the students who received positive directive guidance feedback maintained or increased the number of words 2.9 times more than those who received positive-only feedback in observation 2 in model 1. This result supports H1b.

Observation photo data quantity

Table 8.5 shows the regression analysis results when dependent variables are data quantity of observation photo (i.e., the number of photos). In column Observation 1, there is no significant effect. In column Observation 2, we see that the students contributed 1.59 times more tree photos than bird photos in model 1. This result supports H3a. According to the QICC of each model, model 2 (QICC = 110.82) with interaction terms is better than model 1 (QICC = 111.35). In model 2, we found a significant interaction effect between working alone/together and type of feedback (Figure 8.2). The dashed lines in Figure 8.2 are the average number of photos taken by the students who worked alone (black) and in a pair (gray) (mean$_{alone}$ = 0.75, mean$_{together}$ = 0.97) respectively in observation 1. When working together, the students took more photos after they received feedback, regardless of the type of feedback. However, when working alone, the students who received positive directive guidance feedback took more photos than those who received positive-only feedback. Those who received positive-only feedback contributed fewer photos compared with their contribution in observation 1.

In column Change between observations 1 and 2 in Table 8.5, we see that the students who received positive directive guidance feedback maintained or increased

TABLE 8.4 Results of six generalized estimating equation analyses for (1) the sheet data quantity in observation 1 depending on working alone/together and task difficulty; (2) the sheet data quantity in observation 2 depending on working alone/together, task difficulty, and type of feedback; and (3) the change of sheet data quantity between observations 1 and 2 depending on working alone/together, task difficulty, and type of feedback

Dependent variable: *Data quantity of observation sheet*

Predictors	Observation 1				Observation 2				Change between observations 1 and 2			
	Model 1		Model 2		Model 1		Model 2		Model 1		Model 2	
	B (S.E.)	Exp(B)	B (S.E.)	Exp(B)	B (S.E.)	Exp(B)	B(S.E.)	Exp(B)	B (S.E.)	Exp(B)	B(S.E.)	Exp(B)
Main effects												
Working alone/together	0.04 (0.09)	1.04	0.06 (0.12)	1.07	0.07 (0.10)	1.07	0.11 (0.16)	1.15	0.39 (0.52)	0.67	0.00 (0.87)	1.00
Task difficulty	**0.14 (0.07)***	1.15	0.16 (0.10)	1.18	0.004 (0.08)	1.00	−0.02 (0.17)	1.02	−0.50 (0.39)	0.615	−1.45 (0.79)	0.24
Type of feedback					**0.34 (0.10)****	1.4	0.30 (0.16)	1.6	**1.07 (0.49)***	2.9	0.46 (0.83)	1.59
Interactions												
Working alone/together × Task difficulty			−0.04 (0.13)	0.96			0.03 (0.18)	1.03			1.24 (0.92)	3.45
Working alone/together × Type of feedback							0.08 (0.28)	1.09			0.57 (1.32)	1.77
Task difficulty* Type of feedback							0.08 (0.20)	1.19			1.57 (1.15)	4.79
Working alone/together × Task difficulty* Type of feedback							−0.38 (0.29)	0.68			−2.01 (1.61)	.133
QICC	289.60		291.37		317.29		314.14					

*p < 0.05; **p < 0.01

QICC, quasi-likelihood under the independence model criterion.

TABLE 8.5 Results of six generalized estimating equation analyses for (1) the photo data quantity in observation 1 depending on working alone/together and task difficulty; (2) the photo data quantity in observation 2 depending on working alone/together, task difficulty, and type of feedback; and (3) the change of photo data quantity between observations 1 and 2 depending on working alone/together, task difficulty, and type of feedback

Dependent variable	Data quantity of observation photo				Observation 2				Change between observations 1 and 2			
Predictors	Model 1		Model 2		Model 1		Model 2		Model 1		Model 2	
	B (S.E.)	Exp(B)	B (S.E.)	Exp(B)	B (S.E.)	Exp(B)	B (S.E.)	Exp(B)	B (S.E.)	Exp(B)	B (S.E.)	Exp(B)
Main effects												
Working alone/together	0.26 (0.35)	1.30	0.26 (0.64)	1.30	0.17 (0.25)	1.19	1.03 (0.63)	2.80	−0.37 (0.48)	3.02	−0.47 (0.64)	0.63
Task difficulty	0.18 (0.29)	1.19	0.18 (0.58)	1.20	**0.46 (0.22)***	1.59	0.47 (0.29)	1.60	0.43 (0.35)	1.54	−0.47 (0.63)	0.63
Type of feedback					0.48 (0.26)	1.61	0.98 (0.54)	2.67	**1.50 (.47)**	4.46	1.38 (.74)	3.99
Interactions												
Working alone/together × Task difficulty			−0.01 (0.60)	0.99			−0.47 (0.55)	0.63			0.99 (0.80)	2.69
Working alone/together × Type of feedback							**−1.61 (0.78)***	0.20			−0.77 (1.17)	0.47
Task difficulty* Type of feedback							0.02 (0.42)	1.02			0.99 (0.99)	2.69
Working alone/together × Task difficulty* Type of feedback							1.03 (0.75)	2.79			0.18 (1.53)	1.20
QICC	97.89		99.89		111.35		110.82					

*$p < 0.05$; **$p < 0.01$; ***$p < 0.001$.

QICC, quasi-likelihood under the independence model criterion.

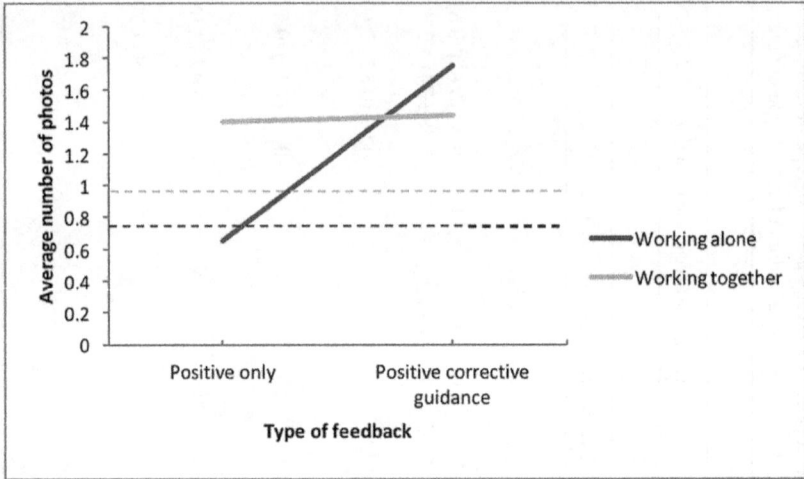

FIGURE 8.2 Interaction effect between working alone/together and type of feedback on the quantity of bird photos in observation 2.

the number of photos 4.46 times more than those who received positive-only feedback in model 1. H1b is supported by this result. However, this result is not robust; when we add interaction terms in model 2, this effect is no longer significant.

Observation sheet data quality

Table 8.6 shows the regression analysis results when dependent variables are data quality (i.e., the number of useful descriptive statements) on the observation sheet. The column Observation 1 shows that the students' data quality on the easy task is better than on the difficult task; there are 1.22 and 1.30 times more useful descriptions on the easy task than on the difficult task in model 1 and model 2, respectively. As model 1 has smaller QICC than model 2, model 1 is better fitted than model 2. These results support H3b.

In column Observation 2, in model 1, we see that students who worked in a pair contributed 1.06 times the number of useful descriptions compared with those who worked alone, with the useful descriptions on the easy task numbering 1.14 times more than those on the difficult task; and the students who received positive directive guidance feedback contributed 1.09 times more useful descriptions than those who received positive-only feedback. These results support H1c, H2c, and H3b. However, when interaction terms are added, these significant results disappear, and there is no significant interaction effect. According to the goodness of fit for model 1 (QICC = 20.53) and model 2 (QICC = 28.27), the model 1 without interaction terms is a better model.

In column Change between observations 1 and 2, we see that there is significant difference in the quality of text observations as judged by the number of useful

TABLE 8.6 Results of six generalized estimating equation analyses for (1) the sheet data quality in observation 1 depending on working alone/together and task difficulty; (2) the sheet data quality in observation 2 depending on working alone/together, task difficulty, and type of feedback; and (3) the change of sheet data quality between observations 1 and 2 depending on working alone/together, task difficulty, and type of feedback

Dependent variable	Data quality of observation sheet											
	Observation 1				Observation 2				Change between observations 1 and 2			
	Model 1		Model 2		Model 1		Model 2		Model 1		Model 2	
Predictors	B (S.E.)	Exp(B)	B (S.E.)	Exp(B)	B (S.E.)	Exp(B)	B (S.E.)	Exp(B)	B (S.E.)	Exp(B)	B (S.E.)	Exp(B)
Main effects												
Working alone/together	0.05 (0.04)	1.05	0.13 (0.09)	1.13	**0.06 (0.03)***	1.06	0.11 (0.09)	1.11	0.86 (0.46)	2.36	0.58 (0.85)	1.80
Task difficulty	**0.20 (0.05) ***	1.22	**0.26 (0.09)***	1.30	**0.13 (0.03)***	1.14	0.16 (0.09)	1.18	**−0.90 (0.41)***	0.41	**−1.43 (0.72)***	.24
Type of feedback					**0.08 (0.03)***	1.09	0.09 (0.09)	1.10	**1.48 (0.46)***	4.40	0.21 (0.81)	1.23
Interactions												
Working alone/together × Task difficulty			−0.14 (0.09)	0.87			−0.08 (0.10)	0.93			−0.23 (1.05)	.79
Working alone/together × Type of feedback							−0.02 (0.10)	0.98			1.90 (1.48)	6.71
Task difficulty* Type of feedback							−0.004 (0.10)	0.10			1.77 (1.01)	5.87
Working alone/together* Task difficulty × Type of feedback							0.005 (0.11)	1.05			−1.65 (1.67)	.19
Type of feedback												
QICC	54.58		55.78		20.53		28.27					

*p < 0.05; **p < 0.01; ***p < 0.001.

QICC, quasi-likelihood under the independence model criterion.

descriptions between the easy task and the difficult task. In observation 2, the quality of text observations on the easy task stayed the same or increased 0.41 and 0.24 times compared with the quality of observations for the difficult task in model 1 and model 2, respectively. We also see that the students who received positive directive guidance feedback maintained or increased the textual data quality 4.40 times compared with those who received positive-only feedback in model 2. This result supports H1c.

Observation photo data quality

Since the sample size of the students who took tree and bird photos in both observations is too small, regression analysis was not performed. We analyzed the descriptive results for photo quality change. The results show a trend that, regardless of whether the students worked in a pair or alone, those who received positive directive guidance feedback took better tree photos in observation 2. This result is consistent with supporting H1c.

Qualitative analysis results

We supplement the quantitative results with the interview results so that we understand better the underlying reasons for the students' behavior.

Pre-interest in the trees and birds

Interviewees' pre-interest helped explain the students' relatively low intrinsic motivation and identified regulation scores in the motivation results. Of the 26 interviewees, all except one said that they didn't have much interest in trees or birds. The exception was a student whose family had many bird feeders, and who said he liked birds.

Different difficulty levels for tree and bird observations

All the interviewees reported that they felt collecting bird data, especially bird photos, was much more difficult than collecting tree data, and thereby confirming prior research (Preece et al., 2016) that supported the different task difficulties in this study (e.g., "It's pretty difficult to observe the bird. A bird is a moving animal. They fly away before you get . . . too close to them" – P7; "The trees were a lot easier to do; I mean, they are standing still" – P24). Further, due to the limitations of the smartphone camera, it is very difficult to take a good photo of a bird. The interviewees complained most about the zoom, light, and focus issues of the smartphone camera (e.g., "My phone camera doesn't have good enough zoom, because the birds maybe like are at the top of the tree, and it's hard to zoom and get a picture of them" – P21).

Reasons for choosing to work alone or together

The following findings help explain why the students who worked in pairs perceived the observation tasks to be more interesting and important to them than the
students who worked alone when they were first exposed to this kind of nature
observation activity. We found that students had different reasons for their decisions to work alone or with another student. The decision to work in a pair was
driven by the desire to satisfy the following needs: (1) *companionship* – wanted to
have company (e.g., "not lonely, there is somebody you can discuss with when you
are observing [trees and birds]" – P17); (2) *fun* – felt more enjoyable and especially
made the observation tasks that they did not think very interesting more appealing to them (e.g., "if you could not have company around, it wouldn't appeal to
me to go to trees and take notes and take pictures. If someone was there, it was a lot
more appealing and more fun" – P19); and (3) *assistance* – helped decrease students'
feelings of uncertainty about undertaking unfamiliar outdoor observation activities, made them feel that the tasks were easier, gave them confirmation from their
partners, and gave them more confidence in their answers, especially for bird observation (e.g., "If it's a bird, with two people, there is more chance to see it" – P12).

The students who chose to work alone emphasized their needs for (1) *concentration
and calm* – they did not want to be distracted by other people and waste time and
energy on keeping the communication going between partners (e.g., "I like to do
things at my own pace, not to wait for other people. Because you can think about it
more, you don't have to always communicate your thoughts" – P26); and (2) *serious-
ness* – they considered this activity as a serious science project rather than something
for their enjoyment (e.g., "Some of the other people in the class don't take it as
seriously as I might like to. It's kind of de-motivational being with others" – P7).

The effects of individualized feedback

The following interview findings help explain why the students who received positive directive guidance feedback felt they had a better understanding of the purpose
of collecting tree and bird data, and why they were asked to do the observation, as
well as why their data quantity and quality significantly increased in observation 2.

All interviewees, no matter what type of feedback they received, conveyed a
general positive feeling about receiving feedback emails. Echoing Rotman et al.'s
findings (2012), volunteers' needs for recognition and attribution were gratified.
All interviewees said that they were happy that their contributions were appreciated and recognized by the researchers (e.g., "I really like it [the feedback]; it
means they care, we are not just some tiny parts of a thing, it makes us feel like we
did something" – P16).

Two new needs, *verification* and *do it right and better*, emerged at this point in
the interviews. The students expressed that it was beneficial for them to know
whether they did the data collection tasks correctly or not, and how to do the data

collection tasks right and better. Simply informing the students that their data was received, and praising and thanking them for their contribution, is not enough, especially when researchers expect them to contribute again, and contribute more and better data. All interviewees expressed their desire to know whether their contributions in observation 1 were right and helpful (e.g., "I didn't expect myself to get everything right on the first try and I'm pretty sure no one really would" – P18). The positive component in the feedback met their needs for *verification* that their contributions were appropriate in observation 1 (e.g., "For the people that are doing it [observation task], the best is the feedback really in the verification, because in that way you know you got something right or wrong" – P12).

However, students who received only the positive components of the feedback could not satisfy the need to *do it right and better*. As one interviewee pointed out, "I really appreciate that a scientist thanked me for investing my time . . . but I also want to know how to improve the observations, how to make it better, and more useful for them"– P5, which was echoed by many other interviewees who received positive-only feedback. They also expressed that, although they felt happy to receive the positive feedback, it did not have much influence on their motivation and performance in observation 2. This explains why many students who received positive-only feedback did not collect more data, or even collected less data in observation 2.

On the contrary, interviewees who received positive directive guidance feedback had better ideas about what to do and were less confused about how to collect the right and better data in observation 2. They reported that they tried harder in observation 2 because of the directive guidance in the feedback (e.g., "I tried hard enough to get a better picture, that takes a lot of time, cause it was my phone camera, it was not easy . . . I definitely tried harder the second week" – P21). The interviewees also "had a better idea about what I was supposed to offer [in the second activity]" – P25 and felt "more motivated to do it right" – P3. It was important for them to know that they provided good contributions or else their help would be meaningless (e.g., "Because if I want to help it, I want to actually give my right observations to the scientists, so I want their feedback to know what they actually like and what actually helps them" – P13).

Additionally, all interviewees expressed that they were interested in participating in other citizen science projects in the future and said that they would expect to receive feedback. They especially emphasized that the feedback was crucial for them to come back and contribute again: "If in the first one they did not give me feedback, I would probably forget about it. Because they wouldn't be there to remind me. If they gave me feedback, I would want to keep on doing it" (P17).

Discussion

The results answered the three questions and partially confirmed the hypotheses we had for incorporating a citizen science project in a university class. For Q1, providing students participating in a citizen science project with individualized feedback containing both positive and directive components increased the students' situational motivation, and also improved contribution quantity and quality more effectively than providing feedback that included only a positive component. Hypotheses 1a, 1b, and 1c were supported.

For Q2, the students who chose to work together had higher situational motivation than those who worked alone during their first-time citizen science experience. After they received feedback, students who worked together turned in observation sheets that were judged to be of higher quality than those of students working alone. However, neither condition – working alone or together – was associated with contribution quantity. Hypotheses 2a and 2c were partially supported, yet hypothesis 2b was not supported. There is an interesting moderator effect of working alone vs. together on the effect of type of feedback on the quantity of photo contribution. The type of feedback influencing the students who chose to work alone differed from the type of feedback influencing those in a pair.

For Q3, it is not surprising that the students contributed more and better data in response to the easy task than the difficult task. Hypotheses 3a and b were supported. However, after receiving feedback, the quality of the students' written descriptions on observation sheets improved more for the difficult task than for the easy task. Hypotheses 3c and d were not supported.

These results allow us to have an in-depth understanding of students' motivation, performance, and the effects of influential factors when conducting a citizen science inquiry activity in university instructional environments. These results provide valuable insights for professors and researchers seeking to combine different citizen science projects and inquiry learning in university settings in the future.

Although the citizen science project used in this study focused on observing trees and birds, the results of students' motivation and performance on doing these two tasks could apply to various biodiversity monitoring tasks. On the one hand, the data we asked the students to collected are essential data elements needed to ensure the quality of biodiversity monitoring data (i.e., the date, time, location, and description of the observation and digital vouchers) (He et al., 2016). On the other hand, a fundamental difference among all biodiversity monitoring tasks is whether the observation targets are static or moving organisms, which leads to different data collection experiences and strategies (Preece et al., 2016; Wiggins & He, 2016). Trees and birds can be considered as the two most typical static and moving organisms respectively. Therefore, when a citizen science project focused on biodiversity monitoring is incorporated in university settings, students may have to do similar observation tasks and they may have similar reactions to those who participated in this study.

This study demonstrated the feasibility of combining biodiversity monitoring citizen science projects and inquiry-based learning elements in university class field environments. Unlike many citizen science project training workshops in which participants are directly asked to learn to do exactly what a protocol describes to ensure the data quality (Cohn, 2008), we encouraged students to choose the way of working they preferred and try out how to collect data by themselves first, then helped them improve their data collection skills and understand the quality of their data by sending them individualized feedback. By drawing on aspects of semi-formal learning (i.e., the students' performances on the project task were not graded; there was no structured curriculum), we successfully encouraged university students with little existing knowledge of, or interest in, citizen science to engage in a project. The students in our study reported that they did not feel reluctant to try this kind of citizen science project again in their classes. The relatively short duration of the study and the lack of pressure of formal evaluation of their performance helped the students to be more relaxed and open-minded in learning and experiencing how to participate in citizen science, rather than to have negative feelings and experiences, as found in previous studies conducted in formal learning contexts (Moss, Abrams, & Kull, 1998; Sadler, Burgin, McKinney, & Ponjuan, 2010; Wormstead, Becker, & Congalton, 2002). Doing citizen inquiry in class first helps prepare them to be prospective citizen scientists and participate in other citizen science projects as volunteers in the future.

Last but not least, the results revealed the importance of providing feedback on citizen inquiry in formal learning environments. Feedback that is individualized and contains both positive and directive components appears helpful in enhancing the commitment and improving the contributions of the students to the citizen science project. Without helpful feedback, they may be more likely to become discouraged and find less meaning in participating in the citizen science project, which therefore might have a negative effect on their learning. It is worthwhile for researchers, project designers, and instructors to put more effort into studying and developing new strategies and technologies to facilitate direct communication between scientists and university students.

Conclusion

This study provides a distinct citizen inquiry example conducted in a university class. It explored several factors that might influence students' motivations and contributions to citizen science: the type of feedback they received, whether they worked alone or in pairs, and whether the task was relatively easy or difficult. First, we found that receiving prompt, individualized feedback, including appreciation, verification, and guidance, was effective in increasing the students' motivation as well as the quantity and quality of their contributions. Second, working together was associated with higher motivation on students' first-time participation in citizen science compared to working alone, and there was an interesting moderating effect of working alone or together on the relationship between type of feedback and contribution quantity. Third, different types of feedback led to different amounts of improvement in students' contribution on easy tasks versus difficult tasks. This study contributes to an understanding of young adults' motivation for participating in citizen science tasks in a class field environment as well as factors affecting their performance. It should provide designers of citizen science projects, as well as professors who wish to involve students in them, with evidence about ways in which experiential learning through citizen science projects may be incorporated effectively in a university classroom, including building in opportunities for collaboration and feedback.

Acknowledgments

We thank the faculty and students who participated in our study.

Note

1 Students received class participation credit regardless of whether they signed the IRB and how well they did on data collection.

References

Aristeidou, M., Scanlon, E., & Sharples, M. (2013). A design-based study of Citizen Inquiry for geology. In: Katherine, M., & Tomaž, K. (Eds.), *Proceeding of the Doctoral Consortium at the European Conference on Technology Enhanced Learning, Co-Located with the EC-TEL 2013 conference*. Paphos, Cyprus: CEUR, 7–13.

Bonney, R., Ballard, H., Jordan, R., McCallie, E., Phillips, T., Shirk, J., & Wilderman, C. C. (2009). *Public Participation in Scientific Research: Defining the Field and Assessing its Potential for Informal Science Education*. A CAISE Inquiry Group Report. Washington, D.C.: Center for Advancement of Informal Science Education (CAISE).

Brossard, D., Lewenstein, B., & Bonney, R. (2005). Scientific knowledge and attitude change: The impact of a citizen science project. *International Journal of Science Education, 27*(9), 1099–1121.

Cohn, J. P. (2008). Citizen science: Can volunteers do real research? *BioScience, 58*(3), 192–197.

Cutraro, J. (2016, September 29). *Finding the First Project For Your Classroom*. Retrieved October, 2016, from http://blogs.discovermagazine.com/citizen-science-salon/2016/09/29/finding-the-first-project-for-your-classroom/#.WBvUmuErJsN.

Deci, E. L., & Ryan, R. M. (1985). *Intrinsic Motivation and Self-Determination in Human Behavior*. New York: Plenum.

Devictor, V., Whittatker, R. J., & Beltrame, C. (2010). Beyond scarcity: Citizen science programmes as useful tools for conservation biogeography. *Diversity and Distributions, 16*, 354–362.

Finarelli, M. G. (1998). GLOBE: A worldwide environmental science and education partnership. *Journal of Science Education and Technology, 7*(1), 77–84.

Fleiss, J. L. (1981). *Statistical Methods for Rates and Proportions* (2nd ed.). New York: John Wiley.

French, L. R., Walker, C. L., & Shore, B. M. (2011). Do gifted students really prefer to work alone? *Roeper Review, 33*(3), 145–159.

Guay, F., Vallerand, R. J., & Blanchard, C. (2000). On the assessment of situational intrinsic and extrinsic motivation: The Situational Motivation Scale (SIMS). *Motivation and Emotion, 24*, 175–213.

He, Y., Preece, J., Hammock, J., Weber, M., McKeon, S., & Wiggins, A. (2016). A journey of citizen science data in an online environment. In *Proceedings of the 19th ACM Conference on Computer Supported Cooperative Work and Social Computing* Companion. San Francisco, CA: ACM Press. 289–292.

Herodotou, C., Villasclaras-Fernández, E., & Sharples, M. (2014). The design and evaluation of a sensor-based mobile application for citizen inquiry science investigations. In *European Conference on Technology Enhanced Learning*. Graz, Austria: Springer International Publishing, 434–439.

Locke, E. A., & Latham, G. P. (2002). Building a practically useful theory of goal setting and task motivation. *American Psychologist, 57*(9), 705–717.

Locke, E. A., Shaw, K. N., Saari, L. M., & Latham, G. P. (1981). Goal setting and task performance: 1969–1980. *Psychological Bulletin, 90*, 125–152.

Moss, D. M., Abrams, E. D., & Kull, J. A. (1998). Can we be scientists too? Secondary students' perceptions of scientific research from a project-based classroom. *Journal of Science Education and Technology, 7*(2), 149–161.

Nov, O., Arazy, O., & Anderson, D. (2010). Scientists@home and in the backyard: Understanding the motivations of contributors to digital citizen science. Retrieved March, 2016, from https://www.researchgate.net/profile/Ofer_Arazy/publication/228279944_ ScientistsHome_and_in_the_Backyard_Understanding_the_Motivations_of_ Contributors_to_Digital_Citizen_Science/links/09e41509bfc3a80135000000.pdf.

Patrick, J. H., & Strough, J. (2004). Everyday problem solving: Experience, strategies, and behavioral intentions. *Journal of Adult Development, 11*(1), 9–18.

Preece, J., Boston, C., Yeh, T., Cameron, J., Maher, M., & Grace, K. (2016). Enticing casual nature preserve visitors into citizen science via photos. In *Proceedings of the 19th ACM Conference on Computer Supported Cooperative Work and Social Computing Companion*. San Francisco, CA: ACM Press, 373–376.

Rotman, D., Preece, J., Hammock, J., Procita, K., Hansen, D., Parr, C. S., Lewis, D., & Jacobs, D. (2012). Dynamic changes in motivation in collaborative ecological citizen science projects. In *Proceedings of the ACM Conference on Computer Supported Collaborative Work*. Seattle, WA: ACM Press, 217–226.

Ryan, R. M. & Deci, E. L. (2000). Self-determination theory and the facilitation of intrinsic motivation, social development, and well-being. *American Psychologist, 55*, 68–78.

Sadler, T. D., Burgin, S., McKinney, L., & Ponjuan, L. (2010). Learning science through research apprenticeships: A critical review of the literature. *Journal of Research in Science Teaching, 47*(3), 235–256.

Strauss, A., & Corbin, J. M. (1997). *Basics of Qualitative Research: Grounded Theory Procedures and Techniques*. Beverly Hills, CA: Sage Publications.

Strough, J., Cheng, S., & Swenson, L. M. (2002). Preferences for collaborative and individual everyday problem solving in later adulthood. *International Journal of Behavioral Development, 26*(1), 26–35.

Vallerand, R. J. (1997). Toward a hierarchical model of intrinsic and extrinsic motivation. In M. P. Zanna (Ed.), *Advances in Experimental Social Psychology* (Vol. 29, pp. 271–360). New York: Academic Press.

Vallerand, R. J. (2012). From motivation to passion: In search of the motivational processes involved in a meaningful life. *Canadian Psychology, 53*, 42–52.

Vallerand, R. J., & Ratelle, C. F. (2002). Intrinsic and extrinsic motivation: A hierarchical model. In E. L. Deci & R. M. Ryan (Eds.), *Handbook of Self-Determination Research* (pp. 37–69). Rochester, NY: University of Rochester Press.

Wal, R., Sharma, N., Mellish, C., Robinson, A., & Siddharthan, A. (2016). The role of automated feedback in training and retaining biological recorders for citizen science. *Conservation Biology, 30*(3), 550–561.

Wiggins, A., & Crowston, K. (2011). From conservation to crowdsourcing: A typology of citizen science. In *2011 44th Hawaii International Conference on System Sciences (HICSS)*. Hawaii: IEEE, 1–10.

Wiggins, A., & He, Y. (2016). Community-based data validation practices in citizen science. In *Proceedings of the 19th ACM Conference on Computer-Supported Cooperative Work & Social Computing*. San Francisco, CA: ACM Press, 1548–1559.

Wormstead, S. J., Becker, M. L., & Congalton, R. G. (2002). Tools for successful student–teacher–scientist partnerships. *Journal of Science Education and Technology, 11*(3), 277–287.

Zhu, H., Kraut, R.E., Wang, Y.-C., & Kittur, A. (2011). Identifying shared leadership in Wikipedia. In *Proceedings of the SIGCHI Conference on Human factors in Computing Systems*. Vancouver: ACM Press, 3431–3434.

Zhu, H., Zhang, A., He, J., Kraut, R. E., & Kittur, A. (2013). Effects of peer feedback on contribution: a field experiment in Wikipedia. In *Proceedings of the SIGCHI Conference on Human Factors in Computing Systems*. Vancouver: ACM Press, 2253–2262.

9

HIGH MOTIVATION AND RELEVANT SCIENTIFIC COMPETENCIES THROUGH THE INTRODUCTION OF CITIZEN SCIENCE AT SECONDARY SCHOOLS

An assessment using a rubric model

Josep Perelló, Núria Ferran-Ferrer, Salvador Ferré, Toni Pou and Isabelle Bonhoure

Introduction

Schools are privileged scenarios to test, improve, perform and upscale citizen science (CS) projects. Teachers can support students in, for example, the process of data collection and analysis (Dickerson-Lange *et al.*, 2016; Eick *et al.*, 2008; Rock & Lauten, 1996). Schools also allow the performance of CS projects over quite a long period of time without having to maintain heavy engagement infrastructures (Dickerson-Lange *et al.*, 2016). The school context also provides a large number of volunteers that can easily participate in a single experiment such as, for instance, in the case of mass experiments (Kasperowski & Brounéous, 2016).

However, these compelling arguments are not consistent with the fact that the presence of CS in schools (understood as pre-university levels) is still anecdotal and, to the best of our knowledge, always deals with a single and particular project. These projects, for historical and feasibility reasons, are indeed mostly constrained to biodiversity and ecology studies (Bonney *et al.*, 2009; Eick *et al.*, 2010; Phillips *et al.*, 2014; Zoellick *et al.*, 2012). Therefore, the methodology described therein is quite specific to a given project or topic and it is generally not easily transferable to a wider variety of scientific disciplines.

Similarly, the evaluation of students' learning competencies during these processes is generally scarce and, if it does exist, is most often qualitative (Bingaman & Eitel, 2010; Dickerson-Lange *et al.*, 2016; Schon *et al.*, 2014). For example, Silva et al. (2016) evaluated the educational and motivational outcomes of their "Cell Spotting" project and Sharples *et al.* (2015) conducted an extensive comparative evaluation of learning of topic knowledge and science inquiry skills. However, questionnaires were only delivered after the experiment and they were not compulsory, thus in some way limiting the significance of the study.

Perhaps the most interesting perspective is reported by the prescriptive essay "Lessons learned from citizen science in the classroom" (Gray *et al.*, 2012), since it puts the spotlight on the class group and the positive learning outcomes in a much broader perspective. We can also add that embedding CS in university-level (undergraduate) classrooms has been shown to be effective for active learning and has enhanced engagement with science (Coleman & Mitchell, 2014; Freeman *et al.*, 2014; Powell & Harmon, 2014). By using both quantitative and qualitative methods, Vitone *et al.* (2016) have found that engagement with science increased thanks to the introduction of the "School of Ants" project in college.

This chapter aims to contribute to the existing literature by presenting empirical results evaluating the impact of introducing CS at schools with up to five different CS projects. We wanted to do so by proposing a ready-made rubric model that can be generalised to any CS project introduced in formal education. The methodology was identically applied in all five CS projects obtaining data from more than 500 secondary school students (between 12 and 15 years old). When designing the study, we had in mind three different goals. The first goal was to create and test an easy-to-follow methodology, capable of introducing a diverse typology of CS projects in formal education. The second goal was to develop a common strategy to evaluate the impact of the several CS projects in order to obtain a set of homogeneous results ready to be analysed and compared. Finally, the third goal was to harness quantitative and robust results regarding the impact of CS in schools by testing the acquisition of knowledge, skills and attitudes among 11 different schools and through the rubric model proposed.

The chapter therefore proposes a rubric model for CS projects to assess the acquisition of competencies and attitudes in schools. We test the tool in five different CS projects in a common way and present the results of these rubrics. Data from our study are analysed not only by aggregating all five CS projects but also by comparing their rubrics to find differences due to the peculiarities of each CS project. Finally, we provide a general discussion linking the observed impact on students' competencies and attitudes with the methodology used, the intrinsic characteristics of the projects introduced in schools and the potential of CS introduction in school.

Methodology

Background and tools

Within the frame of a given local and shared concern, students as a group needed to explain what was observed, to conduct experiments, to collect and analyse data, to interpret observations, to draw conclusions from data and to communicate findings (Hattie, 2009). The study involved a total of 547 students and 17 teachers from 11 different secondary schools, five scientific research groups and 19 scientists. The methodology chosen to evaluate the pilots was quantitative with pre- and post-questionnaires addressed to students, teachers and researchers. Rubric tools (Allen & Tanner, 2006) were designed to help teachers set the goals and assess homogeneously students' acquisition of competencies and attitudes in the 11 different schools and five different CS projects. The rubric model is a very common practice for collecting evidence in learning processes of formal education as well as for assessing the performance of students in a standardised and transferable manner. Rubrics also help teachers to give a clear idea about their expectations and the level of performance for each competency and how to assess these competencies. In this chapter, we present the results based on a rubrics tool while detailed description of results from questionnaires and materials created by each school will be left for future publications.

Our approach has a very specific motivation in a quite unique scenario in the CS world. In 2012, five different research groups from Barcelona (Spain), and from quite diverse collection of disciplines, founded the Citizen Science Office with the support of the Culture Institute of Barcelona (City Council). This emergent initiative already hosts, in 2017, 16 projects from different universities and research centres of the Barcelona metropolitan area. This sort of community of practice is understood by all members as a way of aligning strategies, sharing best practices, organising events or even planning common actions in the field of CS. One of these actions started in March 2014 and was precisely aimed to explore education by means of a common experimental approach. Since all groups already had experience in running their projects in informal contexts, it was decided to look into schools. The main reason was that formal education was seen by the different groups as a difficult space to be explored by each project on its own.

Citizen science projects

Each research project was introduced as a pilot in at least two schools (see Table 9.1 for further details on schools and students). Projects introduced into the schools were:

1. *Plant*tes* (or *Urban Flora and Allergies*), by Aerobiology Information Point (PIA) and Institute of Environmental Science and Technology (ICTA-UAB). They offer a protocol to report and geo-tag allergenic plants to improve the quality of life of people suffering from allergies.
2. *Bee-Path*, by OpenSystems Research Group of the Universitat de Barcelona, by Institute of Complex Systems (UBICS) and by Dribia-Data Research. They provide a tool that allows the study of human mobility through a mobile application in a critical and collaborative way.
3. *Mosquito Alert*, a project coordinated by the Movement Ecology Lab associated with Centre of Advanced Studies (CEAB-CSIC) and Ecological and Forestry Applications Research Centre (CREAF). They offer a platform for participating in research and management of mosquito vectors of disease.

4. *Observadors del Mar* (*Sea Watchers*, in English), by Institute of Marine Sciences (ICM-CSIC). They provide a meeting point between citizens and scientists to investigate the current state of the sea.

5. *RIU.net*, by Research Group Freshwater Ecology and Management (FEM) of the Universitat de Barcelona. They offer an application for mobile phones that allows for an intuitive and easy way to assess the ecological status of a river.

An inquiry-based learning approach

The inquiry-based learning approach fits into the five CS projects since they all build knowledge, skills and attitudes through hands-on learning activities. Students can become active learners and may improve both their perceptions and attitudes towards science (Bingaman & Eitel, 2010; Wee *et al.*, 2004). Following the process established by the National Institute for Health (2005), we were indeed able to

TABLE 9.1 Distribution of citizen science projects among the schools participating in the pilots

Name of the school	Typology	Citizen science project	Number of teachers	Number of students	Age (grade)
FEDAC Sant Andreu (Barcelona)	Private	Urban Flora and Allergies	1	54	12 (1st ESO)
Institut XXV Olimpíada (Barcelona)	Public	Urban Flora and Allergies	1	82	12 (1st ESO)
SI Bosc de Montjuïc (Barcelona)	Public	Urban Flora and Allergies	1	23	12 (1st ESO)
Col·legi Sant Gabriel (Viladecans)	Private	Bee-Path	2	24	15 (4th ESO)
Institut Enric Borràs (Badalona)[1]	Public	Bee-Path	3	19	15 (4th ESO)
Regina Carmeli Horta (Barcelona)	Private	Bee-Path	2	24	15 (4th ESO)
Escola Garbí Pere Vergés (Esplugues de Llobregat)	Private	Mosquito Alert	2	67	12 (1st ESO)
Institut de Tordera (Tordera)	Public	Mosquito Alert	2	56	12 (1st ESO)
Institut Enric Borràs (Badalona)[1]	Public	Sea Watchers	3	34	14 (3rd ESO)
Maristes Champagnat (Badalona)	Private	Sea Watchers	1	86	14 (3rd ESO)
Escola Sant Gervasi (Mollet del Vallès)	Private	RIU.net	1	27	15 (4th ESO)
FEDAC Cerdanyola (Cerdanyola del Vallès)	Private	RIU.net	1	51	12 (1st ESO)

[1]The same teachers were involved in Bee-Path and Sea Watchers projects

ESO, Educación Secundaria Obligatoria (Compulsory Secondary Education).

differentiate two types of inquiry-based projects in our introduction process of CS in schools. Some projects followed a *guided inquiry* while others followed an *open inquiry*. The *guided inquiry* learning projects (i.e. *Mosquito Alert*) provided schools with research questions. Students and teachers were responsible for designing and following their own procedures to respond to those questions and deliver their results and findings. Other projects were quite open (i.e. *Bee-Path*) in the sense that students were encouraged to formulate their own research questions, design and follow through with a developed procedure and communicate their findings and results. That is to say that students had to drive their own investigative questions and the CS project was just a tool to enable their tasks. *Open inquiry* projects are only successful if students are motivated by intrinsic interests and if they are equipped with the skills to conduct their own research study (Bell *et al.*, 2010; Turner & Patrick, 2008). In order to support the experience, learning resources were provided to offer (if needed) guidance to knowledge acquisition (Kirschner *et al.*, 2006) to teachers. However, only upon request were teachers aided by researchers in the process of identifying and better shaping the research questions for each school project.

An important factor that has been incorporated in our study is the relation of CS projects to the community's concerns. In that sense, we have also wanted to respond to those claims by asserting that CS does not go far enough to resolve the concerns of communities and environments. Along these lines, those claims also consider that CS practices need to be considered holistically, by including many non-scientific aspects in the project and without restricting the activity to data gathering and data delivery to scientists (see, for instance, Mueller *et al.*, 2012). Schools in our study were challenged to observe and question real phenomena from their own neighbourhood and thus respond to shared concerns at a very local and situated level (Callon, 2009). The results and scientific conclusions raised by each school were therefore aimed to be materialised as argued proposals to improve the quality of life in their neighbourhood from different perspectives. We believe that community concerns need to be incorporated into the equation on how CS practices can be part of the existing list of innovative mechanisms in science, technology, engineering and mathematics (STEM) education. This is how our approach includes multidisciplinarity and even transdisciplinarity in an organic manner.

Students' profile and dynamics of the pilot studies

Secondary school students, from first to fourth Educación Secundaria Obligatoria (ESO: Compulsory Secondary Education) (mostly from 12 to 15 years old, 13 years old on average) were specifically chosen for this study as it is a life stage when Spanish students decide whether to orient their studies to scientific and information and communication technologies (ICT) careers. We thought that this was the most adequate life stage to promote scientific careers by actively engaging students in real scientific processes able to raise their own concerns as citizens.

The choice is also supported by some studies which, at this life stage, report a decline in science motivation in students (Potvin & Hasni, 2014) and in both academic performance and science self-concept (Grabau, 2016). Table 9.1 synthesises data related to students jointly with other information. Gender balance is quite strong for each class group, with the aggregated proportion of girls around 54%.

All experiences aimed to follow very similar dynamics: lasting 2–3 months and amounting to 10–20 hours. Since all class groups wanted to go further and study their projects in greater depth, they generally dedicated more time to them. The pilots sought collaborative work and the empowerment of the class group with autonomy so as to learn to function with specific and limited support from researchers. Students were encouraged to explore, design and analyse research questions and become active participants in the scientific inquiry process rather than being passive learners.

Specifically, all pilots followed an identical sequence:

1. A scientist, being an expert, introduced the specific CS project in the classroom (about an hour).
2. Students and teachers worked together autonomously. Some of the tasks were distributed within the class group in a way that some of the students took more responsibility in some tasks than in others. Tasks during this phase were:

    a) To define experiments, their location and the outcome that the class group wants to reach.
    b) To run fieldwork based on a given research question and with a given experiment.
    c) To analyse data collected and discuss results in the classroom. Some resources are supplied by scientists to optimise this part of the work.
    d) Results and conclusions took shape in different ways. These forms were decided by the class group. There was also a public presentation in Cosmocaixa where all schools shared their results. There was some media coverage by the national press.

Learning activities and educational resources

Each school could choose the CS project in which they wanted to be involved. For each of the projects, a proposal of learning activities and a set of educational resources were publicly available on the study website (https://cciutadana.wordpress.com, in Catalan). Each project description also included the specific parts of the educative curricula in which the project can be circumscribed. These parts belonged to subjects such as science, biology and geology, physics and chemistry, maths, arts or social studies. However, the final decision on the educational approach was left to teacher interests and school constraints. Teachers also decided in a quite spontaneous way to work with other colleagues at their own school. Some schools worked on natural and physical science courses, others technology or maths and some even introduced the projects in visual arts, social science or humanities.

Pilot evaluation

All teachers received the same rubric model to analyse the acquired competencies of their class group. Competencies and attitudes being evaluated are applicable to all the five CS projects and for the 11 schools. The tool was designed to provide:

1. Indicators of learning acquisition. Prior to the learning process in November 2015, as the researchers and observers of the whole process, we defined the whole rubrics matrix. The existence of the rubrics was mentioned to teachers before they enrolled in the pilots and their contents were briefly discussed.
2. Assessment support tools for teachers. After the learning process and starting from February 2016, all teachers were required to fill in the rubrics and evaluate their own class group. Data gathering was done at an aggregate level and no individual data were taken.
3. A quantitative, homogeneous, transferable and standardised approach to analyse data. The rubrics model delivered to teachers follows the standards established by both the Catalan and Spanish education law and curricula regarding knowledge, skills and attitudes of ESO students of science, communication and technologies. Different grades and different projects are quantified using the same rubrics, being at least valid from firsst to fourth of ESO (from 12 to 15 years old). Rubrics are however general enough to be applied at least to other European countries since they have very similar standards.
4. A guarantee that an inquiry-based learning process is being followed. The process includes creating questions, obtaining supporting evidence to answer those questions, explaining the evidence collected and connecting explanations to existing knowledge and to social contexts.

The rubric model provided scaled levels of achievement for a set of quality criteria and for a given type of performance (Huba & Freed, 2000). We selected communication, ICT and scientific competencies. We also included the *participation and motivation* attitudes as a crucial aspect in formal education, inquiry learning and CS (Jennett *et al.*, 2016; Rotman *et al.*, 2012). We generated four rubrics, one for each competency and for the attitudes. For each case, we provided a set of subcategories and each of them provided a scaled level of achievement with three-level quality gradation. Level 1 assesses the acquisition of basic competencies, level 2 increases the requirements, while level 3 acknowledges that excellent acquisition of the evaluated competencies has been reached.

The descriptions of the competencies and attitudes, the subcategories and the three levels for each category of performance were sufficient for an appropriate judgement. The rubrics were indeed used by the teachers themselves as a self-reflection tool to evaluate the experience of the pilots. Besides this, we added the motivation attitude regarding participation, as this is seen in the literature as a crucial aspect in relation to engagement with CS projects (Jennett *et al.*, 2016; Rotman *et al.*, 2012). These are the categories of analysis of the rubrics:

1. Scientific competencies: necessary for a critical analysis of the reality that surrounds us based on scientific methods.
2. Communication competencies: necessary to communicate on different channels and at different levels and contexts.
3. ICT competencies: necessary for the safe and critical use of technology, including different purposes.
4. Participation and motivation attitudes: necessary to evaluate engagement within the CS project.

Table 9.2 shows the English version of the rubrics and includes in detail the items being evaluated. This is the version that teachers had to fill in.

Results

Student participation and engagement

The CS activities allowed students to participate actively in all the steps that define a scientific investigation and in some cases the activity was entirely designed by the students. The activities carried out in schools were very diverse, since they depended on the design by teachers and, in many cases, by the students themselves. The degree of intervention of the students also varied in each case.

In all cases, the students were involved in the collection and analysis of data. Some of the groups also took part in the choice of the main question (how would people move in pursuit of specific goals? how is the tiger mosquito breeding in our school/in our town?); in the design of the experiment (how will we explain to the participants what they need to do? how will we collect data? what will we consider a positive point?) and in the definition of the hypothesis. There were groups directly involved in all the steps of their scientific investigation. For example, through the use of *Bee-Path*, some students designed a mobility study in an urban environment, while others decided to use it in the study of the mobility pattern of people pursuing specific goals. In the case of *Mosquito Alert*, one school decided to focus its analysis on their buildings, while another one extended the analysis to the entire town. All of these decisions were taken between the teachers and their students.

In this sense, these CS projects were not used (or even viewed) as a "closed" experiment, but as tools to use in their own designed experiment. Moreover, some groups of students decided to communicate their results to their communities and administrations, taking on the role of science communicators and activists. For example, a group decided to develop a mobile panel to increase the awareness of their neighbourhood about beach pollution; other students decided to invite the Mayor and his team to their classroom and show them the tiger mosquito breeding sites map they had developed, so that the administration could communicate these data, and evaluate appropriate actions to reduce the presence of this invasive species.

TABLE 9.2 Rubrics provided to teachers

Scientific competencies

	Level 1	Level 2	Level 3
#1	He/she explains the aim of the scientific research project in which he/she has been involved	He/she explains and justifies the aim of the scientific research project in which he/she has been involved	He/she explains and justifies the aim and repercussions of the scientific research project in which he/she has been involved
#2	He/she lists the steps needed to collect data	He/she lists the steps needed to collect data and justifies their relevance	He/she lists the steps needed to collect data and justifies their relevance and asks questions that improve this process
#3	He/she shows the results obtained	He/she analyses and provides an explanation of the results obtained individually (or in a group)	He/she analyses and provides an explanation of the results obtained individually (or in a group) and participates in the analysis of results obtained by other groups
#4	He/she identifies the results as part of a larger project	He/she identifies and locates the results as part of each citizen science research project	He/she identifies and locates the results as part of each citizen science research project and analyses them taking into consideration the rest of the projects
#5	He/she understands the social significance of the results obtained	He/she understands and defends the social significance of the results obtained with arguments	He/she understands and defends the social significance of the results obtained with ideas on how to improve the context/environment based on the analysis of the results
#6	(If applicable): He/she presents graphs from data	(If applicable): He/she elaborates and explains graphs from data	(If applicable): He/she elaborates and explains graphs from data and uses them as a basis for their arguments
#7	Lists the steps of the scientific process in which he/she was involved	Lists the steps of the scientific process in which he/she was involved and clearly identifies in which step is in at every moment	Lists and describes the steps of the scientific process and participates actively in the design of some of them

	Communication competencies		
	Level 1	*Level 2*	*Level 3*
#1	The final product explains the purpose, steps taken and data collection	The final product explains the purpose, steps taken and data collection and offers a data analysis from data obtained	The final product explains the purpose, steps taken, data collection and offers a data analysis from data obtained. Furthermore, the final product offers possible actions to be taken based on the analysis of data
#2	The wording of the text does not contain misspellings	The wording of the text does not contain misspellings and uses subordinate clauses correctly	The wording of the text is impeccable
#3	(If applicable): Oral explanations are understandable	(If applicable): Oral explanations are understandable and convincing	(If applicable): Oral explanations are understandable and convincing and defend authority
#4	(If applicable): The artwork is sufficient and respects intellectual property rights	(If applicable): The artwork is remarkable and respects intellectual property rights	(If applicable): The artwork is remarkable and respects intellectual property rights and has been edited previously and appropriately

	ICT competencies		
	Level 1	*Level 2*	*Level 3*
#1	He/she uses digital tools for collecting data sufficiently	He/she uses digital tools for collecting data autonomously and safely	He/she uses digital tools for collecting data autonomously and safely and offers explanations about its functioning to colleagues who request it
#2	He/she uses digital tools for presenting the final product sufficiently	He/she uses digital tools for presenting the final product autonomously and safely	He/she uses digital tools for presenting the final product autonomously and safely and offers explanations about its functioning to colleagues who request it

(continued)

TABLE 9.2 (continued)

Participation and motivation attitudes

	Level 1	Level 2	Level 3
#1	He/she listens carefully to the explanations	He/she listens carefully to the explanations and intervenes with pertinent questions	He/she listens carefully to the explanations and intervenes with pertinent questions and clarifies some of their questions to classmates
#2	He/she collects data following instructions and without interfering with the work of the rest of the classmates	He/she participates actively in the data collection	He/she participates actively in both data collection and in its planning
#3	He/she participates in data analysis passively	He/she participates in data analysis actively	He/she participates in data analysis actively coming from his/her team and the rest of the groups
#4	He/she shows respect, but little participation	He/she is actively participating, respecting turns and the opinions of classmates	He/she is actively participating, respecting turns and the opinions of classmates. His/her opinions are respected and most times accepted by the rest of the class
#5	He/she passively participates in the elaboration of the final product	He/she is actively involved in the preparation of the final product (brainstorming and proposing improvements)	He/she is actively involved in the preparation of the final product (brainstorming, proposing improvements and assuming different tasks, etc.)
#6	He/she fills in the forms required for the pilots	He/she fills in the forms required for the pilots. The composition of his/her laboratory notebook is adequate	He/she fills in the forms required for the pilots. The composition of his/her laboratory notebook is exhaustive
#7	He/she participates passively in the final discussion	He/she participates actively in the discussion, listens and supports ideas from colleagues	He/she participates actively in the discussion, listens and supports ideas from colleagues discussing it, and so is respectful of others

Global evaluation results

The rubrics provided a set of subcategory elements to assess homogeneously the learning performance of the 547 students, of 11 schools and five research projects. As stated in the methodology, the competencies analysed were related to science, communication and ICT. Motivation and participation attitudes were also evaluated. Data provided by teachers in the rubrics showed that all students successfully fulfilled the acquisition of the competencies and attitude analysed, although some subcategories did not apply to some of the class groups, as outlined hereafter.

The mean scores, considering the sum of all the projects and the sum of all the competencies or attitudes, are presented in Figure 9.1. The radar chart shown in Figure 9.1 provides the proportion of students (as a percentage) that have reached levels 1, 2 and 3 in four different axes (science, communication, ICT and participation and motivation). Lower values are placed in the centre of the plot while higher values are displaced to the extremes of each axis. Figure 9.1 shows that, for *scientific* and *communication* competencies, the most frequent level reached is level 2, whereas for *ICT* competencies and *participation and motivation* attitudes, the most frequent level reached is level 3. In all cases, level 1 represents a minority of students of no more than 20% for all the types of competencies/attitudes. This finding demonstrates the overall really good results of the CS projects when introduced in formal education. Similarly, averaging all types of competencies/attitudes, most of the students tended to be more in level 2 (41% of students on average) and 3 (40%) rather than the basic level 1 (19%). See Table 9.3 for further details.

If we look at each of the projects, we can also observe from Table 9.3 that *Urban Flora and Allergies* (159 students) has a 2.26 averaged level, *Bee-Path* (67 students) has a 2.25 averaged level, *Mosquito Alert* (123 students) has a 2.11 averaged level, *Sea Watchers* (120 students) has a 2.27 averaged level and *RIU.net* (78 students) has a 2.21 averaged level. This latter finding demonstrated that there are not important disparities in between the projects, in that all of them have received a very good global evaluation.

Scientific competencies

The competencies needed for the critical analysis of the reality that surrounds us were divided into seven different subcategories, provided in Table 9.2. The weighted level among all class groups and subcategories is 2.21. It might indeed be stated that 83% of students were able to make a critical analysis of the reality around them and they are able to use scientific methods at a level at least noticeable (summing up levels 2 and 3 in the aggregate of all class groups), as shown in Table 9.3. Moreover, the level of scientific competency was achieved among all students and 39% of students achieved the top level in scientific competencies. The standard mean error when averaging all categories fluctuates between 3% and 5%, which demonstrates that the categories are robust and provide consistent results among the different items being evaluated.

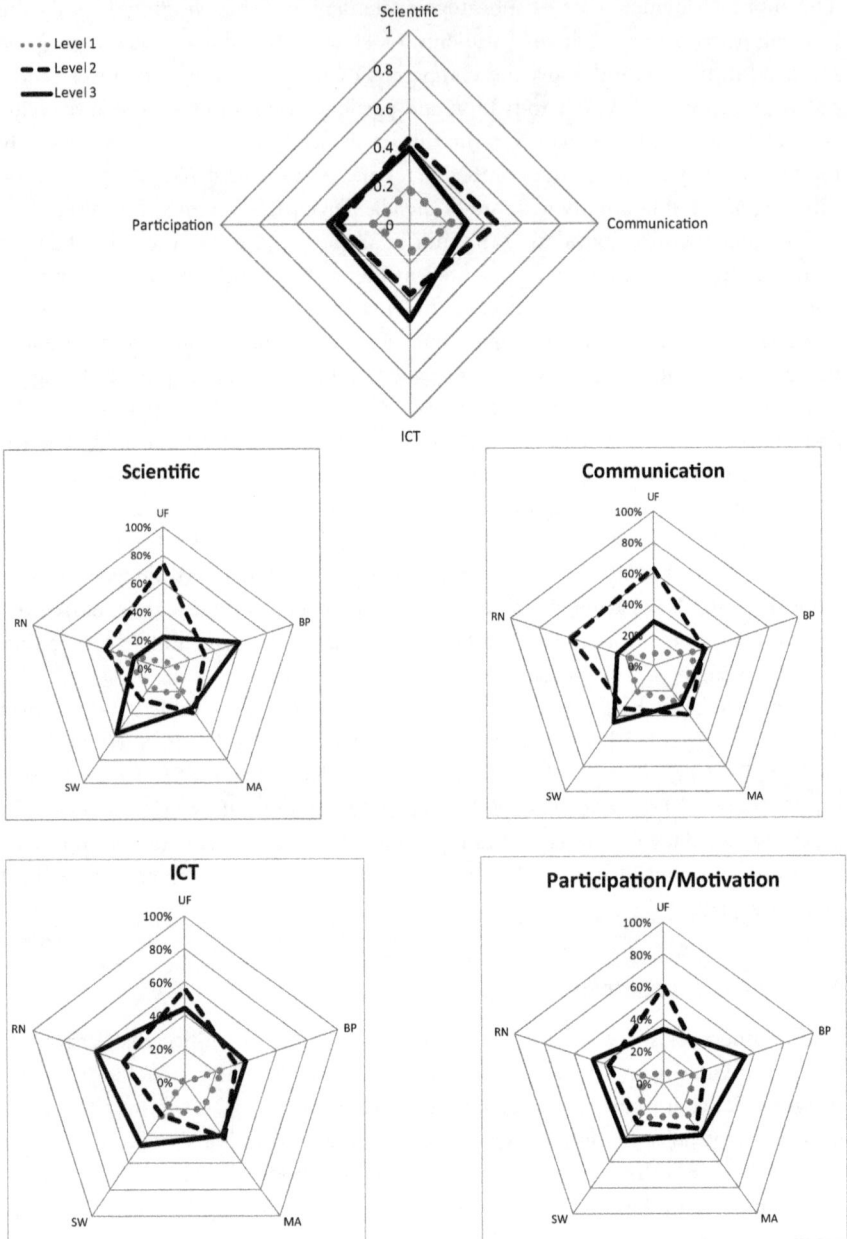

FIGURE 9.1 Mean scores (sum of all projects) by type of competencies and/or attitudes. Number of students being assessed: 547 in total, 159 in *Urban Flora* (UF), 67 in *Bee-Path* (BP), 123 in *Mosquito Alert* (MA), 120 in *Sea Watchers* (SW) and 78 in *RIU.net* (RN). Mean scores by scientific competencies, motivation attitudes and citizen science projects are also shown. More details are reported in Table 9.3.

TABLE 9.3 Averaged values among all students participating and over all different subcategories

	Population (in %)						Weighted level											
	Level 1	SEM	Level 2	SEM	Level 3	SEM	Urban Flora	SEM	Bee-Path	SEM	Mosquito Alert	SEM	Sea Watchers	SEM	RIU.net	SEM*	Average	SEM
Scientific	17%	3%	44%	4%	39%	5%	2.18	0.06	2.49	0.08	2.10	0.19	2.41	0.16	1.89	0.09	2.21	0.12
Communication	23%	3%	46%	3%	30%	5%	2.27		2.35	0.10	2.15	0.19	2.18	0.19	2.33	0.12	2.26	0.04
ICT	14.4%	0.4%	36.3%	0.1%	49.3%	0.4%	2.15	0.07	2.00	0.27	1.97	0.30	2.27	0.10	2.04	0.28	2.09	0.06
Participation/motivation	19%	3%	38%	2%	43%	2%	2.44	0.04	2.15	0.04	2.21	0.09	2.20	0.07	2.56	0.09	2.31	0.09
Averaged	18%	2%	41%	3%	40%	5%	2.26	0.08	2.25	0.12	2.11	0.06	2.27	0.06	2.21	0.17	2.22	0.03

Note: Subcategories averages allow us to estimate the standard error of the mean (SEM) for each competence/attitude. Empty cell corresponds to errors that cannot be computed due to lack of statistics

The averaged results regarding scientific competencies for each CS project are presented in Figure 9.1 and confirm the outstanding results of *Bee-Path* and *Sea Watchers*, as both projects got an average of student level 3 of 59% and 57% respectively. *Urban Flora and Allergies* and *Bee-Path* groups also show the larger proportion of students reaching level 2 and 3. Both CS projects might be qualified as *open inquiry* projects and, although the most extreme one shows better results in level 1, it also obtains less homogeneous results among the group as a side effect.

An even more detailed evaluation is presented in Figure 9.2. The aggregated radar chart highlights that the vast majority of students (91%) acquired in an excellent or very good manner (levels 2 and 3) the competency of analysing results and explaining them in a comprehensive way (subcategory #3; see details in Table 9.2). The majority of the students also reached an excellent level (52%) regarding the competencies on how to justify the purpose of the research project (subcategory #3). Besides, some particular projects obtained very high scores for specific competencies. For example, 83% of students involved in the *Bee-Path* project reached level 3 of the phases of the scientific project (subcategory #7), meaning that the open inquiry design of the project succeeded in involving the vast majority of students in all research phases. Another interesting result shows that 91% of students of *Sea Watchers* class groups reached level 3 when evaluating the competencies related to the general aims of the given project (subcategory #1), probably related to the pedagogic efforts of the scientists and the easy-to-understand purpose of the project when students were asked to collect and report the presence of plastics on the shore close to their school.

It is also worth mentioning that several schools did not develop the competency of data visualisation. This is the case for two of the three schools participating in *Urban Flora and Allergies* (corresponding to 65 students), two of the two schools participating in *Mosquito Alert* (123 students), one of the two schools participating in *Sea Watchers* (30 students) and one of the two schools participating in *RIU.net* (25 students). We strongly believe that this is an aspect that needs to be included in the rubric model and which has to be improved in the Spanish school curricula given that it is directly related to the difficulties of the Spanish school system in increasing ICT competencies (Moreira, 2008).

Communication competencies

Communication competencies are those related with the skills to express ideas and interact orally, written or visually through different channels. We assessed four different subcategories regarding communication competencies which are explicitly described in Table 9.2. Several students were not evaluated on some of the categories mostly due to lack of time for developing the project completely as a whole. *Urban Flora and Allergies* schools just considered one category ("generation of the report") in two schools with 136 students, corresponding to subcategory #1; and "oral presentation" in the third school with 23 students, corresponding to subcategory #3. See Table 9.2 for the full description of competencies.

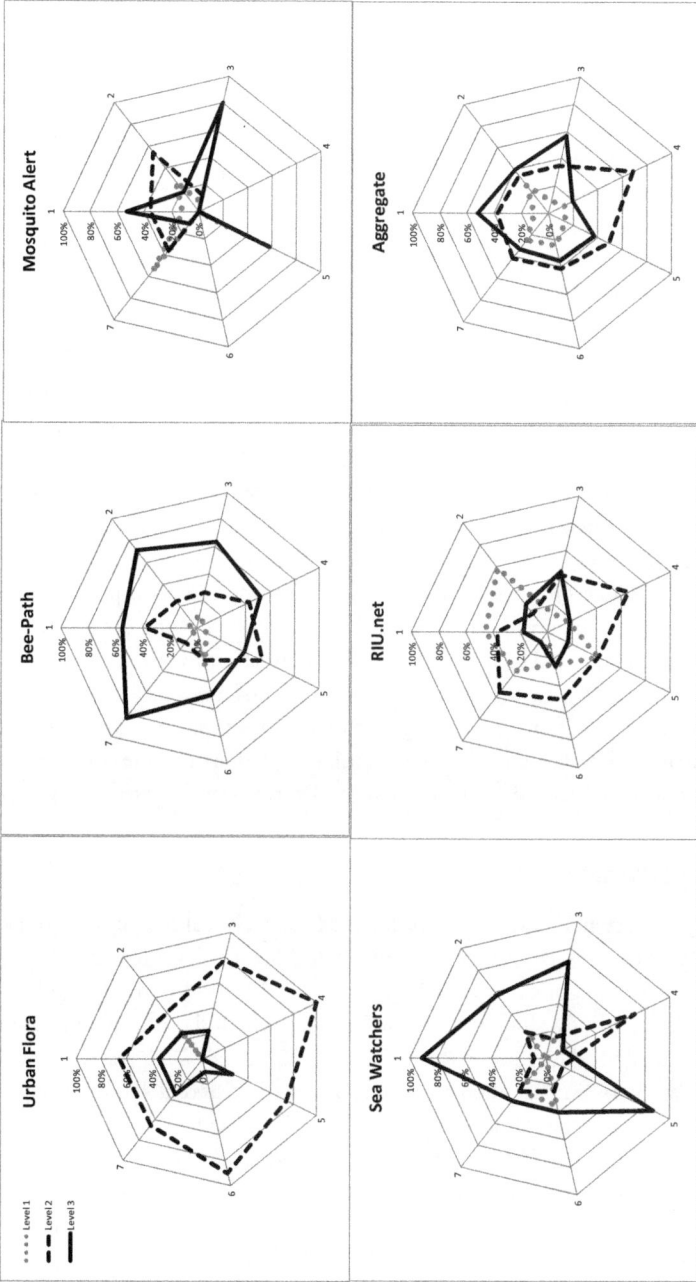

FIGURE 9.2 Detailed scientific competencies for each citizen science project and when all projects are aggregated.

One of the three schools with 24 students participating in *Bee-Path* was able to evaluate all four categories; another one with 24 students was unable to work on the "visual presentation in a final report" (subcategory #3), while the third one with 19 students was only evaluated through the "generation of a final report" (subcategory #1). In the case of *Mosquito Alert* and *Sea Watchers*, one of the schools was susceptible to be evaluated with all categories while the second one limits the evaluation to the category of "generation of a final report" (subcategory #1) with 67 and 34 students respectively. Finally, the two school groups working with *RIU. net* respond to almost all categories (except for "oral expression" in one of the two schools, subcategory #3, which corresponds to 27 students).

However, we still find the results interesting when they are carefully analysed (see Table 9.3). The level established to measure communication achievements was acquired for all students and 76% of them were able to communicate in different contexts and channels in a good manner (that is, summing up level 2 and 3 and all categories). The aggregate shown in Figure 9.3 furthermore reveals that 39% of the students were able to represent data in an excellent manner (subcategory #4). The level of writing (subcategory #2) was solid in 67% (between level 2 and 3) of students, and the remaining 33% were able to write without misspellings. The error behind the aggregated data from all four categories is again small, between 3% and 5%, thus showing once again the robustness of the rubrics being proposed. As shown in Figure 9.3, *RIU.net* reaches a good level of communication competencies for each of the four competencies, the number of level 2 students being always in between 56% and 67%, This could be linked to the important effort by the scientists to explain their projects clearly and their accurate use of several resources. *Sea Watchers* also shows excellent results in generating the final output (subcategory #1) and this can be attributed to their really well-focused objective: to raise awareness about the tremendous amount of plastics across the seafronts of the cities of the schools.

ICT competencies

The ICT competencies are necessary for a safe and critical use of technologies for different purposes, as described in Table 9.2. All school groups developed tasks related to these categories, with the exception of *Bee-Path* (with 19 students) and *Mosquito Alert* (with 67 students) − school groups which did not include the use of ICT in the final product process during their work in class. The results in these two categories are very similar when averaged among the different school groups.

Table 9.3 shows that almost all students (85%) achieved the necessary skills for the safe and critical use of ICT for different purposes and that almost the majority of students reached level 3 in relation to data collection (50%) and data presentation (49%). Figure 9.1 also shows clearly how this competency is the one that gets better results for the highest level (level 1). Therefore, the results are overall very satisfactory and can be related to the compulsory use of ICT tools in some phases of all CS projects included in the current study. For example, in *Urban Flora and Allergies*, geo-located pictures had to be taken; in *Bee-Path*, an App had to be

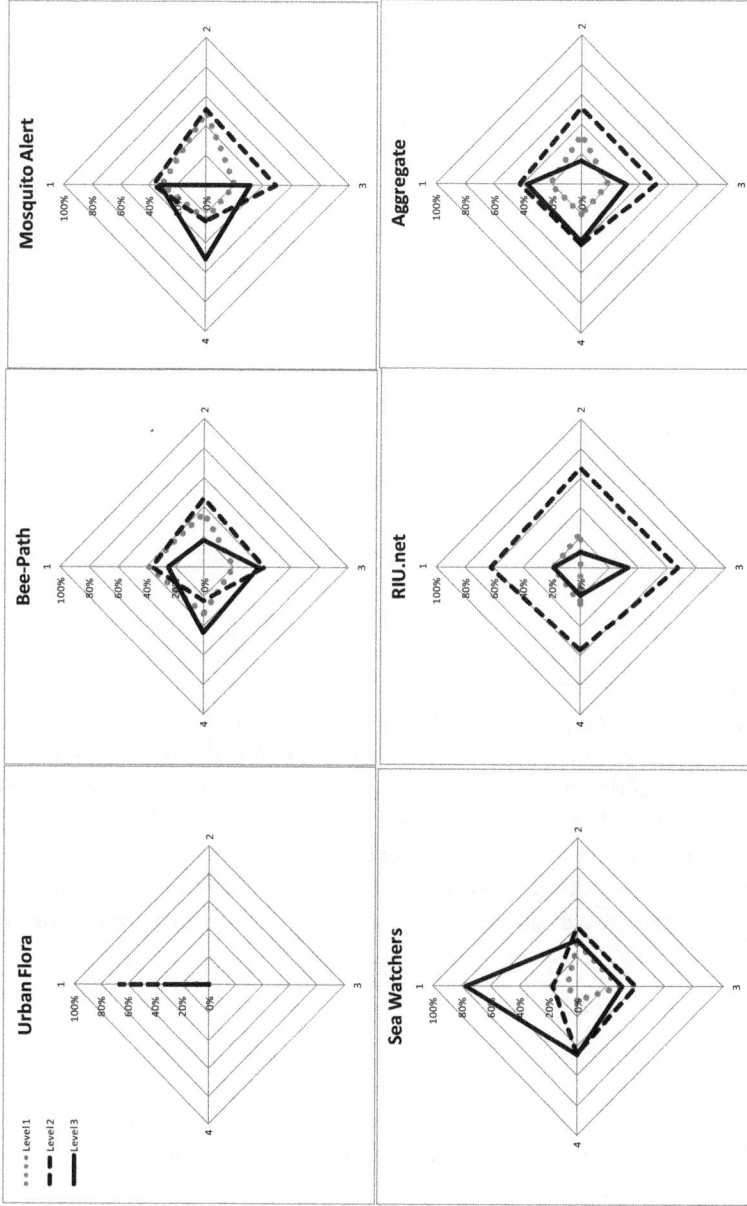

FIGURE 9.3 Detailed communication competencies for each citizen science project and when all projects are aggregated. Results of *Urban Flora and Allergies* that cannot be seen properly for subcategory 1 are: 9% (level 1), 66% (level 2), 25% (level 3). All subcategories and their number are reported in Table 9.2.

used and data treatment and data visualisation were undertaken with sophisticated tools; in *Mosquito Alert* and *RIU.net*, the data collection was done through an App installed on smartphones. If we look closely at Figure 9.4, we can see that *RIU.net* gets the best result concerning the use of ICT for the final output/product of the CS (subcategory #2), and this can be clearly attributed to the fact that this project has a very robust App with a very clear protocol which provides an automatic evaluation of the river based on the different questions that the App formulates to participants. However, if one looks closer at the use of ICT for data gathering (subcategory #1), *Mosquito Alert* and *Sea Watchers* get the best scores. Both work in a very easy manner in geo-locating observations.

Participation and motivation attitudes

Participation and motivation attitudes also reach very high rates in level 3, behind the results obtained for ICT competencies (see Table 9.3 and Figure 9.1). In all, 81% of the students appeared to be very motivated and participative (level 2 and level 3), as shown in Table 9.3. Errors when averaging over all categories are very small (around 3%), thus showing again that rubrics are also robust when evaluating participative and motivated attitudes. Regarding motivation, collecting data reached the highest rate (48%) jointly with data analysis (51%), as shown in the aggregate radar chart from Figure 9.5. It is also worth mentioning that 41% and 46% of the students had respectively shown an excellent attitude in the discussion sessions with a high level of participation. The comparison between projects provided by Figures 9.1 and 9.5 shows that *Bee-Path* reached outstanding results with a majority of level 3 students for all competencies. This can be related to the good scores obtained in scientific competencies and with the *open inquiry* design of the pilots, allowing the students to have a high level of freedom during the whole process.

Finally, the categories that have not been evaluated by all groups are those related to a final reflection (subcategory #7; see again Table 9.2) and to discussion when working with results (subcategory #5), although in very few cases. Subcategory #1 evaluation is only absent in the class groups working with *Urban Flora and Allergies* (with 159 students), while subcategory #5 is only absent in one class group of *Mosquito Alert* (with 67 students).

Discussion

Rubrics have allowed us to evaluate in a quantitative manner the very positive impact of the five interdisciplinary CS pilots when introduced to Catalan secondary school classrooms. An identical methodology has been used in the five CS projects to avoid bias and the very positive results obtained can be attributed to the capacity of CS projects to work in a collaborative manner and co-create a real scientific activity within the class group (Bonney *et al.*, 2009). Namely, students were considered as central actors of their scientific research, being able to decide or to have an influence on several aspects, such as the definition of the research

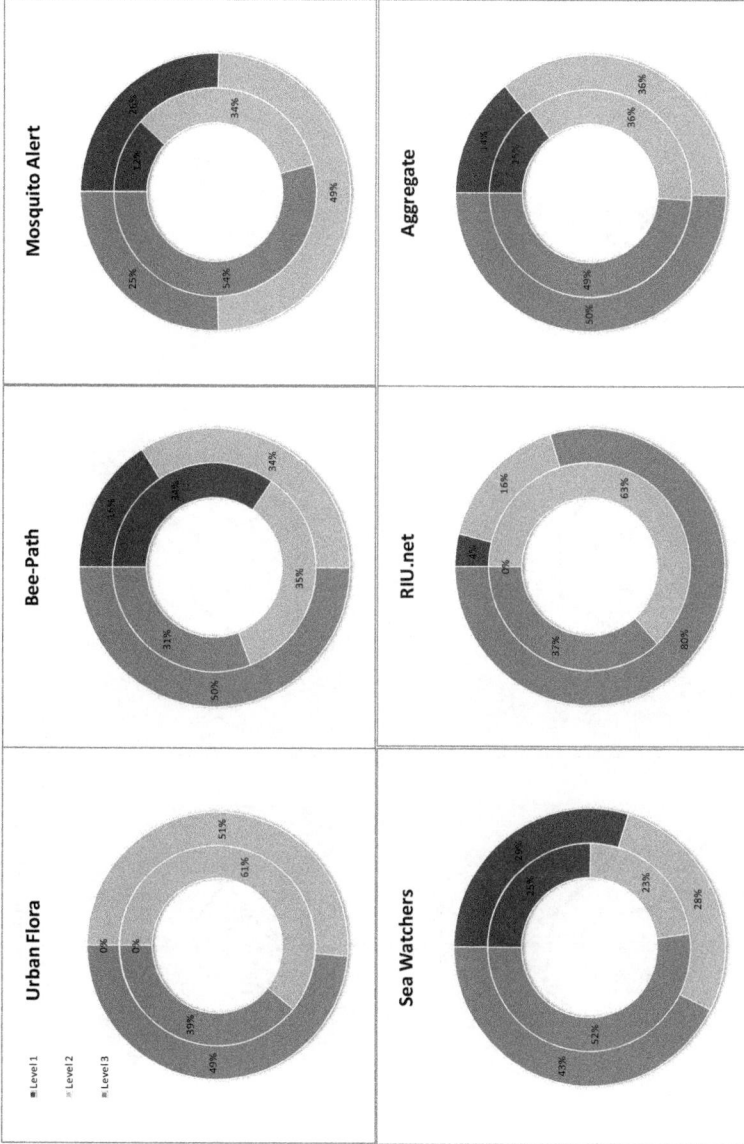

FIGURE 9.4 Detailed ICT competencies for each of five citizen science projects and when all projects are aggregated. Inner circle corresponds to subcategory #1 and outer circle to subcategory #2 (see Table 9.2).

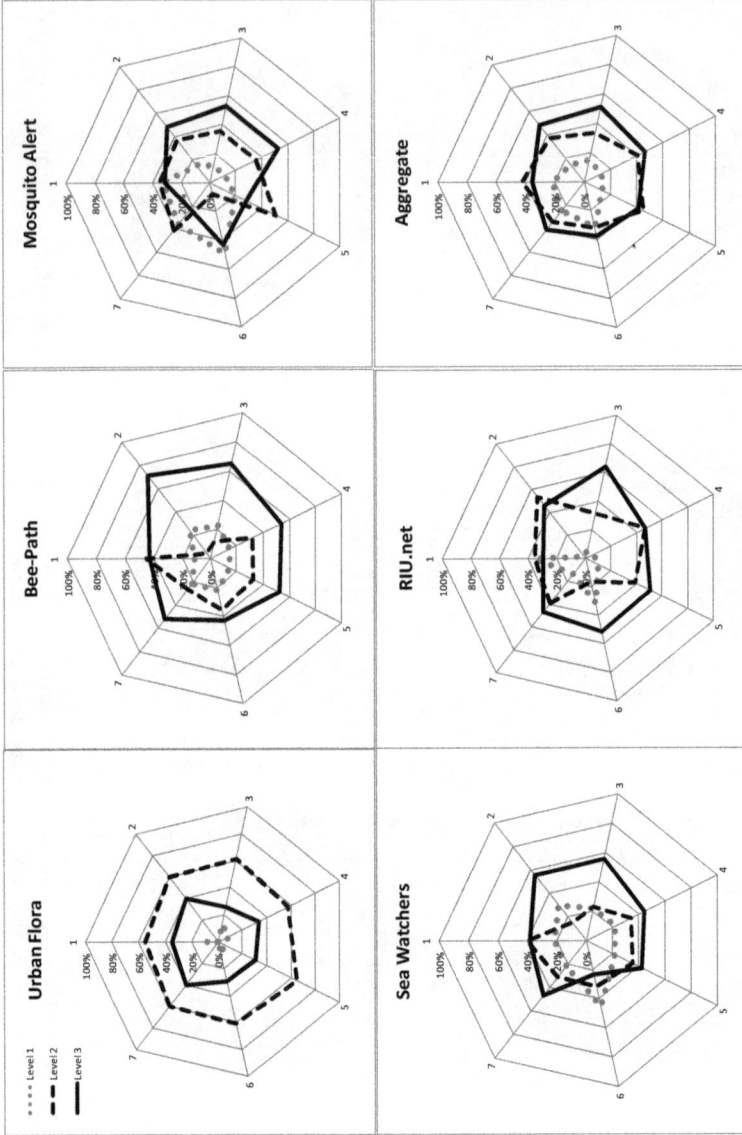

FIGURE 9.5 Detailed participation and motivation competencies for each of five citizen science projects and when all projects are aggregated. All subcategories and their numbers are reported in Table 9.2.

experiment, the protocol used for data collection, the way to report results and the knowledge transfer to the community. Student empowerment, acting as citizen scientists (Gray *et al.*, 2012) and moved by neighbourhood local and shared concerns (Bingaman & Eitel, 2010; Schon *et al.*, 2014), was enabled by the methodology design of the pilots. The experience allowed close contact between curious and active students, engaged teachers and fully committed (most of the time junior) scientists with a CS spirit. We firmly believe that all of these factors contributed to the high motivation of the more than 500 students enrolled in the pilots.

We have to highlight especially that 83% of the students achieved a very good level in scientific competencies, and 39% of them even reached the highest level. Based on these results, we can suggest that the introduction of CS in schools has increased the understanding of the purpose of research from a societal perspective. The results obtained for the scientific competencies are very encouraging and clearly prove that the implementation of CS in secondary schools is a powerful strategy to introduce students to different aspects of the scientific methods (Trumbull *et al.*, 2000). In this way students develop cognitive processes that are related to their new ability to think and work as scientists.

As far as we know, direct comparison with the evaluation of other CS projects at school is not possible, since this is the first time that rubrics have been used for this purpose. One of the closest experiences is probably the one described by Powell and Harmon (2014) that introduced a research experience to 2-year college university students. Their work concluded on the need to mentor students toward a deeper understanding of the complex nature of the scientific process. In our case, this competency was acquired through a "learning by doing" process as the students were directly embedded within the research projects, in that they were independent actors able to take their own decisions in the framework provided by the CS projects.

When we look at the *communication* competencies, we can highlight that the advantages of the introduction of the CS project in secondary schools overtakes the direct benefits in STEM disciplines and has an additional positive impact in other disciplines where writing, reporting, arguing opinions or exposing are key competencies. We advocate a multidisciplinary approach regarding the introduction of CS at schools. Some of these projects had many different perspectives and could be introduced through visual arts, social science or humanities disciplines, as has been the case in one of the schools working with *Bee-Path* and *Sea Watchers*. Results thus encourage working on CS projects in a multidimensional way as a transversal project that can be explored starting from several subjects of the school curricula.

Together with the very good results on scientific competencies acquisition, we shall also highlight *participation and motivation* attitudes, since 43% of the students reached the highest level. Those values are very high in comparison to ordinary activities performed in class, as highlighted by teachers in the online questionnaires provided after the experience. Seventeen teachers answered the survey: 63% of teachers considered CS projects to be as useful as "traditional" activities while over

30% considered them more than useful. All of them considered that the activity has had a positive impact on students: a 94% rating points to the fact that students have been fully engaged and 71% stated that students were highly motivated. We therefore consider that the high level of attitudes towards motivation and participation is one of the two main results of the current study. It contradicts the classical perception that European students are not motivated regarding STEM disciplines (Sjøberg & Schreiner, 2010); however, it is in agreement with previous studies that, using CS as part of regular classroom activities, an increase in student motivation and a positive impact in their attitudes towards science are observed (Silva et al., 2016; Vitone et al., 2016).

The origin of this excellent result concerning participation is probably multi-causal but one can hypothesise that, by participating in CS projects, the students are naturally "forced" to go outside of their comfort zone and act as young activists related to scientific citizenship positioning (Elam & Bertilsson, 2003) and regarding issues affecting their close neighbourhood. In this way, the empowerment of the students is almost immediate, as they have the ability to decide from the very early steps in the research project and their participation and motivation are then strongly increased. The close contact with scientists, the perception of their ability to solve important issues for the community and their empowerment as true owners and disseminators of the projects surely do play a key role too.

In this way, we fully support the conclusions made by Gray et al. (2012) claiming that creating a dialogue with experts and fostering the ability of the public to critique information and evidence are successful factors to be taken into account in order to introduce CS in schools. Our approach and results support this view: an open-minded co-design of the educational activity between teachers, researchers and students led to an increase in intrinsic motivation, the first stone of meaningful learning, as described by Omrod (2014). Once again, the benefits of the CS projects have a wider impact than the STEM disciplines, since an increase in motivation is beneficial for student learning as a whole. Motivation positively affects cognitive processes, leads to increased effort and energy, strengthens persistence in challenges or problem-solving activities and enhances performance.

These very good results in *participation and motivation* attitudes are especially remarkable in *open inquiry* projects such as *Bee-Path* which contrast with other projects such as *RIU.net, Mosquito Alert* or *Sea-Watchers,* which, by following a *guided inquiry* process, get the best results concerning the use of ICT. This can be clearly attributed to the fact that these CS projects have a robust and easy-to-follow protocol in data gathering or evaluation thanks to the use of user-friendly Apps or web-based digital interfaces.

Conclusions

A rubric model to assess the introduction of CS to secondary schools has been designed and applied to a diverse set of CS projects for secondary schools and formal education using a common strategy. The four types of competencies included were *scientific, communication and ICT* and *participation and motivation* attitudes. The rubrics have shown to be easy to follow and to have robust methodology when implemented and tested by 11 secondary schools and with 547 students.

The strategy to provide a multifaceted experience to students and teachers, not exclusively focused on any specific STEM subject, has been proved to be successful. By asking for a very complete cognitive and organisational effort, students acquired not only very good but also excellent *scientific* competencies. Thinking and acting as researchers also improved their *communication* and *ICT* competencies and some of the teachers have also included humanities and arts classes into the pilots to enhance reflection and creativity.

Based on the results obtained, we advocate the use of rubrics for CS project evaluation, allowing for a multidimensional perspective. We also strongly encourage the aggregation of CS projects and their approach to schools in a coherent manner. In this way, efforts made on the methodological and organisational aspects would become more sustainable. By pursuing a context-based learning and moving research to students' everyday life, schools will be able to produce real research and even contribute to reinforce the connections among CS projects, citizenship and democracy within the frame of so-called *action research* (Mills, 2000). While looking for an impact on local communities close to each of the schools, not only does it increase student motivation and competencies in STEM formal education but it also favours innovation in it. We therefore hope that this contribution enriches the toolbox of those who wish to encourage participation and collaboration which can drive social changes and help to face major societal challenges by situating formal education inquiry learning at its core.

Acknowledgements

We would like to acknowledge the 17 teachers and 547 anonymous students who have made this research possible. Teachers who generously engaged in this study are Magda Jimenez, Alicia García, Virginia Camps, Josep López, Miquel Molinas, Eva Mateo, Carmen Olivares, Olga Montañá, Carlos Gimenez, Ángel Lucas, Meritxell Formiga, Sílvia Zurita, Àlex López-Duran, Genís Cedrés, Quique Vergara, Mercè Tarragó and José Carreto. We also especially want to thank all CS projects participating in this study and the researchers behind them.

This work was mostly funded by the Recercaixa grant *Citizen Science: Research and Education* by "la Caixa" Bank Foundation with the collaboration of the Catalan Association of Public Universities (ACUP). Additional support has been received from the European Union's Horizon 2020 research and innovation project STEMForYouth (grant agreement no. 710577, JP and IB), MINECO (Spain) through grants CSO2014-52830-P (NF), FIS2013-47532-C3-2-P (JP and IB), FIS2016-78904-C3-2-P (JP and IB); Generalitat de Catalunya (Spain) through contract no. 2014 SGR 608, JP and IB). The authors also acknowledge the collaboration of the Barcelona Citizen Science Office, an initiative promoted by the Barcelona Institute of Culture (Barcelona City Council).

References

Allen, D., & Tanner, K. (2006). Rubrics: Tools for making learning goals and evaluation criteria explicit for both teachers and learners. *CBE-Life Sciences Education, 5*(3), 197–203.

Bell, T., Urhahne, D., Schanze, S., & Ploetzner, R. (2010). Collaborative inquiry learning: Models, tools, and challenges. *International Journal of Science Education, 32*(3), 349–377.

Bingaman, D., & Eitel, K. B. (2010). Boulder Creek study: Fifth graders tackle a local environmental problem through an inquiry-based project. *Science and Children, 47*(6), 52–56.

Bonney, R., Ballard, H., Jordan, R., McCallie, E., Phillips, T., Shirk, J., & Wilderman C. C. (2009). *Public Participation in Scientific Research: Defining the Field and Assessing its Potential for Informal Science Education.* Washington, DC: Center for Advancement of Informal Science Education (CAISE).

Callon, M. (2009). *Acting in an Uncertain World.* Cambridge, MA: MIT Press.

Coleman, J. S. M., & Mitchell, M. (2014). Active learning in the atmospheric science classroom and beyond through high-altitude ballooning. *Journal of College Science Teaching, 44*(2), 26–30.

Dickerson-Lange, S. E., Eitel, K. B., Dorsey, L., Link, T. E., & Lundquist, J. D. (2016). Challenges and successes in engaging citizen scientists to observe snow cover: From public engagement to an educational collaboration. *Journal of Science Communication 15*(01), A01–1.

Eick, C., Deutsch, B., Fuller, J., & Scott, F. (2008). Making science relevant: Water-monitoring programs help students study science while protecting local waterways. *The Science Teacher, 75*(4), 26–29.

Elam, M., & Bertilsson, M. (2003). Consuming, engaging and confronting science the emerging dimensions of scientific citizenship. *European Journal of Social Theory, 6*(2), 233–251.

Freeman, S., Eddy, S. L., McDonough, M., Smith, M. K., Okoroafor, N., Jordt, H. & Wenderoth, M. P. (2014). Active learning increases student performance in science, engineering, and mathematics. *Proceedings of the National Academy of Sciences 111*(23), 8410–8415. doi.org/10.1073/pnas.1319030111.

Grabau, L. J. (2016). *Aspects of Science Engagement, Student Background, and School Characteristics: Impact on Science Achievement of US Students.* Advisor: Xin Ma. University of Kentucky, Educational, School, and Counseling Psychology. Paper 51. doi.org/10.13023/ETD. 2016.275.

Gray, S. A., Nicosia, K., & Jordan, R. C. (2012). Lessons learned from citizen science in the classroom. *Democracy & Education, 20*(2), article 14.

Hattie, J. (2009). *Visible Learning: A Synthesis of Over 800 Meta-Analysis Relating to Achievement.* New York, NY: Routledge.

Huba, M. E., & Freed J. E. (2000). Learner centered assessment on college campuses: Shifting the focus from teaching to learning. *Community College Journal of Research and Practice 24*(9): 759–766.

Jennett, C., Kloetzer, L., Schneider, D., Iacovides, I., Cox, A., Gold, M., & Talsi, Y. (2016). Motivations, learning and creativity in online citizen science. *Journal of Science Communication, 15*(3), A05.

Kasperowski, D., & Brounéus, F. (2016). The Swedish mass experiments – a way of encouraging scientific citizenship?. *Journal of Science Communication, 15*(01), Y01.

Kirschner, P. A., Sweller J., & Clark, R. E. (2006). Why minimal guidance during instruction does not work: An analysis of the failure of constructivist, discovery. *Problem-Based, Experiential, and Inquiry-Based Teaching, Educational Psychologist, 41*(2), 75–86. doi.org/ 10.1207/s15326985ep4102_1.

Mills, G. E. (2000). *Action Research: A Guide for the Teacher Researcher.* Upper Saddle River, NJ: Prentice-Hall.

Moreira, M. A. (2008). La innovación pedagógica con TIC y el desarrollo de las competencias informacionales y digitales. *Investigación en la Escuela, 64,* 5–18. Retrieved from: http://www.investigacionenlaescuela.es/articulos/64/R64_1.pdf.

Mueller, M. P., Tippins, D., & Bryan, L. A. (2012). The future of citizen science. *Democracy & Education, 20*(1). Retrieved from: http://democracyeducationjournal.org/home/vol20/iss1/2/.

National Institute for Health. (2005). *Doing Science: The Process of Science Inquiry.* Retrieved from: https://www.uwyo.edu/scienceposse/resources/nih_doing-science.pdf.

Omrod, J. E. (2014). *Educational Psychology: Pearson New International Education: Developing Learners.* Harlow, Essex: Pearson Higher Education, 384–386.

Phillips, T. B., Ferguson, M., Minarchek, M., Porticella, N., & Bonney, R. (2014). *User's Guide for Evaluating Learning Outcomes in Citizen Science.* Ithaca, NY: Cornell Lab of Ornithology.

Potvin, P., & Hasni, A. (2014). Analysis of the decline in interest towards school science and technology from grades 5 through 11. *Journal of Science Education and Technology, 23*(6), 784–802.

Powell, N. L. & Harmon, B. B. (2014). Developing scientists: A multiyear research experience at a two-year college. *Journal of College Science Teaching, 44*(2), 11–17.

Rock, B. N., & Lauten, G. N. (1996). K-12th grade students as active contributors to research investigations. *Journal of Science Education and Technology, 5*(4), 255–266. doi.org/10.1007/BF01677123.

Rotman, D., Preece, J., Hammock, J., Procita, K., Hansen, D., Parr, C., & Jacobs, D. (2012). Dynamic changes in motivation in collaborative citizen-science projects. In *Proceedings of the ACM 2012 Conference on Computer Supported Cooperative Work* (pp. 217–226). New York: ACM.

Schon, J. A., Eitel, K. B., Bingaman, D., & Miller, B. G. (2014). Big project, small leaders. *Science and Children, 51*(9), 48–54. doi.org/ 10.2505/4/sc14_051_09_48.

Sharples, M., Scanlon, E., Ainsworth, S., Anastopoulou, S., Collins, T., Crook, C., Jones, A., Kerawalla, L., Littleton, K., Mulholland, P., & O'Malley, C. (2015). Personal inquiry: Orchestrating science investigations within and beyond the classroom. *The Journal of the Learning Sciences, 2*(2), 308–341.

Silva, C. G., Monteiro, A., Manahl, C., Lostal, E., Holocher-Ertl, T., Andrade, N., Brasileiro, F., Mota, P. G., Serrano, F., Carrodeguas, J. A., & Brito, R. M. M. (2016). Cell spotting: educational and motivational outcomes of cell biology citizen science project in the classroom. *Journal of Science Communication, 15*(01), A02.

Sjøberg, S., & Schreiner, C. (2010). *The ROSE project. An overview and key findings.* University of Oslo, March 2010. Retrieved from: http://roseproject.no/network/countries/norway/eng/nor-Sjoberg-Schreiner-overview-2010.pdf.

Trumbull, D. J., Bonney, R., Bascom, D., & Cabral, A. (2000). Thinking scientifically during participation in a citizen-science project. *Science Education, 84*(2), 265–275.

Turner, J. C., & Patrick, H., (2008). How does motivation develop and how does it change. Reframing motivation research. *Educational Psychologist, 43,* 119–131.

Vitone, T., Stofer, K. A., Sedonia Steininger, M., Hulcr, J., Dunn, R., & Lucky, A. (2016). School of Ants goes to college: Integrating citizen science into the general education classroom increases engagement with science. *Journal of Science Communication, 15*(01), A03.

Wee, B., Fast, J., Shepardson, D., Harbor, J., & Boone, W. (2004). Students' perceptions of environmental based inquiry experiences. *School Science and Mathematics, 104*(3), 112–118.

Zoellick, B., Nelson, S. J., & Schauffler, M. (2012). Participatory science and education: Bringing both views into focus. *Frontiers in Ecology and the Environment, 10*(6), 310–313. doi.org/10.1890/110277.

10

CULTURAL CITIZEN INQUIRY

Making space for the "everyday" in language teaching and learning

Koula Charitonos

Introduction

The contributions to this volume make a compelling case for the potential, value and significance of citizen inquiry. They also include references to numerous and considerable challenges that exist in supporting citizen inquiry, defined as the intersection between citizen science and inquiry learning. To date, much attention is placed on applications of citizen inquiry in informal learning settings, particularly in relation to science. The study presented in this chapter is distinct because it focuses on the field of community languages, defined as "languages in use in a society, other than the dominant, official or national language" (McPake et al., 2007, p. 7), and addresses one specific challenge, namely the need to support processes of citizen inquiry within and beyond the classroom.

This chapter presents a small exploratory study undertaken in two community schools in the UK that draws on a blended approach to learning and utilises methods of inquiry learning (e.g. observation, data collection, reflection) and mobile technologies to facilitate young people's engagement in citizen-led inquiry with a focus on social and cultural issues. This chapter puts forward the idea of cultural citizen inquiry by examining how young people can engage with web and mobile technologies and grasp challenging concepts such as identity and heritage. It proposes that there is scope for young people to engage meaningfully with such concepts through means of citizen-led inquiry, not only to develop a sense of wonder about our world but also to develop their understanding and process skills along with an ability to inquire.

At the outset of this study is a recognition that formal education is seen as "detached" from rapid socio-technological change, whereas informal learning is "sidelined" or "ignored" when it could be used as a resource or a way to discover more about evolving personal and social motivations for learning (Kukulska-Hulme, 2015). This study builds upon formal instruction in the language classroom and gives attention to the blend of the physical and the digital contexts with the aim of bringing the digital world into the physical world of the classroom and at the same time representing real everyday experiences directly in the digital domain.

The focus of the study is on a language programme taking place in Greek Supplementary Schools, which largely operate as language schools, and cater for the Greek diaspora community in the UK. Along with the term community language, the term heritage language (HL) is used in this chapter to mark a distinction from the field of first- or second-language acquisition. HL is being used to refer to immigrant languages, indigenous and colonial languages (Fishman, 2001), thus pointing to a language that has broader cultural associations and significance for members of a particular community. The intention in this study is to move beyond a view of language simply related to acquiring grammar and vocabulary (see e.g. Kramsch, 1998) and instead consider the learners' "lived experience" (Anderson & Chung, 2012, p. 262) of their language and heritage as a resource, upon which they draw to create and share meanings of their everyday social and cultural engagements.

The study sets to explore the idea of cultural citizen inquiry as a method that may: (i) allow young learners to situate themselves in relation to other learners and places (i.e. school, home, community); (ii) allow young learners to create and articulate meanings attributed to actions, objects and places; and (iii) facilitate young learners' engagement with their social and cultural contexts. Particularly in the field of community language education this method may validate young HL learners' search for identity, usually intertwined with heritage and culture, and also support them to engage critically with their everyday experiences. The main research question is: How does cultural citizen inquiry provide the means to support young people's learning and development of personally resonant explorations of their heritage and culture? To begin with, this chapter will provide a description of the term cultural citizen inquiry, followed by literature related to HL learning.

Cultural citizen inquiry

This chapter describes a study that aimed to engage young learners with principles of citizen-led inquiry and examine applications to cultural issues. One way to conceptualise cultural citizen inquiry is that it is a learner-centred pedagogical approach characterised by activities that ask students to think about themselves and others in the world, initiating and asking questions about the social and cultural contexts they are embedded in, gathering evidence and then seeking possible explanations and interpretations that may provide responses to those questions. It may also allow for personal meanings and connections to be formed and developed respectively. In this sense, cultural citizen inquiry is seen as a tool to make people attentive, and to frame their engagement with everyday contexts in ways that may foster forms of participation and agency that can be made visible and accessible due to the spread of digital and networked technology. As in inquiry learning, this approach to learning involves learners engaging in reasoning and problem-solving skills and gaining a better understanding of social sciences methods and approaches. It is further seen as helping individuals to build competences drawing on shared values and respect, appreciate diversity, share global awareness and develop cross-cultural skills. Finally, whilst inquiry-based literature tends to be more closely associated with the acquisition of science process skills and science content knowledge or "the thinking patterns that scientists use to construct knowledge" (Chiappetta, 1997; cited in Bunterm et al., 2014, p. 1939), what may be deemed as important outcomes of the cultural citizen inquiry is the construction of narratives related to the social and cultural contexts people are embedded in and identify with, and importantly, a form of learning that guides an individual to be a socially responsible person and "mobilizes . . . people's deeply felt interests and identities in the service of achieving . . . civic voice" (Ito et al., 2015, p. 12).

This chapter presents an exploratory study located within the field of community education. It proposes cultural citizen inquiry as a way of supporting young language learners to get involved in social science research and bring them "closer to the idea of participant observer of their own lives and a new reading of the world around them" (Purdam, 2014. p. 377).

Heritage language speakers and heritage language education

As Fishman (2001) observes, the term HL refers to immigrant languages, indigenous and colonial languages, thus pointing to the language used at home or familiar contexts (Campbell & Peyton, 1998) with an emphasis on its family relevance and broader cultural associations. For Valdés (2001), it is precisely the historical or personal connection to the language that is "salient" (p. 47) and not a speaker's actual proficiency in the language. Indeed, Carreira's (2004) analysis points to identity, language and family background as the primary elements of a definition of HL. The field of HL learning is distinct from first- or second-language acquisition, resulting in traditional foreign language classes being seen as inappropriate for HL learners (Carreira, 2004), as they fail to resource the linguistic and cultural competencies that HL learners have gained in their own learning contexts. This is the reason why Anderson (2009) expresses a concern in relation to HL teaching about how best to address the needs of a highly diverse group of learners for whom neither a "foreign language" approach nor a "mother tongue" approach is appropriate. The chapter explores the unique needs of these particular learners.

In the UK, a great deal of HL or community language education takes place in supplementary/community schools, which offer educational support (i.e. language, core curriculum, faith and culture) and other out-of-school activities to children of ethnic or other minority backgrounds (Evans & Gillan-Thomas, 2015).

These schools are set up "to enable . . . children to learn about their cultural heritage, history and language, encouraging them to develop a positive sense of identity and belonging, confidence and self-esteem" (Evans & Gillan-Thomas, 2015, p. 3). It is estimated that there are approximately 3,000–5,000 such schools in England (NRCSE, 2015), often established by members of the community on a voluntary basis. These schools operate in community centres, youth clubs, religious institutions and mainstream schools with lessons taking place in weekend schools, weekday afternoon schools and evening classes. Supplementary schools may develop students' language proficiency to high levels, but at the same time these schools face a number of challenges, including funding and space to meet, maintaining a pool of qualified teachers and perceived value and relevance of the HL. Their operation is further influenced by a decline in the take-up of languages (British Academy, 2013), associated with a general lack of emphasis on development of multilingual skills within the general population and the education system in the UK (Speak to the Future, 2015). Another issue well recognised within this context is that English tends to become the dominant language for students from ethnic or other minority backgrounds, with patterns of intergenerational language loss being increasingly observed in families.

In the study presented in this chapter, the focus is on a language programme in Greek Supplementary Schools in the UK. At the outset of this study is the author's observation that the schools largely fail to recognise and support the individual goals and needs of HL students, thus resulting in an increasing lack of interest in the HL classes and a decreasing number of students enrolling in the schools over the years. Along with this comes a recognition that the greatest resource of these schools is the community itself, i.e. parents, volunteers and young learners, who hold a shared sense of their origin, have shared experiences and maintain links to their heritage and culture. Similarly to Carreira (2004), this study suggests that the learners' personal and cultural connections to their language should be at the core of HL education. In other words, it should begin with the learners and their immediate reality, and allow them to become meaningfully involved in their learning, whilst as educators we need to become more attentive to the ongoing interconnection between HL learning and identity. This study explores these issues through the lens of cultural citizen inquiry.

Context of the study

Aims and objectives

The research design involved a classroom intervention with a focus on HL learning to examine the integration of mobile and web-based citizen inquiry technologies in the language classroom. The aim of the project was to engage young people with methods of citizen inquiry and give them access to cultural experiences such as object-based activities in a museum and in the school, with an aim of capitalising on these to develop speaking and writing skills as well as digital skills.

Participants

The participants were learners of Greek language attending pre-GCSE, GCSE and A level lessons (13–17 years old) in two Greek Supplementary Schools in Buckinghamshire ($n = 11$) and Leicestershire ($n = 10$). The participants were attending language lessons once a week for an average of 3 hours in total. All the participants had personally owned mobile devices or access to tablets owned by their parents. An initial assessment determined that their perceived familiarity with their use was ranked from good to excellent.

The Greek Supplementary Schools are run under the auspices of three institutions: the Cyprus High Commission in the UK (as a branch of the Ministry of Education and Culture in Cyprus), the Embassy of Greece in the UK and the Greek Orthodox Archdiocese of Thyateira and Great Britain. There are approximately 70 Greek Supplementary Schools in the UK, which follow a course of study that is based on a curriculum for Greek language teaching and learning in diaspora community schools.

In this chapter the analysis will focus on the data collected from the school in Buckinghamshire.

Tools

For the purposes of this study the online citizen inquiry platform nQuire-it was employed. This platform has been designed as part of the project nQuire: Young Citizen Inquiry, coordinated by the Open University in the UK. The aim of the platform is to assist citizens in conducting their own science investigations, enhancing the social investigation aspect and promoting scientific thinking and exploration of the world. The nQuire-it platform offers three types of mission that make use of different methods of data collection: (i) Spot-it missions use uploaded pictures as the method of data collection; (ii) Win-it missions have a research question which requires text as an answer; and (iii) Sense-it missions are connected to the Sense-it Android application and require sensor-based data from mobile devices. In the study presented in this chapter only the first two types of missions were used. For the purposes of the project presented in this chapter, the interface to the platform was translated into Greek.

Activities

To date, the study has consisted of a series of designed lessons involving face-to-face and online activities at participating schools with specific goals that span several sessions. Whole-class sessions in the classroom focused on aspects of the curriculum (e.g. vocabulary, i.e. nouns, connectives, adjectives; speaking, i.e. talk about routines and habits, describe objects; Figure 10.1). The project also involved organisation and attendance at an intergenerational object-handling workshop run by educators based at the British Museum at each of the two participating schools around the theme of "Object Journeys", and also a joint visit to the British Museum around the theme of "People's Journeys". The online missions that were created on the nQuire-it platform involved questions related to learners' everyday life (e.g. "ItsAHabit"), their material environment heritage (e.g. "Looking for #AllThingsGreek", "My very own museum") or their immediate environments (e.g. "Picturing Cultures"). These missions were initiated by the two teachers, but future plans include providing a general topic (e.g. "Discovering your High Street") and giving students control over the missions, the design and how to carry out the investigation. Students used the nQuire-it platform at home due to lack of internet connectivity in the schools.

Participants in both schools were aware of the collaborative nature of this project and the joint online missions, and could see each other's uploads on the platform. This aspect of the project received positive response from the students.

The analysis section that follows is based on observations made by the author at the school in Buckinghamshire. The observation notes were recorded in a research diary immediately after the lessons.

The analysis focuses on two topics: the first topic involves an inquiry related to students' material environment and spanned four lessons over 6 weeks. All lessons were classroom-based and each lasted approximately an hour, apart from lesson 4 that was a 2-hour lesson. Lesson 1 provided a description for an object with a focus on adjectives and endings of adjectives and nouns. It involved a whole-class teaching session around a replica from an iconic cruciform figurine from Cyprus (Figure 10. 1). Lesson 2 involved students moving outside the classroom into the school grounds, exploring the school and identifying objects that remind them of Cyprus and Greece and explaining why. The initial lessons were seen as scaffolding the first online mission that the teacher created and which was titled "Looking for #AllThingsGreek". Due to delays in development of the Greek version of the nQuire-it platform, lesson 3 involved students bringing their mobile devices

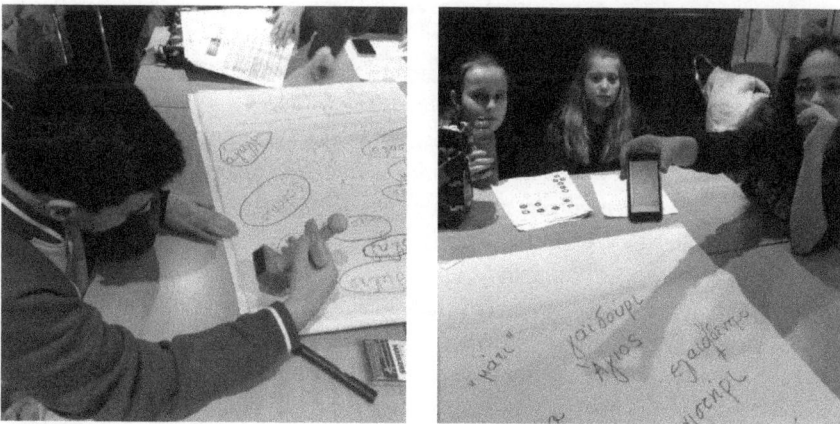

FIGURE 10.1 Activities in the classroom.

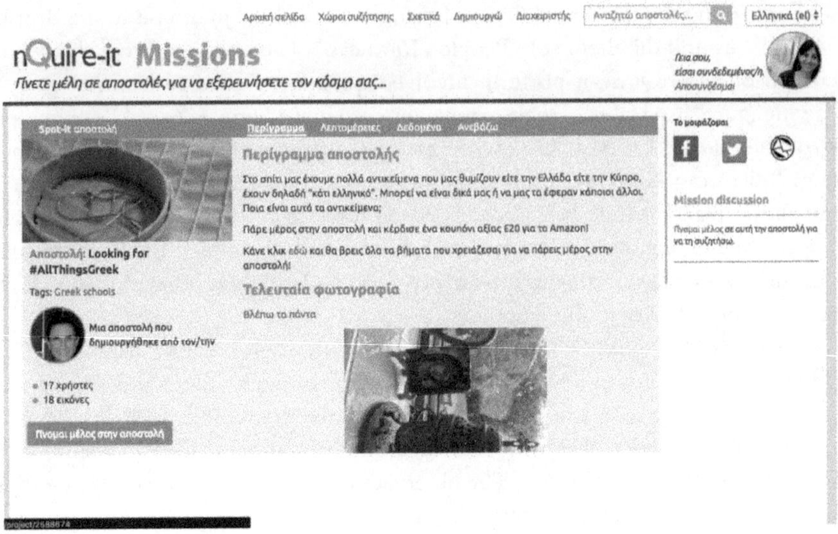

FIGURE 10.2 Mission on the nQuire-it platform: Looking for #AllThingsGreek.

to school and talking about the first set of pictures they had taken (Figure 10. 1). What followed was the launch of an online Spot-it mission on the nQuire-it platform (Figure 10.2), joined by students in both schools. Participants had to explore their home environment and spot objects that they associate with Cyprus or Greece. Participants could upload photos on the platform and write captions in Greek (Figure 10.3). Once this online mission was closed and the winner of the top photograph was announced (based on number of likes), lesson 4 followed, which provided the context for collecting the data that is discussed below. A spiral of the steps based on the inquiry cycle (Scanlon et al., 2013, p. 22) (see Figure 10.5 below) along with printouts of the photographs that were uploaded online were used as the main resources in this lesson to trigger observations and reflections regarding the data collected.

The second topic in the analysis is related to the participants' habits, and spanned three classroom-based lessons over a month. Lesson 1 involved a whole-class teaching session examining a number of photographs the teacher took and brought in, which were related to her everyday routine activities. This was intended as a scaffolding exercise, as it involved students observing and describing visual resources and practising vocabulary (i.e. basic verbs, endings in verbs and routine expressions, expressing opinion). Lesson 2 built upon this and required students to work on a worksheet around "Habits". Their task included creating short texts for their own, family or friends' habits, and then reflect on and discuss these habits. Finally, lesson 3 invited students to "Storyboard your [their] photos" (Figure 10. 4). This resource was created as a response to students expressing difficulty regarding how to capture a habit on a photograph. In parallel with the three lessons an online mission was launched and was entitled "#ItsAHabit".

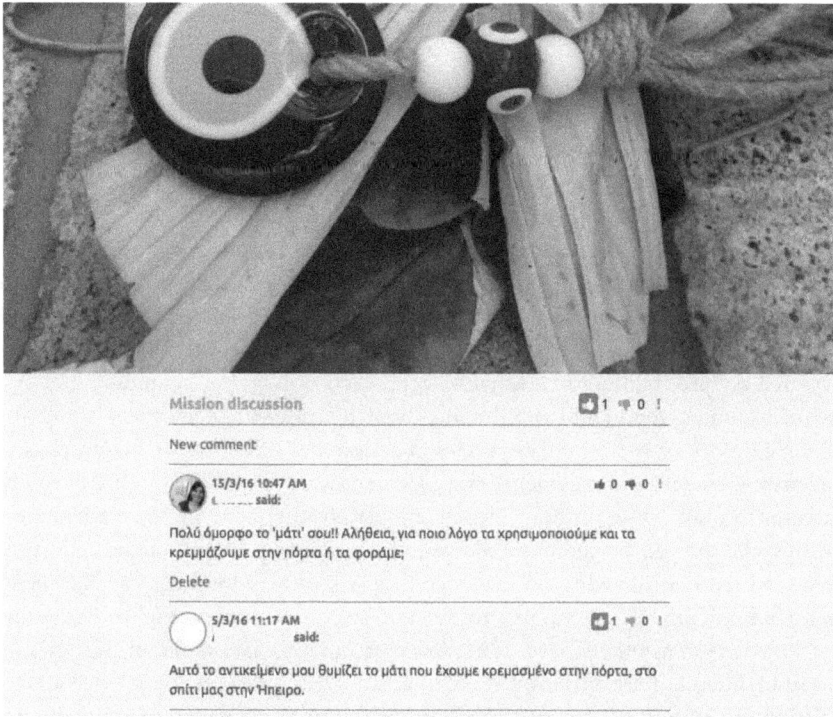

FIGURE 10.3 An example of a participant's post on nQuire–it.

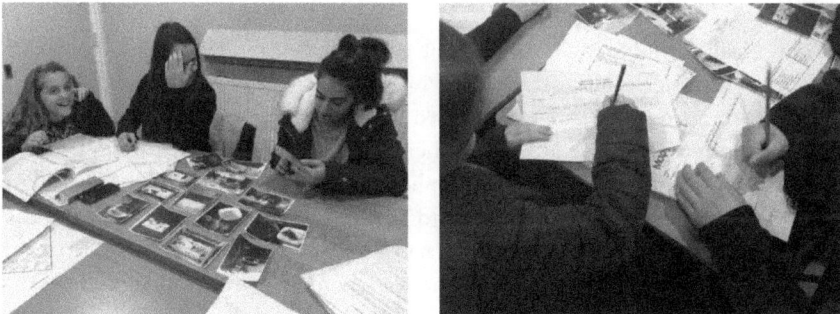

FIGURE 10.4 Classroom lessons around the mission #ItsAHabit.

Methods and data collected

Action research

The research study was partly driven by the author's interest in examining how to create learning designs to incorporate effective use of mobile technologies and methods of citizen inquiry within language learning and teaching and partly motivated by her own desire to shape positively the experiences of her students attending community language education and change their "habits of mind" related to learning spaces and tools. As a result, the study presented in this chapter is firmly located in the realm of a practitioner who looks to "improve the rationality and justice of their own practices, their understanding of these practices, and the situations in which the practices are carried out" (Carr & Kemmis, 1986, p. 162), and as such it demonstrates "inquiry-in-action" (Reason & Bradbury, 2008). The intention is to link practice and ideas with the aim of investigating an inquiry in which questions examined are brought to bear on significant practical issues regarding blended approaches to teaching and learning. The approach, drawing on Lewin's (1946/1948) definition of action research as "proceed[ing] in a spiral of steps, each of which is composed of a circle of planning, action and fact finding about the results of the action" (p. 206), involved more or less systematic cycles of action and reflection. In action phases, practices were tested and evidence was gathered, whilst the reflection involved my attempt to make sense of the evidence and plan further actions. My contribution to this volume can be therefore viewed as a tangible outcome of the reflection stage, where I am drawing on evidence that was gathered but also on the many ways of knowing as a practitioner to open up and share my learning. In doing this I acknowledge, as others have done, that this inquiry "had different purposes, is based in different relationships, has different ways of conceiving knowledge and its relation to practice" (Reason & Bradbury, 2008, p. 8) compared to conventional academic research.

Data collection and analysis

In this chapter, the focus is on content generated by the participants (i.e. photographs) and rich observation notes by the teacher/author to examine how students engaged with and experienced the innovative pedagogic practices in the classroom. Qualitative analysis of the data involved repeated consideration of whole-class data, together with online photos and observation notes. The analysis involved a process of moving backwards and forwards through notes and time, trying to make sense of events and interactions. The data presented here are drawn predominantly from two lessons in the classroom which served as vehicles for exploring issues of interest.

Discussion and findings

Mission: Looking for #AllThingsGreek

In this section, descriptions and extracts from students' interactions in a classroom setting are presented to illustrate how a small group of students ($n = 7$) followed classroom instruction with a focus on the ways the inquiry task helped them to reach insights. During this lesson (lesson 4) students were split into two smaller groups: the first group consisted of three members and the second group of four members (student 1–student 7). They were first asked to examine the printouts of the photographs that were uploaded on the nQuire-it platform and then to classify them. Students wrote their tags on sticky notes, and in turn stuck the photographs on their classroom wall (Figure 10. 5). During this process a physical display of the data was created in the classroom. Table 10. 1 shows their initial classification.

Use of the two languages

This first part of the activity allowed the students to discuss among themselves, elicit and agree upon ideas and make these visible to the rest of their group. Students' regular practice in situations where group work is required is to use English as the main language. The terms were translated into Greek (e.g. every-day things, tradition) and written on sticky notes (Figure 10.5). Students were instructed to describe briefly the photograph and explain in the target language why they made the specific association, and were further prompted to express agreement or disagreement with others' suggestions by using opinion statements in the target language. As this was prior knowledge the teacher wrote these expres-sions on the whiteboard for students to use as reference (e.g. I agree/disagree with what you are saying . . ., In my opinion this . . .). However, early on in this activity the teacher realised that the students' competency in the target language was limiting their ability to respond to her instructions and level of questioning, especially in a natural and spontaneous manner. Importantly, this was seen as hin-dering their engagement with the inquiry process. Therefore, a key decision made by the teacher was to allow students to use English to communicate and share their ideas in this process.

Use of photographs as data

Apart from one case (i.e. photo A1, Table 10.1), the captions had no influence on the classification process. It was observed that, rather than reading the captions in the photographs, the students were classifying the photographs based on recollec-tions and personal associations with the visual representations. For example, student 4 made a comment about photograph D6 (Table 10.1): "I have one, the same. I buy these whenever I go to Cyprus", hence the personal connection was very strong and inevitably determined how a photograph was tagged. Another example was category C (Table 10.1) which they simply called *to mati* (i.e. charm) as the link to their own experience with objects similar to the ones depicted in the three photographs was very strong. It could be argued that students failed to use the text as evidence or acknowledge the person who took/crafted and uploaded the photo-graph in this process. An additional follow-up activity could have been for students to analyse the captions, tag them and classify the photographs based on this analysis and then to compare and contrast these with their own classification. It is noted

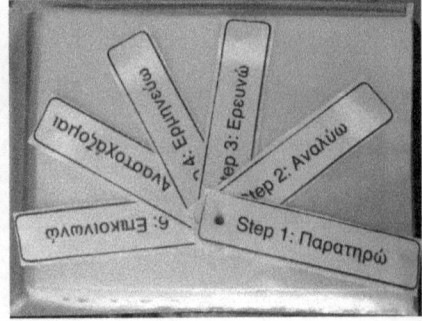

FIGURE 10.5 Working through the data in the classroom.

TABLE 10.1 Initial classification of photographs ($n = 17$)

Tags	Photos					
A. Family						
B. Church / tradition						
C. Charms						
D. Souvenirs						
	1	2	3	4	5	6

that the analysis below will illustrate that some of their initial ideas shifted during the lesson. A comparison of Tables 10.1 and 10.2 (see below) shows how the classification changed over time.

Challenge and refinement of ideas

This process revealed concepts for which students appeared to have a vague understanding. An example of this is the term "tradition", which, as shown in Table 10.1 is grouped together with "church". A discussion about this term was triggered when student 2 assigned photograph B6 (Table 10. 1) to the category "tradition" by saying: "We use this every day to make coffee". To give some contextual information about photograph B6, it depicts a small pot, called *briki* in Greek, which is usually used to make coffee. It is noted that all the students knew what this is and what it is called. Once the photograph was placed against this category, student 1 commented "but this is not a religious tradition, it's a cultural tradition". Student 3 then pointed to the photograph that depicts Greek books (B2, unclassified, Table 10.1) and said: "It is also tradition, they go to school". A subsequent conversation around this remark followed:

Teacher: You are also going to school every day. Would you call this a tradition? [to student 3]

Student 3: . . . not really, going to the English school is not a tradition.

Teacher: So what is a tradition?

Student 6: Music is tradition.

Student 2: It means something which is going on for generations and generations . . .

Teacher: So does this [photograph E2] show a traditional object?

Student 3: It's an everyday object.

The teacher's question (line 1) challenged student 3. Whilst student 3 rejected the idea of English school as a tradition, her response may imply that Greek school is perceived as a tradition. This sheds light on her earlier comment about photograph B2 (i.e. it depicts Greek books), as these can only be used at the Greek school, which presumably is seen as "tradition". Following the teacher's next question (line 3), it was the response by student 2 that got the teacher's attention. The teacher linked back to the original photograph (B6) as this remained an unresolved issue in the course of this interaction to ask whether they would call the *briki* a traditional object (line 6). Student 3's response provided a temporary solution (line 7) and led to the creation of a new sticky note with the term "everyday things" on it, which student 3 placed against the wall along with the two photographs (row E, Table 10.2). Her response, however, is admittedly vague, as it does not clarify whether everyday objects could also be called "traditional objects" and vice versa. To address this issue, subsequent investigations could introduce the term "tradition" as a concept-in-focus for new missions.

TABLE 10.2 Refinement of the classification of photographs ($n = 17$)

Tags	Photos				
A. Family					
B. Church / tradition					
C. Charms					
D. Souvenir/ touristic					
E. Everyday things/only for Greeks/ you only buy it in Cyprus/ Greece					
F. Jewellery bracelets					
	1	2	3	4	5

What followed in this conversation was student 2 adding: "It's [*briki*] an object only for Greeks". The teacher challenged this idea by referring to a personal example, as demonstrated by the following extract:

Teacher: I have a Polish friend who has one [*briki*]. I gave it to her as a gift, she loves it and she is using it regularly. So, is it really only for Greeks?

Student 2: But she only knows about it because you gave it to her . . .

Student 1:   She couldn't have bought it somewhere else other than Greece or Cyprus.

Teacher: Yeah . . . but is it only for Greeks?

Student 1:   It is the country of origin, it is a "country-unique" object.

As shown in Table 10. 2, two new tags were added next to "everyday things": the first, "only for Greeks" and the second, "you only buy it in Cyprus or Greece", that reflect the conversation above.

Teaching features of language and culture

The classification process gave the teacher an opportunity to direct students to category C (Table 10. 1), which includes photographs that depict objects intended to bring protection to their owner (i.e. "charms") (Figure 10.3). All students knew the name of the object – which also gave the name of the group – and recalled that they had a few at home. Drawing on the caption of the nQuire-it post on Figure 10. 3, i.e. "This object reminds me of a charm that is hung on the door of our house in Epirus" (translation), the teacher asked them why this object is displayed in our homes but the students could not articulate why they possess them and what they signify. Through discussion, a few key terms, such as "protection", "luck" and "keep evil away" emerged. The teacher also used this opportunity to teach proverbs that exist in Greek and are related to these particular objects. Despite the teacher's explanations, it is noted that students did not associate these objects with religious practices, and the category was kept in its original form and name (category C).

Opening up, revisiting and reflecting

It was observed that students were gradually opening up to others' ideas and views. An example is related to photograph D3 (Table 10.1), which depicts personal memoirs. Student 4 initially assigned this photograph under the tag "souvenirs", but was challenged by student 1 as illustrated by the following: "I disagree with [student 4], because this picture does not show souvenirs" (in Greek). She carried on by pointing to other photographs in category D to explain her rationale: "These [souvenirs] are things that everyone could go to Greece or Cyprus in touristic shops and buy them. The others [photograph D3] are not! Someone brought them with them here [UK]" (in English).

This explanation seemed sufficient to student 4, who "on the spot" re-assigned the photograph to category A, family (photograph A2, Table 10.2) and went back to category D to add the term "touristic" on to another sticky note. A subsequent activity could have been for the teacher to use this comment as an "anchor" and encourage further discussion regarding the reasons people bring objects with them and stories students could share from their family memoirs. This could also frame the topic of another investigation.

Towards the end of lesson 4 the teacher asked the students to consider a different classification for the photographs, even though the general consensus among students was that what they had in front of them was a final product. The teacher challenged them by moving initially one photograph (B4, Table 10. 1) into a new unclassified category, with students responding and moving three more photographs into this new category, which they termed "Jewellery/bracelets" (category F, Table 10. 2). Further sorting out and refinement of ideas could follow in this process to encourage new interpretations and perspectives to arise in the analysis of the photographs (e.g. symbols).

A final question was posed by the teacher to prompt reflection about the photographs: "Looking at these photographs, what do they show? What do they tell about us? What do they tell someone else about you?" Responses pointed to symbols included in the photographs (e.g. cross), the dominant colour in the photographs, which is blue, "as in the Greek flag and the sea", and the representations of the landscape (i.e. sea, white houses, blue doors/windows), which are considered as "too typical Greek", hence pointing to stereotypes of representations. An important comment by student 1 was noted: "They don't really tell much about us to a foreigner, apart from the souvenir things. But for us they are all Greek stuff". Her comment reveals a collective understanding about, and connection to, the objects depicted in the photographs, apart from the souvenirs that do not seem to carry much weight. She also appears to make a distinction between "us [students with Greek heritage]" and "foreigners", in a statement that highlights a bond shared among this group but also marks the completion of an activity that arguably led to personal understanding and fulfilment.

Mission: #ItsAHabit

The Spot-it mission #ItsAHabit was related to students' everyday routine activities. In this section insights from the classroom setting are presented to illustrate how a group of students ($n = 8$) perceived the use of the nQuire-it platform in terms of posting content online and the usability of the platform.

"I don't want to put anything there that is not right"

Throughout the intervention many participants expressed concerns related to writing text in Greek and posting comments online that may include mistakes. This is related to their perceived competence in the target language. The following conversation illustrates this point:

Student 1: I joined the mission but I don't want to put anything there [nQuire-it] that is not right.

Teacher: It's OK if things are not 100% correct.

Student 1: No, I don't want to have things wrong.

To address similar concerns as the one expressed above the teacher created a worksheet titled "Storyboard your photos" (Figure 10.4), where work in the classroom would proceed to structure the online activity. For example, student 1 used this worksheet as a way to correct the spelling and syntax mistakes for captions she would include in her online posts for the mission #ItsAHabit. It is noted that, even though students responded well in classroom activities, and took photographs of their habits on their mobile phone ($n = 2$ each), the mission had no content uploaded online in the duration of the three lessons.

"Is there an app?"

A few delays in the launch of the nQuire-it platform in Greek and issues related to social log-ins at the beginning of the project seemed to have had a lasting impact on students, who were thinking that "things are not working". Further to this, two students were persistently asking about an app that they could use to take and upload photographs directly from their mobile phone. Related to this point, the steps required to upload content on the platform (i.e. take picture, send/upload it on computer, log on the platform) were a source of frustration for a few participants. This is seen as being associated with certain expectations due to participants' every-day engagement with commercial apps. Technical breakdowns at the early stages of the project along with a perceived lack of an app are seen as two main factors influencing their online participation. It may also be that students approached the task of using the platform from a "schooling" perspective as it was seen as homework. Finally, the lack of necessary infrastructure in the school (i.e. no wi-fi or 4G connection) certainly had an impact on the design of lessons and participation.

Implications and conclusion

This chapter presented examples of a blended approach to citizen-led inquiry investigations that were centred on realistic and relevant contexts to "encourage students to take advantage of their knowledge . . . and in reasoning about their findings" (McElhaney & Linn, 2013, p. 52). The analysis showed that instruction in the classroom prompted students to think of ideas, gave them opportunities to share and refine ideas and also challenged – to an extent – misconceptions they may have had. Firming the instruction in personal experiences and cultural connection to the HL (Carreira, 2004) is seen as allowing students to connect to their prior knowledge or ideas and can help them monitor their own understanding so that they can identify gaps in their knowledge. Evidence was also provided that, despite limited online interactions among students, the creation of a physical display in the classroom of data collected from a joint investigation among students from two schools became a "resource and an arena for students' reflections" (Pierroux et al., 2011, p.34) that have authentic photographs as points of departure. It was interesting to note that, despite being allowed to use English in the discussion, the nature of the activity made it possible for students to choose the situations where they felt they could use the target language. It is argued that this reflects an authentic rather than an instructional approach to language learning.

A number of challenges arose from integrating cultural citizen inquiry in the context of schools, including students not completing their tasks; the quality of data collected and how manageable it is – especially considering the prospects of mass participation; technology working in a systematic way; the range of devices used by students; anxiety among students for content generated online; and arguably a lack of control on the teacher's side during the presentation and facilitation process. In hindsight, it could be said that students took part in the investigations and the classroom discussions with no clear understanding of the relationship between the topic, the task and intended outcomes. They did not seem yet to have fully developed strategies to negotiate "the rules for participation" (Wells; quoted in Ash, 2002, p. 395) in the context of a citizen inquiry. In fact, they were developing skills "on the go", and through their engagement in the activity and the interactions in the classroom – as mediated by a teacher-as-expert – the negotiation of meaning and considerations of new ideas were encouraged and emerged.

It was observed that students were reaching insights from the interactions with their groups and the teacher, partly enhanced by the design of the teacher's instruction and partly due to the methods of citizen inquiry that allowed for students' own contexts to have a presence in the HL classroom. That said, cultural citizen inquiry with young people requires scaffolding, resource and support to guide students toward designing and conducting investigations, and still, this does not ensure that students will adequately distinguish and refine ideas or clarify misconceptions around the issues-in-focus. The two investigations that were presented in this chapter are seen as the starting points towards this process of gaining the skills of being engaged in research of their everyday contexts. Related to this is a major challenge that this study highlights: how to allow students to take on the role of an active investigator and let go of their "schooling" perspective, especially when the investigation is taking place in a formal education setting. That said, for young people, their role as investigator and their involvement with methods of social science research may allow them to be more attentive to their everyday life and develop new perspectives of the world around them.

Finally, it is recognised that this chapter presents a small exploratory study which provides little scope for any generalisations. However, it is seen as paving the way for further research in the field of cultural citizen inquiry. The study – initiated by practitioners and firmly situated in the practical context of two schools – shows how principles of citizen-led inquiry were taken into account in a learning design in HL education with young people. The engagement with a small group of learners is an attempt to work toward practical outcomes, and also about creating new forms of understanding. The exploratory nature of this study and the example it provides of a joint inquiry-led investigation with a focus on culture certainly guides work in similar contexts. Importantly, it informs future projects that may involve multiple schools and students joining in inquiry-led investigations on a national and international scale which over time would lead to the accumulation of a substantial evidence source.

Acknowledgements

Special thanks to the British Academy for providing the funding for this study through the British Academy Schools Language Awards. I am grateful for the support that was provided by the Open University in the UK and the British Museum in London. The parents, teachers and children in the two Greek Supplementary Schools also deserve my greatest appreciation.

References

Anderson, J. (2009). Relevance of CLIL in developing pedagogies for minority language teaching. In: Marsh, D., Mehisto, P., Wolff, D., Aliaga, R., Asikainen, T., Frigols-Martin, M. J., Hughes, S., and Lange, G. (Eds.), *CLIL Practice: Perspectives from the Field*. Jyväskylä: CCN: University of Jyväskylä, 124–132.

Anderson, J., and Chung, Y.-C. (2012). Community languages, the arts and transformative pedagogy: Developing active citizenship for the 21st century. *Citizenship Teaching & Learning*, 7(13), 259–271.

Ash, D. (2002). Negotiations of thematic conversations about biology. In Leinhardt, G., Crowley, K., and Knutson, K. (Eds.), *Learning Conversations in Museums*. Mahwah: NJ, Lawrence Erlbaum, 357–400.

Bunterm, T., Lee, K., Ng Lan Kong, J., Srikoon, S., Vangpoomyai, P., Rattanavongsa, J., et al. (2014). Do different levels of inquiry lead to different learning outcomes? A comparison between guided and structured inquiry. *International Journal of Science Education*, 36(12), 1937–1959.

British Academy (2013). *Languages: The State of the Nation*. Retrieved September 10, 2016 from http://www.britac.ac.uk/publications/languages-state-nation.

Campbell, R., and Peyton, J. K. (1998). Heritage language students: A valuable language resource. *The ERIC Review*, 6(1), 38–39.

Carr, W., and Kemmis, S. (1986). *Becoming Critical: Education Knowledge and Action Research*. Lewes: Falmer.

Carreira, M. (2004). Seeking explanatory adequacy: A dual approach to understanding the term "heritage language learner". *Heritage Language Journal*, 2(1), 1–25.

Evans, D., and Gillan-Thomas, K. (2015). *Supplementary education. Descriptive analysis of supplementary school pupils' characteristics and attainment in seven local authorities in England, 2007/08–2011/12*. Paul Hamlyn Foundation. Retrieved July 10, 2015 from http://www.phf.org.uk/publications/supplementary- schools-research-report/.

Fishman, J. A. (2001). 300-years of heritage language education in the United States. In Peyton, J. K., Ranard, D. A., and McGinnis, S. (Eds.), *Heritage Languages in America: Preserving a National Resource*. Washington, DC: Center for Applied Linguistics & Delta Systems, 81–98.

Ito, M., Soep, E., Kligler-Vilenchik, N., Shresthova, S., Gamber-Thompson, L., and Zimmerman, A. (2015). Learning connected civics: Narratives, practices, infrastructures. *Curriculum Inquiry*, 45(1), 10–29.

Kramsch, C. (1998). *Language and Culture*. Oxford: Oxford University Press.

Kukulska-Hulme, A. (2015). Language as a bridge connecting formal and informal language learning through mobile devices. In Wong, L.-H., Milrad, M., and Specht, M. (Eds.), *Seamless Learning in the Age of Mobile Connectivity*. Singapore: Springer, 281–294.

Lewin, K. (1946/1948). Action research and minority problems. In Lewin, G.W. (Ed.), *Resolving Social Conflicts*, pp. 201–216. New York: Harper & Row.

McElhaney, W. K., and Linn, C. M. (2013). Orchestrating inquiry instruction using the knowledge integration framework. In Littleton, K., Scanlon, E., and Sharples, M. (Eds.), *Orchestrating Inquiry Learning*. Abingdon: Routledge, 58–68.

McPake, J., Tinsley, T., Broeder, P., Mijares, L., Latomaa, S., and Martynuik, W. (2007). *Valuing All Languages in Europe*. Graz: European Centre for Modern Language. Retrieved July 10, 2015 from www.ecml.at/mtp2/publications/Valeur-report-E.pdf.

NRCSE (2015). *Supplementary Education*. Retrieved July 10, 2015 from http://www.supplementaryeducation.org.uk/supplementary-education-the-nrc/.

Pierroux, P., Krange, I., and Sem, I. (2011). Bridging contexts and interpretations: Mobile blogging on art museum field trips. *MedieKultur Journal of Media and Communication Research, 50*, 30–47.

Purdam, K. (2014). Citizen social science and citizen data? Methodological and ethical challenges for social research. *Current Sociology, 62*(3), 374–392.

Reason, P., and Bradbury, H. (2008). *The SAGE Handbook of Action Research: Participative Inquiry and Practice* (2nd ed.). London: SAGE Publications.

Scanlon, E., Anastopoulou, S., and Kerawalla, L. (2013). Inquiry learning reconsidered: Contexts, representations and challenges. In Littleton, K., Scanlon, E. and Sharples, M. (Eds.), *Orchestrating Inquiry Learning*. Abingdon, Routledge, 7–30.

Speak to the Future (2015). *RT news report on poor UK language skills*. 14 April 2015. Retrieved May 25, 2015 from http://www. speaktothefuture.org/rt-news-report-on-poor-uk-language-skills/.

Valdés, G. (2001). Heritage language students: Profiles and possibilities. In J. K. Peyton, D. A. Ranard, & S. McGinnis (Eds.), *Heritage Languages in America: Preserving a National Resource*. Washington, DC: Center for Applied Linguistics & Delta Systems, 37–80.

11

EDUCATIONAL BACKGROUNDS, PROJECT DESIGN AND INQUIRY LEARNING IN CITIZEN SCIENCE

Richard Edwards, Diarmuid McDonnell, Ian Simpson and Anna Wilson

Introduction

Two overlapping currents of research and practice influence this chapter. The first current is the massive growth of citizen science around the world – the participation of volunteers in authentic scientific research projects. There is a huge diversity of citizen science project designs and the possible contributions of volunteers vary accordingly. Arguably, these volunteers can be said to be engaged, to different degrees, in inquiry-based learning simply through the practices in which they participate. The second current is the ongoing work to promote inquiry-based learning in science education and beyond. It might seem strange that such work is necessary, given that many might assume that learning science entails learning scientific methods – to do science is to inquire into phenomena. However, over recent decades and in many countries, there has been a tendency for the teaching of science to move away from teaching the practices of scientific method to learning *about* science and the scientific method, or learning about the history of science. In this situation, learning science does not entail developing the practices of scientific inquiry. Engaging volunteers in citizen science, therefore, might be positioned as an alternative route through which people can learn science and the practices of science, rather than learning about it, thus the interest of those researching inquiry-based learning in citizen science.

Drawing upon an empirical study of the educational backgrounds and learning outcomes of volunteers in two citizen science projects in the UK, this chapter explores the rippling of these two currents and the extent to which people do learn inquiry-based practices through engagement in citizen science activities, where these projects do not necessarily have an explicit pedagogical purpose. In other words, we examine how inquiry-based learning might be said to be implicitly embedded as a pedagogy as part of what we might term the hidden curriculum of citizen science as a social practice.

The primary impetus behind citizen science projects has been in relation to public participation in science and the contribution of volunteers to authentic scientific research. However, increasing attention has been given to the learning outcomes arising from participation in citizen science and its wider educational potential to stimulate an interest in science. Citizen science is identified as, potentially or actually, offering new ways to engage in scientific research, new ways through which to engage the public in this research, and, with that, offering new possibilities for science learning (Bela et al., 2016; Phillips, Ferguson, Minarchek, Porticella, & Bonney, 2014). Central to this is the exploration of the relationship between the design of projects – how they are organised and the types and degrees of volunteer engagement they support – and learning outcomes and the ways to attract people from different demographic and educational backgrounds into citizen science (e.g. Bonney et al., 2009a, 2009b; Garibay Group, 2015). While the projects themselves are primarily designed to enable the scientific research to be undertaken, there is recognition increasingly that such decisions also implicitly – and sometimes explicitly – impact upon the possibilities for volunteers' learning. One aspect of this is in relation to developing the practices of inquiry, bearing in mind that volunteers may also have existing expertise upon which they might draw from prior forms of study or work.

The chapter is in four parts. First, we outline briefly some of the notions of inquiry-based learning and their relationship to the practices of scientific method. Second, we explore some of the existing research on the relationship between educational background and learning outcomes in citizen science. Third, we provide background information on the study undertaken and the two citizen science projects we surveyed, and present relevant data from the analysis of the survey, which has allowed us to explore some of the complex relationships between participant attributes, citizen science project design and inquiry learning outcomes. Account needs to be taken of the fact that the study reported was not explicitly focused on inquiry-based learning through citizen science, but science learning more generally. Fourth, we outline some of the possible implications of this study for further research and practice in citizen science and inquiry-based learning.

Inquiry-based learning

Inquiry-based learning is one of a number of overlapping pedagogical framings that have been developed in response to what are considered the limitations of more instruction-based transmission approaches of memorisation, recall and rote learning in science education. Framed somewhat interchangeably as, for instance, problem-based learning, learning by doing, experiential learning, student-centred learning, active learning, they all point to the active role that people can play in constructing knowledge and understanding. Different traditions of research from, for instance, Deweyian pragmatism and Marxist Vygotskyian psychology flow through these framings and their uptakes and mixings usually have more to do with the specific domains within which they are articulated than the overall broad domain of learning theory.

While not bound by a specific domain, inquiry-based learning sits within a tradition of research in science education that seeks to move beyond a pedagogy of instruction and recall of facts to enhance or introduce a pedagogy of engagement and practice. In inquiry-based approaches, learners are supported to engage in practices such as identifying their own questions, identifying and evaluating evidence relevant to the question and being able to explain and communicate the results (Bell, Urhahne, Schanze, & Ploetzner, 2010). More broadly, the National Science Education Standards (1996) in the USA influentially identified a number of characteristics integral to inquiry learning in science education. For instance, learners need to know that science entails more than memorisation and have the opportunity to develop new knowledge, add new data and reframe previous understanding of an issue. Integral to this are student-centredness and peer learning and success is measured by the transferability of their science learning into broader life contexts.

Similar lists pepper the literature. For instance, the US National Institute for Health (2005) identified inquiry learning as entailing the development of questions, making relevant observations, doing research to establish existing data, developing methods and instruments for experiments and data collection, collecting, analysing and interpreting data, outlining possible explanations and exploring implications for further study. Analytically exploring the similarities and differences of such characterisations of inquiry learning could take up much time, but its fruitfulness would be questionable. And it is the family resemblance of such characterisations rather than a single closely defined understanding of the concept which might be considered one of its weaknesses. Inquiry-based learning can mean many things and result in different approaches. Despite this possible conceptual weakness, implicit in many of these characterisations are certain conceptions of scientific method and content knowledge.

Within the discussion of inquiry-based learning, learner engagement has been differentiated into various levels to reflect different forms that such learning might take based upon the nature and extent of the inquiry practices in which learners are involved. For instance, Banchi and Bell (2008) clearly outline four levels of inquiry: confirmation inquiry, structured inquiry, guided inquiry and open inquiry. Confirmation inquiry entails the learner following a procedure to address a question, both of which are established by a teacher. With structured inquiry, the learners are provided with a question and procedure but are supported in developing explanations on the basis of the data collected. Guided inquiry entails the teacher providing a question to learners, but them developing procedures to answer it and communicate their findings. With open inquiry, learners formulate their own questions as well as engaging in all other components. Open inquiry might be considered the closest to practicing the scientific method, and the other forms could be used to scaffold learners into developing these practices. As we will see, these levels of inquiry-based learning resonate with certain typologies of citizen science project based upon the nature and extent of volunteer participation and provide one of the possible ripples between the two.

Inquiry-based learning is a generic pedagogical approach that can be utilised in a range of ways and in different contexts. In engaging in such processes, learners are expected to develop the capacities associated with these practices. As such, there is a range of learning outcomes that are developed through such a pedagogical approach. It is inquiry-based learning expressed as learning outcomes that we witness in part in the discussion of learning through citizen science.

Citizen science and learning outcomes

Citizen science projects take many different forms, using different types of engagement and encouraging the participation of different groups. Some are more local, and some, increasingly mediated by computer technologies, are more global. Some target and involve specific groups, such as school children, while others are more open, increasingly using crowdsourcing and other forms of technology. Some are disciplinary-based, while others are more problem-focused and multidisciplinary. Although referred to as citizen science, the majority focus on environmental and ecological issues and engage volunteers in field science. While most are instigated by professional scientists working in both public and third-sector organisations, there is increasing interest in more collaboratively developed and citizen-initiated projects. Their importance is reflected in the increasing support citizen science projects have from government organisations, third-sector groups and other public bodies, including schools, colleges and universities, and the increasing number of guidelines and sets of principles produced on how to develop projects (e.g. Tweddle, Robinson, Pocock, & Roy, 2012).

There has been a significant growth in citizen science projects over the last three decades and, with that, research in areas such as the demographics and motivations of volunteers (e.g. Raddick et al., 2010), the validity of the scientific work undertaken (e.g. Shirk et al., 2012; Wiggins, Newmany, Stevensonz, & Crowston, 2011), the effects of such work on attitudes to science (e.g. Brossard, Lewenstein, & Bonney, 2005) and the learning outcomes they support (e.g. Garibay Group, 2015; Phillips et al., 2014). Increasing attention is being given to researching who contributes to these scientific projects, the forms of knowledge and expertise they draw upon in making their contributions, the knowledge practices in which they engage, what is learnt through participation in such projects and the ways in which these result in science learning, the development of science capital and enhanced participation in science-related activities more broadly (Archer, Dawson, DeWitt, Seakins, & Wong, 2015). Volunteers to citizen science may have different degrees of acquired expertise in scientific inquiry, and thus their learning *of* and *through* inquiry may differ also.

While motivation to contribute to citizen science among volunteers remains an important focus of interest, less is known about those who contribute, their educational backgrounds and the learning arising from their participation in projects.

Where the latter has been studied, the focus has largely been upon science learning outcomes – what is learnt – rather than learning processes – how that learning occurs. These learning outcomes include the learning of inquiry practices. Drawing upon existing work in the USA, Phillips et al. (2014) have produced a framework for evaluating the learning outcomes of citizen science projects. The framework focuses on: interest in science and the environment; self-efficacy; motivation; knowledge of the nature of science; skills of science inquiry; and stewardship and behaviour. We can see how these broad learning outcomes overlap with, but also may go beyond, some of the wider conceptions of inquiry-based learning we discussed above. However, there is then the question of how and to what extent any or all of these learning outcomes are achieved. This in part depends upon citizen science project design and the nature and levels of engagement of volunteers in scientific practices.

In examining the design features of citizen science projects, different areas have often been the focus of attention, in particular, their organisational structure – expert-led/contributory, peer/collaborative, community-defined/co-created – and the nature and extent of the scientific contributions of volunteers – e.g. defining questions, gathering information, developing hypotheses, designing the study, data collection, analysing samples, analysing data, interpreting data, drawing conclusions, disseminating results, discussing results and asking new questions. In their attempt to produce a typology of citizen science, Wiggins and Crowston (2011, 2012) explored approximately 80 facets of projects: project demographics (e.g. age, geographic range, research discipline, stated goals), organisational features (e.g. affiliations, funding sources), participation design (e.g. task types, skills or tools required), educational features (e.g. informal learning resources, curricular materials), outcomes (e.g. publications, protocol revisions, innovations), technologies (e.g. communication tools, website features), processes (e.g. data validation, volunteer management, communication) and data management (e.g. data sharing, ownership, stewardship). From their clustering of projects, they identified five types of citizen science project:

1. action projects: volunteer-initiated participatory action research to encourage participant intervention in local concerns
2. conservation projects: natural resource goals, involving citizens in stewardship
3. investigation projects: focusing on scientific research goals in a physical setting
4. virtual projects: similar goals to investigation projects, but entirely ICT-mediated and differing in a number of other characteristics
5. education projects: education and outreach as primary goals.

Wiggins and Crowston (2012) suggest these are mutually exclusive types, but this seems hard to accept, given the educational dimensions, in particular, informal learning, associated with any such projects. Their sample of projects for their review was also relatively small.

More influentially, for Shirk et al. (2012) it is the degree and quality of volunteer participation that define different types of project and this is more pertinent to the discussion in this chapter, as this may reflect different possibilities for drawing upon and developing inquiry practices. In terms of the degree of participation, they identify five types:

1.   contractual projects: communities ask professional researchers to conduct a specific scientific investigation and report on the results
2.   contributory projects: generally designed by scientists and for which members of the public primarily contribute data
3.   collaborative projects: generally designed by scientists and for which members of the public contribute data but also help to refine project design, analyse data and/or disseminate findings
4.   co-created projects: designed by scientists and members of the public working together and for which at least some of the public participants are actively involved in most or all aspects of the research process
5.   collegial contributions: non-credentialled individuals conduct research independently with varying degrees of expected recognition by institutionalised science and/or professionals.

For Shirk et al. (2012), the quality of participation is evaluated in relation to a number of areas – inputs, activities, outputs, outcomes and impacts. Overall, they suggest this provides a framework for the design of specific citizen science projects. They also point out that different models have strengths and limitations. For instance, contributory projects are more likely to produce robust scientific research outcomes, while co-created projects are more likely to affect policy decisions. Different designs are associated with varying types of volunteer engagement and this impacts upon the possibilities for inquiring and learning the practices of inquiry.

In addition, as we saw above in relation to inquiry-based learning, there have been attempts to characterise participation in citizen science into a number of levels. For instance, Haklay (2012), identifies four levels of participation:

1.   crowdsourcing: citizens as sensors
2.   distributed intelligence: citizens as interpreters
3.   participatory science: citizens as contributing to problem definition and data collection
4.   extreme science: citizens collaborating in problem definition, data collection and analysis.

While not exactly matching on to the framing of confirmation inquiry, structured inquiry, guided inquiry and open inquiry, we witness again resonances and family resemblances in the two currents of research and practice identified at the beginning of this chapter.

With these two currents of research and practice in mind, we now turn to the empirical study of learning through citizen science. While the focus of the research reported was wider than an examination of the development of inquiry-based learning through participation in citizen science, in exploring project design, educational background and learning outcomes, it inevitably offers some pertinent findings on linkages and possibilities.

Educational backgrounds and learning outcomes in two citizen science projects

The empirical research addressed two questions: What are the educational backgrounds of people contributing to citizen science projects? What do volunteers learn informally from participating in citizen science projects? Two citizen science projects were identified by the British Trust for Ornithology (BTO) to be the settings for this research, which was undertaken in 2015. The Wetland Bird Survey (WeBS) is the main monitoring scheme for non-breeding water birds in the UK, providing the data to evaluate the conservation of their populations and habitats. It began in 1947, and in 2015 had around 3,000 volunteers participating in monthly counts at specific locations around the UK. The data collected are used to assess the size of water bird populations, determine trends in numbers and distribution and assess the importance of individual sites. The Nest Record Scheme (NRS) gathers data on the breeding success of UK birds. Project volunteers find and follow the progress of individual birds' nests. The data collected are used to monitor trends in breeding performance among bird populations. These help to identify species that may be declining because of problems at the nesting stage. The NRS started in 1939 and in 2015 had around 660 active volunteers.

The online survey instrument for this project was devised by the project team in discussion with BTO staff. It drew upon existing surveys in the citizen science and informal science learning field, but additional questions were added to gather data on prior subjects studied, the influence of family and friends on participation in citizen science and any impacts upon engagement in wider science-related activities. The survey was piloted with a small number of BTO volunteers and revised in response to feedback. It was made available to volunteers between April and November 2015. A link to the survey was sent by the BTO to all volunteers contributing to WeBS and NRS. Two reminders were sent during the period that the survey was live. The response rate for NRS was around 38% and 23% for WeBS volunteers. While both are respectable response rates for such surveys, caution is necessary in generalising from the results, as it is often the most engaged who respond to surveys.

A range of descriptive and inferential statistical techniques were applied to the analysis of the data. Responses captured on an ordinal scale were mainly treated as if they were interval data. This was considered appropriate as respondents were asked to select a number rather than category. It also facilitated easily interpretable comparisons of mean and median scores between groups of participants. Where appropriate, overall measures of certain variables were created (for example, informal learning): these were constructed by combining the responses to a question's items (statements) and the internal consistency of the overall measure was assessed using Cronbach's alpha. For categorical variables, cross-tabulations were produced and an appropriate measure of association was calculated to assess the strength of the pattern in the table (gamma, Cramer's V); the statistical significance of the association was then determined by the use of a chi-square test. For metric variables, measures of central tendency were calculated and a variety of bivariate statistical techniques were employed to determine whether there were statistically significant differences between groups. For mean scores, independent sample and paired t-tests were conducted and for median scores Wilcoxon Mann–Whitney and Wilcoxon signed ranks tests were employed. Findings were also subject to robustness checks to determine the effect the level of measurement and functional form had on the results.

The numbers of volunteers contributing to these projects increase up to the age of 70 – the biggest proportion being in the age range 61–70 – after which numbers decrease. Almost 83% of respondents were male. Almost 98% were white UK residents. Of useable responses, 53% identified themselves as employed, 46% as retired and 1% as students. Responses were analysed drawing upon the UK Office for National Statistics (2010) employment categories. Of the employed, 57% identified themselves as in professional occupations, 19% as in associative professional and technical occupations and 9% as managers, directors or senior officials. Of the retired, 66% identified themselves as simply retired, while 24% identified themselves as retired professionals. These data suggest that older, white males from higher socio-economic backgrounds are the major contributors to these two projects. Whether this is generalisable or a reflection of who is most likely to respond to such surveys is an important question. However, their current or past occupations may be taken to infer existing expertise in the use of higher-order inquiry practices and the generation and use of data than would be the case among the general population.

Motivation to participate in NRS and WeBS was explored. Volunteers were asked to comment on a scale of 1 (not at all motivating) to 6 (very motivating). In line with other research, enjoying finding out about the natural world and making a contribution to scientific research were major reasons for participating in these projects. Interest in the particular project, the particular scientific domain and science in general all rated highly. It is also interesting that 14% of respondents identified wanting to learn more about science as very motivating (a score of 6). The motivations are similar across both projects, although the overall measure is slightly higher for NRS than WeBS. Statistically, the differences in learning outcomes between projects are not attributable to motivations. In this sense, it appears that the activities in which volunteers engage are more significant in relation to learning outcomes than the motivations for participating in the first place.

The educational backgrounds of respondents in relation to highest level of previous qualifications are reported in Figure 11.1. This shows that almost two-thirds of respondents have university qualifications, which one would anticipate given the higher socio-economic status of most volunteers. The no degree category

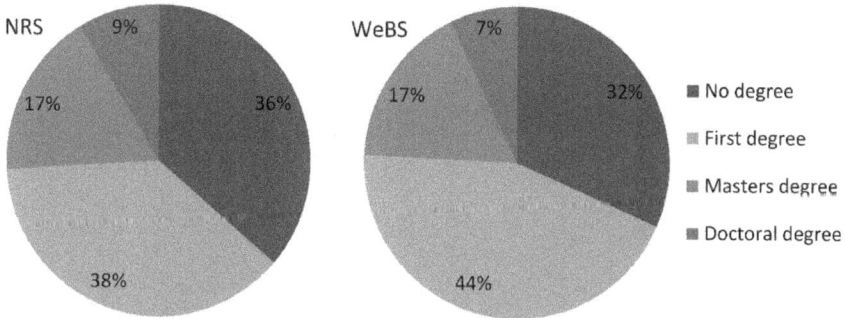

FIGURE 11.1 Educational qualification levels of citizen science volunteers. NRS, Nest Record Scheme; WeBS, Wetland Bird Survey.

refers to individuals who left school at 16 or 18, who may or may not have school qualifications, and individuals who are currently enrolled in undergraduate programmes but have not yet attained a degree.

In addition to exploring volunteers' prior level of qualification, we also explored the subjects they had studied to establish the potential levels and areas of expertise upon which they might draw in contributing to projects. Participants were asked about subjects for which they had received qualifications, their level, as well as subjects they had previously studied but for which they had received no qualifications. These were taken as proxies for existing expertise. This is reported in Table 11.1; percentages are rounded to the nearest whole number. This gives a somewhat complex picture of the prior certificated capability upon which volunteers were able to draw and is suggestive rather than definitive, and therefore requires further research to establish actual levels of existing expertise.

While school-level qualifications in the core sciences of biology, chemistry, mathematics and physics received the highest number of responses, in terms of higher education qualifications, the proportion of responses in these subjects is relatively small. Higher proportions of higher education qualifications are to be found in subjects with fewer responses, such as engineering, environmental science and earth science. This may show in part the ways in which science educational trajectories diversify and shift post-school in the UK. When examining the responses to the other category, there is evidence of the contribution to these citizen science projects of people who have higher education qualifications in a range of social sciences, but, most prominently, education. Teachers and ex-teachers represent an important group contributing to these citizen science projects. While existing scientific expertise would seem to be available to many volunteers, in terms of specific areas of science, the prior knowledge and capability would appear to be diverse.

Given the specific focus of these citizen science projects is ornithology, it is noticeable that only just over 35% of respondents reported previous study of the subject. Of these, only 12% identified school or higher education qualifications in this area. This reflects the lack of formal ornithology qualifications in the UK

TABLE 11.1 Prior subjects studied and school and higher education qualifications

Subjects	n	%			
		Other	Previous study	School	Higher
Aquaculture	53	9	85	2	4
Archaeology	72	8	83	3	6
Astronomy	78	5	86	5	4
Biology	580	3	15	58	24
Chemistry	551	3	13	74	11
Computing	225	29	38	17	16
Earth sciences	187	4	28	33	35
Engineering	166	19	22	9	49
Environmental science	270	12	34	13	41
Mathematics	569	4	5	81	9
Ornithology	332	17	71	3	9
Physics	491	3	12	79	6
Technology studies	149	11	33	44	11
Other subjects	226	12	7	14	68

and suggests that the development of ornithological expertise among volunteers to these projects mostly takes place in less formal ways. It also indicates that people with a variety of educational backgrounds in terms of subjects studied contribute to these projects. Given the nature, level and extent of prior qualifications in the sciences, and age and socio-economic status of volunteers, it might well be considered that a high proportion have good levels of generic inquiry-based expertise to draw upon prior to engaging in these citizen science projects, even if their prior knowledge in the subject domain of ornithology, as measured by qualifications, was more limited. The recentness of their use of such expertise – for instance, in work or other forms of volunteering – prior to participating in these projects was not examined in this research, but would be worthy of further study.

What then of the relationship between educational background and learning outcomes? Participants were asked to self-report on a scale of 1 (less) to 6 (more) the extent to which they had learnt specific outcomes from their participation in the citizen science project. These outcomes were derived from Phillips et al. (2014) – as listed above – and therefore go beyond some of the narrower framings of inquiry-based learning identified above. Here we explore specifically the extent to which inquiry-based characteristics are demonstrated in the science learning outcomes of these citizen science projects. The self-reported nature of the extent of volunteers' learning of specific outcomes and the limited nature of the scale used mean that some caution is necessary in drawing strong conclusions from the survey.

Table 11.2 identifies both the numbers responding to each learning outcome and the proportions who identify themselves as having learnt more and less. This shows large percentages of volunteers identifying themselves as learning in all the

TABLE 11.2 Learning outcomes: 1 (less) to 6 (more)

Learning outcomes	n	%					
		1	2	3	4	5	6
Topic of project	907	4	2	9	15	32	38
Data collection	881	11	8	16	22	23	20
Data analysis	788	28	17	21	16	12	7
Framing a scientific question	734	55	18	15	7	4	2
Scientific method	761	33	21	21	13	7	5
Scientific careers	742	55	14	13	8	6	4
Ethics of scientific research	759	46	15	18	8	7	6
Impact of research on others	765	36	15	16	16	10	7
Evaluation of evidence	754	41	18	20	12	7	3
Purpose of science	782	28	15	20	14	14	9

outcome areas identified – from 77% learning about developing research questions to 95% learning about the topic of the project. However, on closer examination, it is only in relation to 'learning about the topic' and 'learning about data collection', a relatively narrow selection of inquiry learning outcomes, that volunteers identify themselves as learning more. For most outcomes participants indicated that, from their viewpoint, only a little learning took place. This suggests that, from the volunteers' perspective, the educative potential of these particular citizen science projects to develop inquiry-based practices is not being as fully developed as it might be; volunteers are learning less than they might in relation to a range of learning outcomes and may be simply drawing upon existing expertise to contribute to projects.

We examined if there were any statistically significant differences in the importance of learning outcomes to contributors in relation to prior levels of education (Figure 11.2). This shows that volunteers without a degree had higher mean learning scores for eight of the ten learning outcomes compared with those with a degree or above. In others words, the less qualified the volunteers, the more they evaluated themselves as learning across most of the learning outcomes. The lesser numbers of participants with no degree would seem to be learning statistically significantly more through participating in these citizen science projects than those with higher education qualifications. This group would appear to be learning more in relation to inquiry-based outcomes. However, it is noticeable that this is not the case in relation to the learning about the 'topic of project', which is where most volunteers evaluated themselves as learning most. For the more qualified, therefore, it would appear that they are drawing most on their wider expertise in science and maybe their experience of inquiry practices in contributing to citizen science projects. However, this needs further, more detailed study to be confirmed.

Further analysis demonstrated that the NRS survey respondents have higher reported levels of learning outcomes than WeBS participants. We explored the extent to which project design – the types and levels of activity in which volunteers

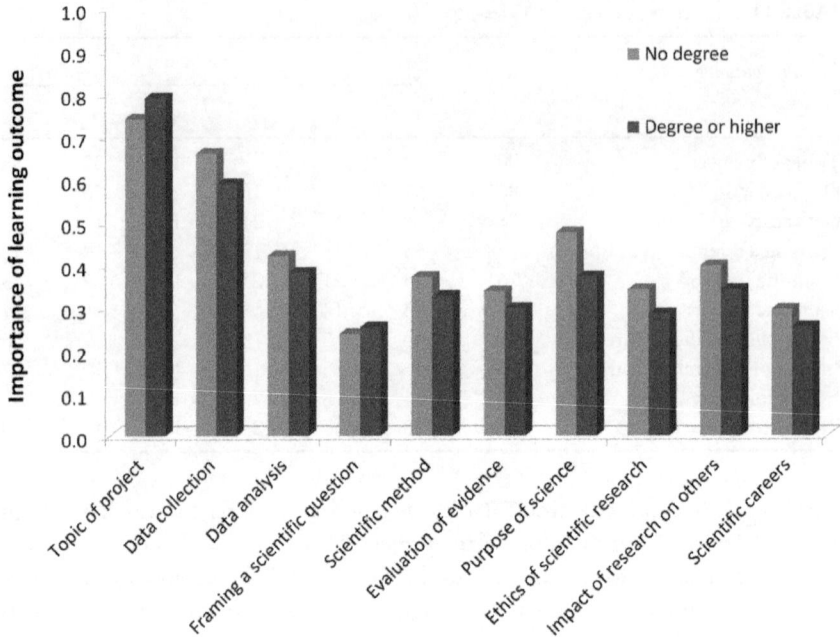

FIGURE 11.2   Importance of learning outcomes to volunteers.

engage – might be related to higher reported levels of learning outcomes. Ostensibly, both projects sit within the contributory category. However, when asked about the activities in which they engaged, there are statistically significant differences in the extent to which participants engage in these activities, especially with regard to analytical tasks. These differences may account for the higher mean learning outcome scores for NRS participants, as it is this project that involves more extensive levels of engagement in most research activities. From respondents to the survey, it would appear that NRS has more aspects of collaborative citizen science projects than WeBS. This demonstrates that the design of citizen science projects seems to have an impact on levels and types of learning outcomes. Further research could explore the extent to which there are also correlations with different forms of inquiry – confirmation, structured, guided and open.

Conclusion

In relation to this study, volunteers are clearly self-reporting learning through their participation in citizen science activities. Tentatively, given the limited nature of the project, the evidence is that this is related in part to their prior levels of education, the nature of the activities in which they participate and the intensity of their engagement in those activities. The context for this, of course, is one where the majority of volunteers have university qualifications and significant numbers have university qualifications in sciences. It may not, therefore, be surprising that we found that those with higher-level qualifications were more likely to be drawing upon some existing level of expertise in making their contributions and learning less, while those with lesser qualifications engaged more fully in activities and learnt more. Both groups identify themselves as learning more in relation to topic-specific knowledge, while the more qualified report themselves as learning less in other areas. However, we would not wish to generalise this to all citizen science projects, as what emerges is the complexity of the factors influencing learning through citizen science and the particularities of project and volunteer demographics in this project.

The focus of this study was on informal science learning through citizen science. There are clearly family resemblances between science learning and inquiry learning, although the range of strategies and topics associated with the latter can be argued to extend beyond the former. There would appear to be some scope for exploring the relationship between some of the typologies of inquiry learning and citizen science project design, as designs that enable volunteers to engage more fully in inquiring practices might be inferred to result in more learning, especially for those with fewer qualifications. However, in the context of citizen science, such practices have to be determined by the scientific purpose of the project; the science may limit the inquiry or science learning for perfectly legitimate reasons.

While a relationship between citizen science project design and some elements of inquiry learning can be argued to be demonstrated in this project, as important are the demographics of the volunteers contributing to citizen science. In the context of this study, the potential of the projects to support more self-reported learning among those less qualified is demonstrated, but these are the minority of volunteers. Citizen science therefore faces the dilemma of many volunteering and adult education organisations and initiatives, as those that participate most tend to have existing educational experiences, expertise and qualification upon which to draw. From a citizen science perspective, there are advantages to this, insofar as fewer resources are required to support individuals in contributing to projects. However, this is a somewhat limited view and could be counter-productive given the need to broaden the support for scientific understanding of issues and the significance of citizen science to society more broadly. On that basis, there is a desire to engage a wider demographic in citizen science projects with the associated requirement to design activities and provide support that enables effective engagement for both scientific and learning outcomes. The projects studied here point to some of the possibilities and challenges associated with this, and how the nature and level of engagement can make a difference.

It is clear that citizen science can contribute to the self-reported inquiry and scientific learning of volunteers. However, the arenas of inquiry learning practice and research are not synonymous with those of citizen science. While the intermingling of their currents may have productive elements, we need also to be wary of the whirlpools of definition and ownership that can develop.

Acknowledgements

We would like to acknowledge the support provided by the BTO for this project, in particular Ben Darvil and Chris Wernham.

Funding for this project was provided by the British Academy.

References

Archer, L., Dawson, E., DeWitt, J., Seakins, A., & Wong, B. (2015). 'Science capital': A conceptual, methodological, and empirical argument for extending Bourdieusian notions of capital beyond the arts. *Journal of Research in Science Teaching*, DOI10.1002/tea.21227.

Banchi, H., & Bell, R. (2008). The many levels of inquiry. *Science and Children*, 46, 26–29.

Bela, G., Peltola, T., Young, J., Balázs, B., Arpin, I., Pataki, G., Hauck, J., Kelemen, E., Kopperoinen, L., Van Herzele, A., Keune, H., Hecker, S., Suškevičs, M., Roy, H., Itkonen, P., Külvik, M., László, M., Basnou, C., Pino, J., & Bonn, A. (2016). Learning and the transformative potential of citizen science. *Conservation Biology*, DOI: 10.1111/cobi.12762.

Bell, T., Urhahne, D., Schanze, S., & Ploetzner, R. (2010). Collaborative inquiry learning: Models, tools, and challenges. *International Journal of Science Education*, 3, 349–377.

Bonney, R., Cooper, C., Dickinson, J., Kelling, S., Phillips, T., Rosenberg, K. & Shirk, J. (2009a). Citizen science: A developing tool for expanding science knowledge and scientific literacy. *BioScience*, 59, 977–984.

Bonney, R., Ballard, H., Jordan, R., McCallie, E., Phillips, T., Shirk, J., & Wilderman, C. (2009b). *Public participation in scientific research: Defining the field and assessing its potential for informal science education. A CAISE inquiry group report*. Technical report. Washington, D.C.: Center for Advancement of Informal Science Education (CAISE).

Brossard, D., Lewenstein, B., & Bonney, R, (2005). Scientific knowledge and attitude change: The impact of a citizen science project. *International Journal of Science Education*, 27, 1099–1121.

Garibay Group. (2015). *Drive to discover: Summative evaluation report*. Minnesota: University of Minnesota Extension.

Haklay, M. (2012). Citizen science and volunteered geographic Information – overview and typology of participation. In D. Sui, S. Elwood and M. Goodchild (Eds.), *Crowdsourcing geographic knowledge: Volunteered geographic information (VGI) in theory and practice*. Berlin: Springer, pp. 105–122.

National Institute for Health. (2005). *Doing science: The process of science inquiry*. http://science.education.nih.gov/supplements/nih6/inquiry/guide/info_process-a.htm.

National Science Education Standards. (1996). Washington, DC: National Academy Press.

Office for National Statistics. (2010). *Standard occupational classification 2010*. London: Palgrave Maxmillan.

Phillips, T. B., Ferguson, M., Minarchek, M., Porticella, N., & Bonney, R. (2014). *User's guide for evaluating learning outcomes in citizen science*. Ithaca, NY: Cornell Lab of Ornithology.

Raddick, M., Jordan, G., Bracey, P. Gay, P., Lintott, C., Murray, P., Schawinski, K., Szalay, A., & Vandenberg, J. (2010). Galaxy zoo: Exploring the motivations of citizen science volunteers. *Astronomy Education Review*, 9, 010103-1, 10.3847/AER2009036.

Shirk, J., Ballard, H., Wilderman, C., Phillips, T., Wiggins, A., Jordan, R., McCallie, E., Minarchek, M., Lewenstein, M., Krasny, E., & Bonney, R. (2012). Public participation in scientific research: A framework for deliberate design. *Ecology and Society*, 17, 29. http://dx.doi.org/10.5751/ES-04705-170229.

Tweddle, J., Robinson, L., Pocock, M., & Roy, H. (2012). Guide to citizen science: *Developing, implementing and evaluating citizen science to study biodiversity and the environment in the UK*. London: Natural History Museum and NERC Centre for Ecology & Hydrology for UK-EOF. Available online: www.ukeof.org.uk.

Wiggins, A., & Crowston, K. (2011). From conservation to crowdsourcing: A typology of citizen science. *Proceedings of the Forty-fourth Hawai'i International Conference on System Science* (HICSS-44).

Wiggins, A., & Crowston, K. (2012). Goals and tasks: Two typologies of citizen science projects. Paper presented at the Forty-fifth Hawai'i International Conference on System Science.

Wiggins, A., Newmany, G., Stevensonz, R., & Crowston, K. (2011). Mechanisms for data quality and validation in citizen science. Paper presented at the Computing for Citizen Science workshop at the IEEE eScience Conference.

12

DESIGN PROCESSES OF A CITIZEN INQUIRY COMMUNITY

Maria Aristeidou, Eileen Scanlon and Mike Sharples

Introduction

As citizen science projects develop and spread, human–computer interaction (HCI) researchers are focusing on how to improve the user experience, attract more members and amplify scientific and learning outcomes in projects with IT infrastructure (Preece, 2016). The need to design and implement user-centred technologies was one response to the high attrition rate (Nov, 2007; Nov, Arazy, and Anderson, 2011; Ponciano and Brasileiro, 2015) and the dabbling behaviour of the members who are not deeply engaged (Eveleigh et al., 2014) noted in these communities. What distinguishes the design of citizen inquiry from citizen science design is its emphasis on advancing the collaborative inquiry learning aspects of the project and supporting citizens to initiate their own investigations. Although the community design focus is on taking engagement and user experience to a greater level, it is also important to realise that we are creating community learning and inquiry spaces. The aim of this chapter is to identify some design features for engaging members in online citizen inquiry communities whilst also supporting inquiry learning within them. This may lead to a design which offers better scaffolding and offers guidance in every inquiry step to support citizen-led investigations within an engaging and sustainable environment. Given the multi-faceted nature of online citizen inquiry communities, this study is framed around four topics: online communities, inquiry learning, design and technology. The organisation of the chapter is as follows. The following section briefly introduces the four aforementioned challenging topics. We then summarise how requirements drawn from these areas were implemented on the nQuire-it platform, tested with an online citizen inquiry community (Weather-it) and compared to another community (Inquiring Rock Hunters). Next, we reflect on the design results and propose guidelines for improving community engagement and inquiry learning in similar citizen inquiry communities, based on the outcomes of the interventions. The last section presents conclusions from this study.

Background

Online communities

The main idea of citizen inquiry is to open up social scientific processes to distributed communities of citizens with shared interests to allow them to conduct and report the results of inquiry-led projects. These communities operate mainly online because their members are geographically distributed. An online community is any virtual social space that has a purpose, is supported by technology and is guided by shared policies (e.g. registration policies, language) (Preece, 2001). What distinguishes online communities, in general, from other software is the interactions among people; they come together to learn, give or receive information and support, and find company. In this chapter, we discuss the nQuire community for citizen inquiry, where members of the public create small-scale science investigations for others to contribute, on topics that have included weather and environmental noise. Other examples of citizen inquiry communities include iSpot (Silvertown et al., 2015) and Zydeco (Lo et al., 2013). What characterises these communities is a prime focus on science learning through shared inquiry.

Activating the majority of the members and trying to get them to be active contributors instead of lurkers (not active contributors) is significant for achieving the critical mass of members and member-generated content in the community. In response to lurking, the commitment to the community is one of the most important motivations that keeps the community going (Bateman, Gray, & Butler, 2010). A theory that supports this work is the *three-component model of commitment* (Meyer & Allen, 1991), which was developed to reflect the different psychological stages that support and attach the members to communities. These correspond to the psychological states of *affective, normative* and *continuance* commitment. In *affective commitment,* members 'want to stay'. This is divided into 'identity-based' commitment, where the member is a part of the community, and 'bond-based' commitment, where the member is close to the other members. In *normative commitment,* members 'ought to stay' and this is associated with commitment to the purpose of the community, the commitment of other members and reciprocity. In *continuance commitment,* members 'need to stay' and this refers to the net benefits people gain from the community, such as information, social support, companionship and reputation (Ridings & Gefen, 2004). Some design examples that strengthen commitment are to increase the sense of co-presence (Slater et al., 2000) and interpersonal interaction (Postmes, Spears, & Lea, 2002) (affective), to highlight the purpose and up-to-date success of the community (Ren & Kraut, 2012) (normative) and to assess motivations for participating in the community (Ghosh, 2005; Nov, 2007) (continuance).

Examining the lifecycle of an online community by observing its activities and growth, such as those we wish to develop for citizen inquiry, helps in monitoring the community and adjusting the approaches used within it in order to keep it active (Iriberri & Leroy, 2009). At each stage the members have different needs and it is necessary to employ different tools, technologies or management activities efficiently. One description of the lifecycle of a typical online community consists of the following stages: potential, coalescing, maturing, stewardship and transformation (Wenger, McDermott, & Snyder, 2002). This is not linear, as the process can be iterative and adaptable to the needs of the members and the purpose of the community (Young, 2013). The stages of the lifecycle are also encountered with different names, such as inception, creation, growth, maturity, death (Iriberri & Leroy, 2009) or with fewer stages, such as pre-birth, early life, maturity, death (Preece, 2000). Although there are suggestions available at every stage of the lifecycle for sustaining the community, the communities never 'run themselves' even if the fundamental design has been set in motion from the early stage of their development. Community leaders interviewed argue that a community is never completely 'built' (Stuckey & Smith, 2004) and research shows that ongoing design and development depend on the individual community and its own community life (Aristeidou, Scanlon, & Sharples, 2015b; Fischer, 2002).

Inquiry learning

In citizen science projects, members of the public take part in scientifically valid investigations and may experience the process of scientific discovery. In this way, they may learn about the research topic and develop scientific literacy. According to evidence-based research by Kloetzer et al. (2013), three levels of learning can be identified in citizen science projects. The first level is related to the mechanics of the activities (activity learning), the second focuses on the project and the science behind it (on-topic learning) and the third is associated with the learning within the community (community learning). This learning occurs both informally, through contributing to the task and interacting with others, and formally, with scientists providing training to members for completing specific tasks.

However, learning in citizen science projects happens mainly as a side effect during the formalised training which aims at successful completion of the scientific goals, rather than as part of an educational design that intends to improve the learning outcomes. This training is focused on the skills required to perform the specific investigation. Only a few projects conduct research to improve learning outcomes, while most focus on the evaluation of scientific outcomes and how to increase contributions. This limited evidence of participant gains in knowledge about science knowledge and process (Bonney et al., 2015), along with a lack of evidence that citizen science projects have been effective in meeting educational goals (Crall et al., 2013), has led to the development of citizen inquiry communities that put a greater emphasis on designing for learning.

Blending inquiry learning with citizen science in a citizen inquiry community leads to the creation of an environment of bottom-up citizen participation, where citizens need a scaffolding mechanism to conduct their own personally meaningful and authentic investigations. Thus, creating an online environment for citizen inquiry requires difficult design decisions, as the interactions need to be supported and guided. An inquiry-led system addresses suggestions from previous studies on learning in citizen science projects, towards putting the material to be presented in the context of the scientific method (Crall et al., 2013; Cronje et al., 2010). For instance, seeing a dynamic representation of the inquiry process could allow members to shape the processes of investigation and understand how these align with inquiry activities. Such a representation conveys a simple navigation that supports the cycle of inquiry, with its phases, tools and activities. An example is the inquiry phase diagram (octagon) (Figure 12.1) from the Personal Inquiry project, designed for structuring inquiry, supporting discussion and enabling sharing of results (Sharples & Anastopoulou, 2012). The inquiry cycle involves the steps 'find my topic', 'decide my inquiry question or hypothesis', 'plan my methods, equipment and evidence', 'collect my evidence', 'analyse and represent my evidence', 'respond to my question or hypothesis', 'share and discuss my inquiry' and 'reflect on my progress'.

Design

As mentioned earlier, the design of a citizen inquiry community should reflect members' needs and experiences. One of the most important concerns is usability design, especially when you have to design for people with different technology experiences. After securing the technology usability, an important task is to

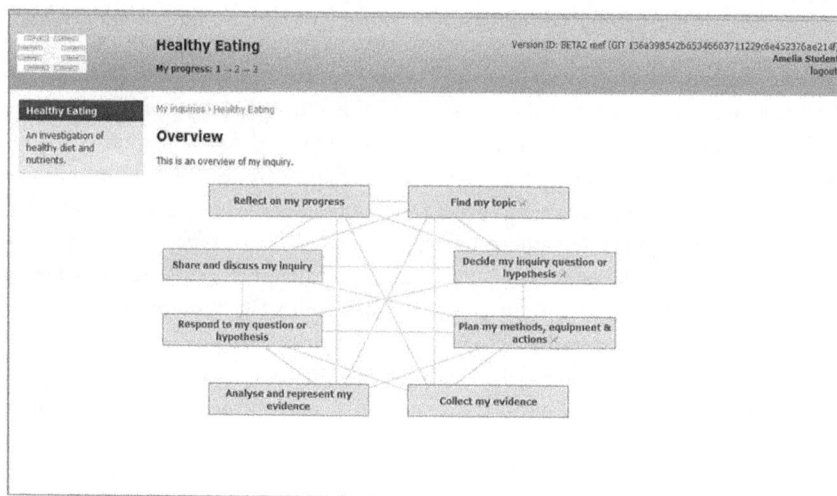

FIGURE 12.1 The inquiry phase diagram from the Personal Inquiry project.

understand how communities form around citizen inquiry projects and how to support community members. Approaches to the creation of technologies that focus on users and their needs are 'participatory design' (Kensing & Bloomberg, 1998; Schuler & Namioka, 1993) 'crowdsourced design' (Grace et al., 2014; Maher et al., 2014) and 'human-centred design' (Sharples et al., 2002; Steen, 2011). Participatory design involves collaboration between technology designers and users in order to place the latter as partners in the centre of design decision making. In crowdsourced design, users are invited to express their opinion about the design and suggest changes that may improve it and meet their own needs. Finally, in human-centred design experts' knowledge of system design, human cognition and social interaction is combined with studies involving typical users, to inform design.

Creating a community for citizen inquiry requires development of tools and practices that can be adopted by diverse groups of people and support the facilitation of inquiries. A starting point for developing such a community is exploring design aspects of online communities and inquiry learning practices mentioned in the previous sections. Therefore, some important steps could be taken for the community pre-birth preparations, such as the selection of technology, community and inquiry requirements, setting up exemplar inquiries and testing the tools used for the investigations. Then, a core group could give life to the community, recruit and welcome new members. Finally, several techniques could be used for making the community more appealing and thereby sustain participation, such as instructions on getting started, prizes, email updates and notifications. The community design can eventually be improved in the next iteration through design contributions submitted by members, who in turn gain social rewards as the system evolves (Fischer, 2011) and become satisfied with a design that meets their needs.

Technology

Networked technology opens the door for broad public participation and facilitates the operation of projects in which members are geographically distributed. The user experience of members taking part in citizen science projects can be enhanced by using integrated platforms that use additional data collection technology, such as camera, sensor and geo-positioning software, distributed by Google Play Store, Apple's App Store and other online app stores. But making good technology choices requires key questions to be answered: What type of project will it be used for (type of data collection/analysis required) and who are the members?

In citizen inquiry communities, as in other online communities, there is a diversity of members, in terms of nationality, language, interests, experience and age. Some members will be familiar with new technologies; others will be experts in the scientific topic. While top-down citizen science projects are grouped into 'active' and 'passive' data collection projects, based on whether they actively involve humans in collecting data (Preece, 2016), citizen inquiry communities engage members in actively conducting their own investigations based on their everyday experience of science. Thus, the technology should not be limited to data collection and analysis, but should offer space for initiation, incubation, sharing, visualisation, discussion and personalisation of science investigations, so that non-expert participants can design and structure inquiries, and recruit other people to take part, assisted by more expert members or through help functions embedded in the technology. Other activities that take place in citizen inquiry communities, similar to citizen science projects, include contributing data to one's own or other investigations, reviewing, discussing and analysing contributions, and re-using data for other purposes such as teaching. Designing technology that supports inquiry and discussions, ensures smooth operation of activities and motivates members is important for enabling learning and engagement.

A team from the UK Open University, inspired by the citizen inquiry approach, created the nQuire toolkit, which supports the idea of having lay people act as scientists (Herodotou, Villasclaras-Fernandez, & Sharples, 2014). The nQuire toolkit, building on previous work on the nQuire platform designed to support inquiry learning in schools (Sharples et al., 2015), scaffolds members in creating, managing, sharing and completing projects of their own interest. It consists of the nQuire-it web platform[1] (Figure 12.2) and the Sense-it Android app[2] (Figure 12.3). Based on the method of data collection, the nQuire-it platform provides three different types of investigation (called 'missions'): Sense-it, Spot-it and Win-it. Sense-it missions use sensor recordings collected from the Sense-it Android application;

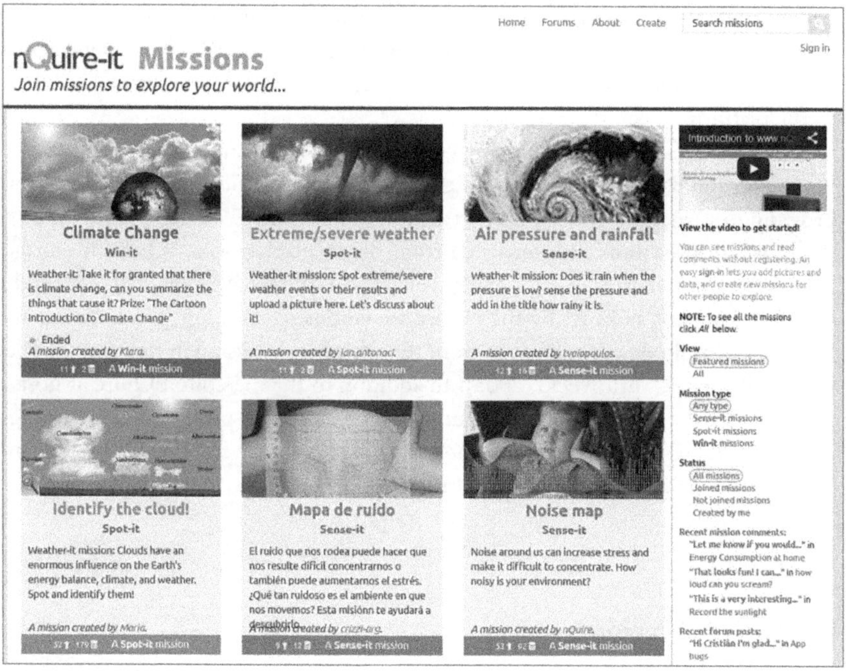

FIGURE 12.2 The nQuire-it platform.

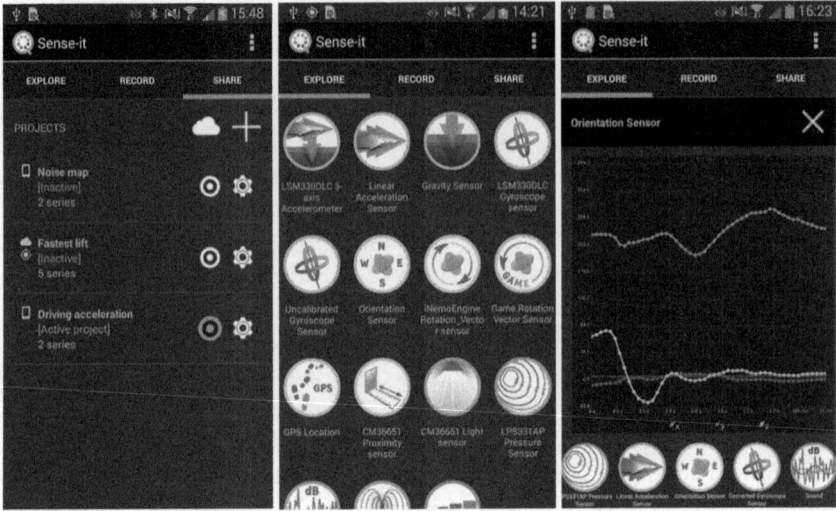

FIGURE 12.3 Screen displays from the Sense–it Android app.

Spot–it missions display user–contributed pictures for discussion and comparison; Win–it missions pose research questions which require text for answers. The Sense–it Android app activates the existing sensors of Android smartphones and tablets, such as light sensor, humidity, pressure and temperature. The Sense–it app profiles connect to Sense–it investigations on the nQuire–it platform. Users record, visualise, store and download the log files on their mobile devices or upload them to the platform.

Initiating a mission is facilitated by visual conceptual organisers who assist creators in naming and describing their investigations, numbering the goals of their mission, providing instructions for taking part in the project and selecting the methods of data collection (sensors, images, text) from the available tools. nQuire–it engages lay people and scientists in an 'open collaboration' model (Vreede et al., 2013), by which the mission tasks set by the owner are completed through combination and synthesis of multiple contributions from the members, utilising in this way 'collective intelligence' (Suriowecki, 2005). In addition to the missions, nQuire–it hosts a forum for further discussion which can be connected to a specific mission through a link to a discussion forum topic. The source codes for the nQuire–it platform and Sense–it app are available[3] for modification and distribution.

Methodology

Design-based research

In this chapter we describe some design features for engaging members in citizen inquiry communities and advancing inquiry learning within them. The current study employs a design-based research methodology (Design-Based Research Collective, 2003). Design-based research stresses the need for design principles that inform and enhance both research and practice in educational contexts, and leads to the development of usable knowledge. A central notion in design-based research is to create an improved practice, while the 'intervention' is a collaborative task of both the research and the participants (Cobb et al., 2003). In this regard, we chose this particular methodology in order to study the interventions through ongoing revisions according to the success of the revisions on levels of engagement and learning, and identify all the aspects that may affect the situation rather than manipulating specific variables (Collins et al., 2004). We have also employed crowdsourced design (Maher et al., 2014) in order to capture participants' perceptions and suggestions about the design and improve it accordingly.

This research employed two design studies around the citizen inquiry communities: 'Inquiring Rock Hunters' and 'Weather-it'. In the first community, members were conducting investigations about rocks and in the second about weather. The first intervention design, Inquiring Rock Hunters, had a more exploratory character and thus allowed room for improvements in the design of the second longer iteration. Results from the first intervention (with 24 participants) showed that there was a low sense of belonging to the community and low levels of engagement (Aristeidou, Scanlon, & Sharples, 2014). Therefore, the main requirements for building the second intervention, Weather-it (with 101 participants), focused on the design of an engaging citizen inquiry community that facilitates inquiry learning. Nevertheless, we can draw implications from both interventions for orchestrating a citizen inquiry community.

Detailed results of the projects have been presented elsewhere (Aristeidou et al., 2014; Aristeidou, Scanlon & Sharples, 2015a, 2015b); this chapter describes design features applied mainly to the Weather-it community (and in comparison to some Inquiring Rock Hunters results) that engage and disengage citizen inquiry community members, and increase inquiry learning within the communities. These prepare other practitioners to advance further online citizen inquiry and other similar communities.

Methods used for data collection

The data collection employed open-ended survey questions and it was aiming at gaining insight into the satisfaction and learning levels of the community members. Qualitative analysis of the data involved consideration of all the responses in the survey questions: 'What did you like the most in Inquiring Rock Hunters/ Weather-it?' ($n1 = 20$, $n2 = 52$); 'Are you still an active member of the Weather-it community (and answer = no), could you please state the reason?'($n = 17$); and 'What, if anything, have you learned new or interesting through your participation in Inquiring Rock Hunters/Weather-it?' ($n1 = 20$, $n2 = 28$). Thematic analysis and inductive coding of the responses from the first two survey questions allowed the development of themes focused on design factors that engage and disengage members from the communities, respectively, while responses to the third question provided insight into the design features, of the particular community, that supported learning. The approach used in orchestrating the design of the communities is described in the next section.

Proposed orchestration of the citizen inquiry community

Our approach to designing the citizen inquiry communities has been guided by the needs of citizen inquiry and advice around online communities, and has been improved through crowdsourced design. Design resources we needed to consider included collaborative inquiry tools, learning content, data collection tools, uses of mobile sensors and social technologies. Building on an already-existing citizen inquiry platform (nQuire-it), some of the requirements had already been included in its design (see 'Existing nQuire-it design' section below), so the focus was on improving it and making it more engaging. Essential requirements to be implemented are listed in Table 12.1, followed by less essential ones, in the 'Design requirements' section below. The section 'Requirements applied to nQuire-it' demonstrates the requirements that were finally implemented.

TABLE 12.1 Essential design requirements

Requirement name	Description	Reference
Notification	to reinforce participation	Kraut & Resnick, 2011
List with recent investigations	to help members find the most active investigations	Resnick & Konstan, 2012
News feed	to convey activity within the community	Resnick & Konstan, 2012
Personal messages	to build stronger relationships	McKenna et al., 2002
Top posters	to build a comparative atmosphere and motivate members	Locke & Latham, 2002
Most popular investigations	to display performance feedback and motivate members	Kraut et al., 2012
Who is currently online	to increase social presence interaction and engagement	Preece, 2000 Beuchot & Bullen, 2005 Brown, 2001
Invitations through other social networks	to attract members to the community	Resnick & Konstan, 2012
Visit profiles	to increase co-presence	Slater et al., 2000
Web analytics	to trace and demonstrate community statistics to the moderator	Resnick & Konstan, 2012
Video tutorial	to introduce new users to the platform	

Existing nQuire-it design

Some principles influencing the initial design of the nQuire-it platform included the following:

- *Attractive professional look.* This is a significant motivation for users to join it (Fogg, Soohoo, & Danielson, 2003) and use it (Heijden, 2003). The buttons should all be findable (big, bold, with images or menu-like) on the home page.
- *Create a profile (username, photo and country/town).* Wenger (2001) argues for the importance of individual identity in a social learning system. The users should be able to express their individual personality in the community by adding personal information and pictures, so as to reflect their identity (Andrews, 2002) and be perceived as real people in mediated communication (Garrison & Arbaugh, 2007).
- *Sign in by using existing username from other platforms.* The integration of the community with other sites, such as Facebook, Google and Twitter, makes user registration easy and fast by using their existing user identifiers.
- *Search, join and start a mission.* Searching, joining and starting missions are essential requirements for citizen inquiry communities and nQuire-it offers easily accessed buttons to facilitate these options.
- *Inquiry-led mechanism.* The platform provides guidance for the investigations through steps and tabs that represent inquiry phases.
- *Comment on data (Figure 12.4).* This feature allows feedback and discussion around the collected data.
- *Content-sharing system in external platforms (Facebook, Twitter, email).* Exporting of content will increase the visibility of the community among the social networks of members (Resnick & Konstan, 2012).
- *Reputation system (rating/like).* Members should be rewarded for their efforts (Iriberri & Leroy, 2009). The current reward system in nQuire-it is based on receiving or giving 'likes' (Figure 12.5).

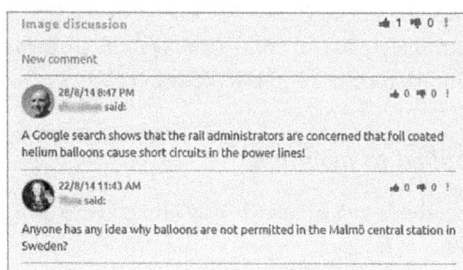

FIGURE 12.4 nQuire-it – comment.

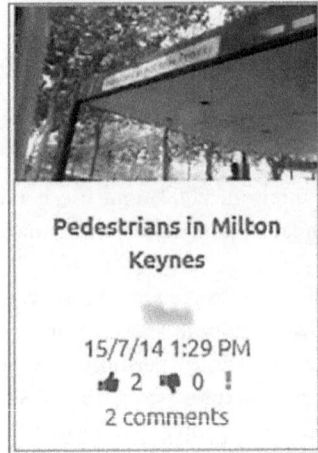

FIGURE 12.5 nQuire–it – thumb up.

- *Links to forums to join the platform forum discussion.* The forums can be used for on-topic and off-topic discussion, and for direct communication between members and moderators.
- *Archive list with all the investigations or by specific type.* A list with all the available investigations makes it easier for members to view and participate in those that reflect their interests.

Design requirements

Table 12.1 presents a list with the essential additional requirements to be implemented:

Other less essential requirements to be implemented, extracted or drawn from literature include *badges* for particular contributions (Anderson et al., 2013) and the *reader-to-leader funnel* (Preece & Shneiderman, 2009), which causes progressive commitment as newcomers move from being reading to having leadership roles within the community; *members' list* and *location map* for social presence; *add friends* for enhanced affective commitment; *subscription* to mailing list for community updates (Kraut & Resnick, 2011); *feedback* in every step of the investigation (Kubey & Csikszentmihalyi, 2013); and a *learning room* for further discussions, as in some online community forums (e.g. UK Weather Watch).

Requirements applied to nQuire-it

Only a subset of the above requirements was implemented on the nQuire-it platform due to limitations of time and resources and privacy and security concerns. The applied features (see list below) were mainly drawn from the above list of essential requirements or emerged from the flow of the community and investigations. The implementation was carried out by the nQuire-it development team at the Institute of Educational Technology of the Open University according to project requirements.

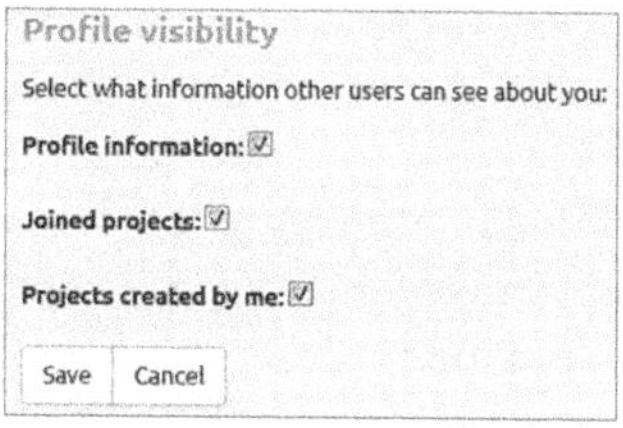

FIGURE 12.6   nQuire-it – profile visibility.

- The investigations displayed on the main page of nQuire-it were sorted by the *most recent ones* and thus members were able to spot the most active investigations.
- One could click on a member's name in order to *visit his or her profile page* and learn more about that person: name, location, description, interests and which projects s/he has joined and created. Members could decide about the degree of privacy for their profiles (Figure 12.6).
- A list at the right sidebar was added displaying *who is currently online* in order to increase visibility and inform members about who else is active.
- One of the nQuire-it moderators uploaded to the right sidebar a *video-tutorial* explaining the basics about the platform.
- *Web analytics* were accessed through the Google analytics page and facilitated monitoring the activity within the community daily and weekly.
- A *learning room* was developed in the forums, where further discussion took place around the investigations and other topic-related issues.
- *Exemplar investigations* of each mission type were set up, with input from topic experts, in order to be used as examples for the creation of other missions.
- A feature that was not included in the requirements list but was spotted later was *merging the accounts* created through nQuire-it and Sense-it. This helped to prevent the existence of two usernames for members who were using both the mobile application and the platform. Furthermore, members could connect their nQuire-it profile with profiles in other social networks (i.e. Google, Facebook, Twitter) (Figure 12.7).
- Another feature which is considered significant for a community for scientific investigations, and was added afterwards to the nQuire-it platform, is the option for *downloading the collected data* in a spreadsheet to make the data analysis easier. A button to download the data in CSV format was made available below the list of collected data.

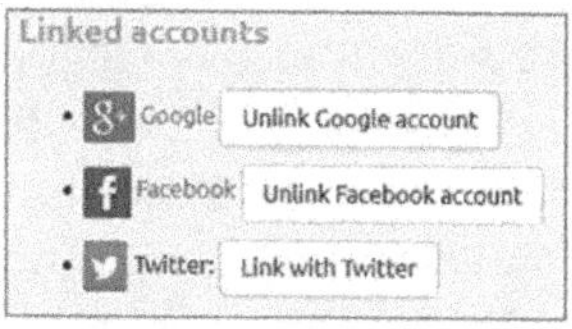

FIGURE 12.7   nQuire-it – linked accounts.

Alternative techniques were sought for other important features that could not be implemented on the platform for this project. These include:

- tangible *awards and prizes* (Amazon coupons and books) for particular contributions, such as monthly prizes for the top contributor, best photographer and the most voted Win-it response
- manual *notifications* to members for any feedback received on their posts
- a *mailing list* with the new activities and weekly updates, and a Facebook group with daily posts which aimed to remind the members to visit the community again.

Reflections on the design

In Inquiring Rock Hunters which was based on an earlier platform, most of the members commented on the difficulty they would have had in using the software without a tutorial. The Weather-it mission on the nQuire-it platform was generally found to be easy to use, with some members commenting on the well-organised structure, and the ease of browsing subjects and creating missions. However, several members spotted software bugs or limitations during or at the end of the project. The feedback allowed ongoing improvements and the creation of a list with further design requirements, related to the user interface, project communication, social and inquiry technologies. The majority of the Weather-it members referred to the technology and software usability either as the reason they liked the project and thus remained engaged, or as the cause for not being active at the time of the survey.

Overall, and beyond technology, the factors that sustained the engagement of members who remained active in the Weather-it community until the end of the project, as identified in the survey responses, were the social aspect, the variety and the concept of citizen inquiry (investigation ownership and interaction). On the other hand, the disengagement of Weather-it members from the community was mainly related to time constraints and secondly to lack of interest in the available topics. Moreover, lack of experience and low self-confidence were also reasons that several members from both Weather-it and Inquiring Rock Hunters gave for their decision to abandon their investigations and the communities.

The majority of Inquiring Rock Hunters stated that, throughout their participation in the community, beyond content knowledge, they also gained knowledge on how to approach an investigation. This knowledge includes the phases of the inquiry process, science field research methods and information about where to collect data from and how, and how to manipulate those data. This self-report is in contradiction to reports from Weather-it members in which they mentioned that they gained domain knowledge, yet they made no reference to learning about research methods and science inquiry process. A strong influence on the Weather-it outcome is likely to be the absence of the visualised inquiry framework used in

Inquiring Rock Hunters. Finally, findings related to the Weather-it evolution and sustainability indicated that the ongoing design and development, based on the individual community and its needs as applied in this work, resulted in eventually having a slightly growing and sustainable community with steady activity fluctuations (Aristeidou et al., 2015b). It is still an open issue as to whether is possible to sustain a community of citizen inquiry in the long term, beyond the period of active design and facilitation.

Implications for the design of a citizen inquiry community

The following design considerations aim to facilitate the creation, improvement and sustainability of online citizen inquiry communities in which members remain engaged and adopt good inquiry learning practices. These do not aim to apply to all contexts, but to improve the design of online citizen inquiry communities and their scaffolding mechanisms for the creation of collaborative, personally meaningful and authentic investigations by citizens.

Support ongoing feedback on software

The importance of the technology usability has been emphasised in this study, as this was reported as the main reason for members staying or leaving the community. It is, therefore, important to address usability concerns by engaging members in the evolving design. Ongoing feedback may reveal bugs and needs, improve the software design and obviate member dropouts.

Support variety in topics and ways of engagement

Community members commented positively on the variety within our citizen inquiry community. In nQuire-it, variety was enriched not only through the data collection methods that missions provided, but also with the diversity in topics, locations and members' level of expertise that made participation more interesting. This idea of multiple forms of contribution acknowledges the many interests of users and motivates members' participation (Bonney et al., 2015).

Provide social technologies

Our findings illustrate that some members sustained participation in the community and developed a sense of belonging due to the interactions they had with other members during their investigations. The nQuire-it toolkit supported interactions between members through an open participation approach, which is suggested to enhance the sense of community and lead to higher levels of engagement (Jennett & Cox, 2014; Jennett et al., 2013). As a result, Weather-it members felt welcome to the community and satisfied with their active roles and the number of new available activities.

Support ownership of collaborative investigations

Members of the citizen inquiry community showed their satisfaction with the option to create their own missions or help others with their missions. Unlike other citizen science projects where volunteers were more interested in solitary experience and independent working (Eveleigh et al., 2014), Weather-it members found interaction a fun way of learning and getting engaged with science.

Update members with to-do lists of smaller or similar tasks

Drop-outs are strongly associated with lack of time and interest. However, some members may revisit the community after they dropped out; lists with small investigation tasks with time duration or tasks similar to the ones they showed some interest in could support their return.

Promote support groups

Another important reason why members stopped engaging with the community was lack of confidence. Members' anxiety about the quality of their contributions may be overcome with the creation of experts supporting groups that discuss the data and comment on contributions.

Design explicit inquiry activities as part of a complete scientific process

Members of Inquiring Rock Hunters indicated higher levels of scientific literacy gains compared to Weather-it members. A design feature that facilitated understanding of inquiry phases and methods was the use of the inquiry framework (Figure 12.1) that allowed members to understand the structure of the inquiry activities. Engaging members with several phases or the entire scientific process requires preparation. It is necessary to provide aim, activity, tools and research method instructions for each phase. This information about the entire scientific process and where each inquiry phase lies may facilitate scientific literacy to a greater extent. However, there may be a tension between providing well-structured activities and supporting easy creation of a broad range of missions and challenges by users. The first may lead to gains in knowledge of scientific processes, but at the expense of user engagement and participation, and the latter may result in lack of scientific rigour.

Concluding comments

In this chapter we have reviewed the literature that frames our work on citizen inquiry communities, with a particular focus on which aspects support engagement and enhance inquiry learning in the community. We have demonstrated design requirements, drawn or borrowed from literature, that aim at improving the orchestration of citizen inquiry communities. Of those requirements, several were implemented and tested on nQuire-it through the Weather-it citizen inquiry community, and the results were compared to Inquiring Rock Hunters. Social aspects, variety and a sense of inquiry were the features that engaged members with the community, while time constraints, lack of interest and experience were the reasons that members dropped out. Technology and software usability had a crucial role in both cases. Furthermore, a comparison between the two communities indicated the importance of illustrating inquiry activities as a part of a complete scientific process for supporting scientific literacy.

In this proposed orchestration of citizen inquiry communities, we combined our own belief in the importance of designing appropriate technologies to support inquiry learning with the needs of our participants. Although a readymade technology was adopted, both usability issues and the broader context of use were taken into account. A challenge to be overcome is how to design technology and social infrastructure that support scaling up. Technologies reported in the 'Implications for the design of a citizen inquiry community section could aid scalability, for instance, by developing a better scaffolding system that automatically guides and informs members at every step of the inquiry process or a recommendation system that delivers to-do lists to individual members according to their interests.

Our aim with this study was to improve user experience and engagement, and support the inquiry learning aspect of citizen inquiry communities. Orchestrating principles from online communities, inquiry learning, design and technology helped in creating an engaging space for community and inquiry learning. The findings of this research have added to the body of current research into how to engage members and support inquiry learning in online citizen inquiry communities with similar conditions. The next substantial step is to explore the efficiency of these design guidelines in further sustaining the communities and supporting inquiry learning.

Notes

1 www.nquire-it.org.
2 https://play.google.com/store/apps/details?id=org.greengin.sciencetoolkit.
3 https://github.com/nQuire.

References

Anderson, A., Huttenlocher, D., Kleinberg, J., & Leskovec, J. (2013). Steering user behavior with badges. In *Proceedings of the 22nd International Conference on World Wide Web* (pp. 95–106). Geneva: ACM.

Andrews, D. (2002). Audience-specific online community design. *Communications of the ACM, 45*(4), 64–68.

Aristeidou, M., Scanlon, E., & Sharples, M. (2014). Inquiring rock hunters. In C. Rensing, S. de Freitas, T. Ley, & P. J. Muñoz-Merino (Eds.), *Open Learning and Teaching in Educational Communities, Proceedings of the 9th European Conference on Technology Enhanced Learning, EC-TEL 2014* (pp. 546–547). Springer International Publishing.

Aristeidou, M., Scanlon, E., & Sharples, M. (2015a). Weather-it missions: a social network analysis perspective of an online citizen inquiry community. In G. Conole, T. Klobučar, C. Rensing, J. Konert, & É. Lavoué (Eds.), *Design for Teaching and Learning in a Networked World* (Vol. 9307, pp. 3–16). Springer International Publishing.

Aristeidou, M., Scanlon, E., & Sharples, M. (2015b). Weather-it: evolution of an online community for citizen inquiry. In S. Lindstaedt, T. Ley, & H. Sach (Eds.), *Proceedings of the 15th International Conference on Knowledge Technologies and Data-driven Business, i-Know 2015,* article no. 13. New York: ACM Digital Library.

Bateman, P. J., Gray, P. H., & Butler, B. S. (2010). Research note – the impact of community commitment on participation in online communities. *Information Systems Research, 22*(4), 841–854.

Beuchot, A., & Bullen, M. (2005). Interaction and interpersonality in online discussion forums. *Distance Education, 26*(1), 67–87. doi:10.1080/01587910500081285.

Bonney, R., Phillips, T. B., Ballard, H. L., & Enck, J. W. (2015). Can citizen science enhance public understanding of science? *Public Understanding of Science, 25*(1), 2–16. doi:10.1177/0963662515607406.

Brown, R. (2001). The process of community-building in distance learning classes. *Journal of Asynchronous Learning Networks 5*(2), 18–35.

Cobb, P., Confrey, J., DiSessa, A., Lehrer, R., & Schauble, L. (2003). Design experiments in educational research. *Educational Researcher, 32*(1), 9–13. doi:10.3102/0013189X032001009.

Collins, A., Joseph, D., & Bielaczyc, K. (2004). Design research: Theoretical and methodological issues. *Journal of the Learning Sciences, 13*(1), 15–42. doi:10.1207/s15327809jls1301_2.

Crall, A. W., Jordan, R., Holfelder, K., Newman, G. J., Graham, J., & Waller, D. M. (2013). The impacts of an invasive species citizen science training program on participant attitudes, behavior, and science literacy. *Public Understanding of Science, 22*(6), 745–764. doi:10.1177/0963662511434894.

Cronje, R., Rohlinger, S., Crall, A., & Newman, G. (2010). Does participation in citizen science improve scientific literacy? A study to compare assessment methods. *Applied Environmental Education and Communication, 10*(3), 135–145. doi:10.1080/1533015X.2011.603611.

Design-Based Research Collective. (2003). Design-based research: An emerging paradigm for educational inquiry. *Educational Researcher, 32*(1), 5–8.

Eveleigh, A., Jennett, C., Blandford, A., Brohan, P., & Cox, A. L. (2014). Designing for dabblers and deterring drop-outs in citizen science. In *Proceedings of the 32nd Annual ACM Conference on Human Factors in Computing Systems – CHI '14* (pp. 2985–2994). New York: ACM Press. doi:10.1145/2556288.2557262.

Fischer, G. (2002). Beyond "couch potatoes": From consumers to designers and active contributors. *Proceedings of Computer Human Interaction 3rd Asia Pacific* (pp. 2–9). Piscataway, NJ: IEEE. doi:10.1109/APCHI.1998.704130.

Fischer, G. (2011). Understanding, fostering, and supporting cultures of participation. *Interactions, 18*(3), 42–53. doi:10.1145/1962438.1962450.

Fogg, B., Soohoo, C., & Danielson, D. (2003). How do users evaluate the credibility of web sites? A study with over 2,500 participants. *Proceedings of the 2003 Conference on Designing for User Experiences* (pp. 1–15). doi:10.1145/997078.997097.

Garrison, D. R., & Arbaugh, J. B. (2007). Researching the community of inquiry framework: Review, issues, and future directions. *Internet and Higher Education, 10*, 157–172. doi:10.1016/j.iheduc.2007.04.001.

Ghosh, R. (2005). *Understanding Free Software Developers: Findings from the FLOSS Study.* Paper presented at the Conference of New Models of Software Development, Harvard Business School. Retrieved September 21, 2016, from http://www.flossproject.org/papers/ghosh-2005.pdf.

Grace, K., Maher, M., Preece, J., Yeh, T., Stangl, A., & Boston, C. (2014). A process model for crowdsourcing design: A case study in citizen science. In J.S. Gero (Ed.), *Design Computing and Cognition 2014* (pp. 263–282). Cham, Switzerland: Springer International Publishing. doi: 10.1007/978-3-319-44989-0.

Heijden, H. Van der. (2003). Factors influencing the usage of websites: The case of a generic portal in The Netherlands. *Information & Management, 40*(6), 541–549. doi: 10.1016/S0378-7206(02)00079-4.

Herodotou, C., Villasclaras-Fernandez, E., & Sharples, M. (2014). Scaffolding citizen inquiry science learning through the nQuire toolkit. In *Proceedings of EARLI SIG 20: Computer Supported Inquiry Learning* (pp. 9–11). Retrieved September 21, 2016, from http://oro.open.ac.uk/42030/1/EARLIsig20meeting_submission_3_final %281%29.pdf.

Iriberri, A., & Leroy, G. (2009). A life-cycle perspective on online community success. *ACM Computing Surveys (CSUR), 41*(2), article no. 11. New York, NY: ACM Digital Library. doi:10.1145/1459352.1459356.

Jennett, C., & Cox, A. L. (2014, October 14). *Eight Guidelines for Designing Virtual Citizen Science Projects.* Paper presented at the Second AAAI Conference on Human Computation and Crowdsourcing. Retrieved September 21, 2016, from http://www.aaai.org/ocs/index.php/HCOMP/HCOMP14/paper/view/9261.

Jennett, C., Eveleigh, A., Mathieu, K., Ajani, Z., & Cox, A. (2013, June 5). *Creativity in citizen science: All for one and one for all.* Paper presented at the ACM Web Science Conference, Websci'13. Retrieved September 21, 2016, from http://discovery.ucl.ac.uk/1395531/.

Kensing, F., & Bloomberg, J. (1998). Participatory design: Issues and concerns. *Computer Supported Cooperative Work, 7*(3–4), 167–185.

Kloetzer, L., Schneider, D., Jennett, C., Iacovides, I., Eveleigh, A., Cox, A., & Gold, M. (2013). Learning by volunteer computing, thinking and gaming: What and how are volunteers learning by participating in virtual citizen science? In B. Kapplinger, N. Lichte, E. Haberzeth, & C. Kulmus (Eds.), *Changing Configurations of Adult Education in Transitional Times, Proceedings of 7th European Research Conference – ESREA* (pp. 73–92).

Kraut, R., & Resnick, P. (2011). *Evidence-based Social Design: Mining the Social Sciences to Build Successful Online Communities.* Cambridge, MA: MIT Press.

Kraut, R. E., Burke, M., Riedl, J., & Resnick, P. (2012). The challenges of dealing with newcomers. In R. E. Kraut, & P. Resnick (Eds.), *Building Successful Online Communities: Evidence-based Social Design* (pp. 179–230). Cambridge, MA: MIT Press.

Kubey, R., & Csikszentmihalyi, M. (2013). *Television and the Quality of Life: How Viewing Shapes Everyday Experience.* New York, NY: Routledge.

Locke, E., & Latham, G. (2002). Building a practically useful theory of goal setting and task motivation: A 35-year odyssey. *American Psychologist, 57*(9), 705–717. doi: 10.1037/0003-066X.57.9.705.

Lo, W., Delen, I., Kuhn, A., McGee, S., Duck, J., & Quintana, C. (2013). *Zydeco: A mobile-based learning system to support science inquiry learning.* Paper presented at the 2013 Annual Meeting of the American Educational Research Association.

Maher, M. L., Preece, J., Yeh, T., Boston, C., Grace, K., Pasupuleti, A., & Stangl, A. (2014). NatureNet: A model for crowdsourcing the design of citizen science systems. In *Proceedings of the 2014 CSCW Companion* (pp. 201–204).

McKenna, K. Y., Green, A., & Gleason, M. E. (2002). Relationship formation on the Internet: What's the big attraction? *Journal of Social Issues, 58*(1), 9–31. doi:10.1111/1540-4560.00246.

Meyer, J., & Allen, N. (1991). A three-component conceptualization of organizational commitment. *Human Resource Management Review, 1*(1), 61–89. doi:10.1016/1053-4822(91)90011-Z.

Nov, O. (2007). What motivates Wikipedians? *Communications of the ACM, 50*(11), 60–64. doi:10.1145/1297797.1297798.

Nov, O., Arazy, O., & Anderson, D. (2011). Dusting for science: Motivation and participation of digital citizen science volunteers. In *Proceedings of the 2011 iConference* (pp. 68–74). New York: ACM digital library. doi:10.1145/1940761.1940771.

Ponciano, L., & Brasileiro, F. (2015). Finding volunteers' engagement profiles in human computation for citizen science projects. *Human Computation, 1*(2), 245–264. doi:10.15346/hc.v1i2.12.

Postmes, T., Spears, R., & Lea, M. (2002). Intergroup differentiation in computer-mediated communication: Effects of depersonalization. *Group Dynamics: Theory, Research, and Practice, 6*(1), 3–15. doi:10.1037/1089-2699.6.1.3.

Preece, J. (2000). *Online Communities: Designing Usability and Supporting Socialbilty*. New York, NY: John Wiley.

Preece, J. (2001). Sociability and usability in online communities: Determining and measuring success. *Behaviour & Information Technology, 20*(5), 347–356. doi:10.1080/0144 9290110084683.

Preece, J. (2016). Citizen science: New research challenges for human–computer interaction. *International Journal of Human–Computer Interaction, 32*(8), 585–612. doi:10.1080/1 0447318.2016.1194153.

Preece, J., & Shneiderman, B. (2009). The reader-to-leader framework: Motivating technology-mediated social participation. *AIS Transactions on Human–Computer Interaction, 1*(1), 13–32.

Ren, Y., & Kraut, R. (2012). Encouraging commitment in online communities. In R. E. Kraut, & P. Resnick (Eds.), *Building Successful Online Communities: Evidence-Based Social Design* (pp. 179–230). Cambridge, MA: MIT Press.

Resnick, P., & Konstan, J. (2012). Starting new online communities. In R. E. Kraut, & P. Resnick (Eds.), *Building Successful Online Communities: Evidence-Based Social Design* (pp. 179–230). Cambridge, MA: MIT Press.

Ridings, C., & Gefen, D. (2004). Virtual community attraction: Why people hang out online. *Journal of Computer-Mediated Communication, 10*(1). doi:10.1111/j.1083-6101.2004. tb00229.x.

Schuler, D., & Namioka, A. (Eds.). (1993). *Participatory Design: Principles and Practices*. Hillsdale, NJ: Lawrence Erlbaum Associates.

Sharples, M., & Anastopoulou, S. (2012). Designing orchestration for inquiry learning. In K. Littleton, E. Scanlon, & M. Sharples (Eds.), *Orchestrating Inquiry Learning* (pp. 69–85). Abingdon: Routledge.

Sharples, M., Jeffery, N., du Boulay, J. B. H., Teather, D., Teather, B., & Du Boulay, G. H. (2002). Socio-cognitive engineering: A methodology for the design of human-centred technology. *European Journal of Operational Research, 136*(2), 310–323. doi:10.1016/S0377-2217(01)00118-7.

Sharples, M., Scanlon, E., Ainsworth, S., Anastopoulou, S., Collins, T., Crook, C., Jones, A., Kerawalla, L., Littleton, K., Mulholland, P., & O'Malley, C. (2015). Personal inquiry: Orchestrating science investigations within and beyond the classroom. *Journal of the Learning Sciences, 24*(2), 308–341.

Silvertown, J., Harvey, M., Greenwood, R., Dodd, M., Rosewell, J., Rebelo, T., Ansine, J., & McConway, K. (2015). Crowdsourcing the identification of organisms: A case-study of iSpot. *ZooKeys, 480*, 125. doi: 10.3897/zookeys.480.8803.

Slater, M., Howell, J., Steed, A., Pertaub, D.-P., & Garau, M. (2000). Acting in virtual reality. In *Proceedings of the Third International Conference on Collaborative Virtual Environments – CVE '00* (pp. 103–110). New York: ACM Press. doi:10.1145/351006.351020.

Steen, M. (2011). Tensions in human-centred design. *CoDesign*, 7(1), 45–60. doi:10.1080/15710882.2011.563314.

Stuckey, B., & Smith, J. (2004). Building sustainable communities of practice. In P. Hildreth & C. Kimble (Eds.), *Knowledge Networks: Innovation through Communities of Practice*. London: Igi Global (pp. 150–162).

Suriowecki, J. (2005). The wisdom of crowds: Why the many are smarter than the few. *Business Economics*, 41(4), 63–65.

Vreede, T. De, Nguyen, C., Vreede, G. De, Boughzala, I., Oh, O., & Reiter-Palmon, R. (2o13). A theoretical model of user engagement in crowdsourcing. In P. Antunes, M. A. Gerosa, A. Sylvester, J. Vassileva, & G. de Vreede (Eds.), *Collaboration and Technology, Proceedings of 19th International Conference – CRIWG 2013* (pp. 94–109). Wellington, New Zealand: Springer. doi:10.1007/978-3-642-41347-6_8.

Wenger, E. (2001). *Supporting Communities of Practice: A Survey of Community-oriented Technologies*. Retrieved June 1, 2017, from https://guard.canberra.edu.au/opus/copyright_register/repository/53/153/01_03_CP_technology_survey_v3.pdf.

Wenger, E., McDermott, R. A., & Snyder, W. (2002). *Cultivating Communities of Practice: A Guide to Managing Knowledge*. Boston, MA: Harvard Business School Press.

Young, C. (2013). Community management that works: How to build and sustain a thriving online health community. *Journal of Medical Internet Research*, 15(6), e119. doi:10.2196/jmir.2501.

INDEX